A CULTISH SIDE OF CALVINISM

Micah Coate

Innovo
Publishing

Published by
Innovo Publishing, LLC
www.innovopublishing.com
1-888-546-2111

Innovo
Publishing

Providing Full-Service Publishing Services for
Christian Authors, Artists & Organizations: Hardbacks, Paperbacks,
eBooks, Audiobooks, Music & Videos

A CULTISH SIDE OF CALVINISM
Copyright © 2011 by Micah Coate
All rights reserved.

All references to Scripture were taken from the NKJV unless otherwise noted.

Library of Congress Control Number: 2011934221
ISBN 13: 978-1-936076-83-3
ISBN 10: 1-936076-83-7

Cover Design & Interior Layout: Innovo Publishing, LLC

Printed in the United States of America
U.S. Printing History

First Edition: July 2011

For my friend and brother, Shane Quezada;

with much gratitude to Hilary Wilcox,

along with those elect few who supported me in this work.

ENDORSEMENTS

"At last, someone has the courage to tie Calvinism into the dark side where it originated. Great book, I enjoyed it!"

Dr. Tim LaHaye
Author, Minister, Educator, and Founder of Tim LaHaye
Ministries in El Cajon, CA

"Micah is a youth pastor who is young himself, but he understands the problems of Calvinism far beyond the great majority of people of his age. I wish I had read this many years ago."

Dr. Earl D. Radmacher
President Emeritus of Western Seminary and Chancellor of
Rocky Mountain Bible Seminary in Englewood, CO

"Micah Coate, in his assessment of Calvinism, issues a warning about a dangerous side of this popular perspective increasingly faced by churches today. I, for one, am grateful for this warning."

Dr. Paige Patterson
President of Southwestern Baptist Theological Seminary in
Fort Worth, TX

"One does not have to agree with everything in Micah Coate's fascinating book to profit from it. He sets before us a much-needed caution, lest we put any man's system of theology over biblical theology. You will find this book helpful to you, regardless of your theological persuasion."

Dr. Jerry Vines
Retired Pastor of First Baptist Church of Jacksonville, FL;
Founder of Jerry Vines Ministries in Woodstock, GA

"I believe we will all be better served if we hear Micah out. If the size and nature of the challenge (or attack) should be factored into a reasonable response or defense, Micah may be onto something. That is why I am going to encourage young and old alike to hear what Micah has to say about the cultish side to Calvinism."

George Bryson
Author of *The Dark Side of Calvinism*, Director of Calvary Chapel
Church Planting Mission, Russia

"Theological traditions are the tramway of intellectual transportation and result in spiritual transformation. Theological traditions are mediated through a theologian's own theoretical and ideological assumptions. However, traditions and assumptions are not to be assimilated automatically nor accepted uncritically. This book does neither."

Dr. Fred Chay
Associate Professor of Theological and Biblical Studies Phoenix Seminary
and President of Grace Line Ministries based in Scottsdale, AZ

"Micah Coate's great contribution is in alerting Christians of many ways in which Calvin and his followers resemble cultic corruptions of Biblical truth. Although he does not accuse Calvinism of actually being a cult, by using the word, 'cultish,' he well documents the harmful impact of Calvinism in its resurgence today."

Dr. C. Gordon Olson
Author of *Getting the Gospel Right* and Professor at
Liberty University, Lynchburg, VA

"Pastor Micah Coate has accurately analyzed and described the astoundingly unscriptural doctrines of Calvinist soteriology. Few people understand how far astray Calvin and his followers have gone from the simple biblical truths of salvation by grace alone through faith alone, but this book should open the eyes of both laymen and theologically trained pastors to dangers inherent in allowing Calvinism the least foothold in a church. Coate has taken a different approach in describing the dark side of Calvinism, comparing its tenets to those found in recognized cults. This approach is interesting and makes it easier to see the faulty and unwelcome side of Calvinism."

Dr. Richard S. Beal
Retired Dean of the Graduate College and Professor Emeritus of Zoology at Northern Arizona University; as an ordained Baptist clergyman he teaches adult Bible classes in Prescott, AZ

"Micah Coate has asked the hard questions. Let the Calvinists respond!"

Dr. Alan Streett
Criswell Endowed Chair of Expository Preaching, Criswell College, Dallas, TX

"While some may take exception to the title of this book, its theological criticisms of extreme Calvinism are true and helpful. Micah Coate exposes theological, historical, and cultural facts about Calvinism that are often ignored or hidden. I hope this book is read widely and thoughtfully."

Dr. Charles C. Bing
President, GraceLife Ministries, Burleson, TX

"Micah Coate has done a remarkable job of exposing the underbelly of Calvinism. Everyone who feels himself drawn into the web of logic served up by Five-Point Calvinism should read this book. Every parent who has a child come home from college espousing Reformed theology should give him this book for Christmas. Like so many cults, Calvinism attracts people with the sweet candy on the apple (the glory of God), usually without ever exposing them to the rottenness inside the apple itself (double predestination)."

Dr. Dave Anderson
Professor of Theology and Biblical Languages and President of Grace School of Theology in The Woodlands, TX

"With great skill, submission and sincerity, Pastor Micah Coate has very faithfully brought to light a much-needed word regarding the pitfalls of a deficient and defiant craze with Calvinism. In this outstanding work, Pastor Coate weaves these victorious patterns through his discerning work to show real life in Christ alone, and through none other! When you read this captivating, clear work, it will bring certainty of conviction. This literary work will greatly mandate, motivate, and matriculate you in maturity serving the Master!!!"

Pastor Eddie Atkinson
Calvary Baptist Church, Beverly Hills, FL

CLARITY

- This book is not claiming that those who believe the theology of Calvinism are members of a cult, nor is it claiming that Calvinism in and of itself is a cult. The book should not be viewed as a personal impugning of Calvinists themselves but rather of their doctrine. Lastly, it is not claiming that Calvinists are outside the household of faith as is true with many Christian cult members.

- This book is not a thorough description of Calvinism or of its five main points. For that, read John Calvin's *Institutes of the Christian Religion*, R.C. Sproul's *What is Reformed Theology?* and George L. Bryson's *The Five Points of Calvinism*.

- This book is not a direct refutation of Calvinism. For that, read Jerry Walls and Joseph Dongell's *Why I Am Not a Calvinist*, Laurence M. Vance's *The Other Side of Calvinism*, and Dave Hunt's *What Love Is This?*

- This book is not a comparison of Calvinism to its long-term rival, Arminianism, to which the author does not subscribe.

- This book is not an attempt to reveal the mystery of how man's free will and God's sovereignty work together.

- This book is a simple and basic comparison between the theology of Calvinism as described by its leaders and classic cults as defined by leading Christian cult apologists. It is also a study of the incompatibility of Calvinism and Scripture. Through these comparisons, I hope you might find as I have found: *the drastic need of reforming the reformed theology.*

Disclaimer

The views within this book are the personal thoughts and reflections of the author and are not necessarily representative of the present church at which he serves.

TABLE OF CONTENTS

PREFACE

As time passes while I write this book, I become more and more convinced that its thesis is true. With increasing momentum, the popularity of Calvinism is spreading. In September 2009, *Christianity Today* celebrated Calvin's five hundredth birthday with the theme titled "John Calvin: Comeback Kid," confirming my thought that Calvinism is a misunderstood theology and practice. My normal and everyday interactions with others also prove this to be true. And though I am not facing obstacles in writing this book, I surely am not receiving an overwhelming amount of encouragement. There seem to be many reasons not to write a book that unveils the popular Christian trend of being "reformed" in faith. Not only because the truth and core of Calvinism—and the consequences of believing it—are so crystal clear to me, but also because its message is so disturbingly blurred; nothing less than my passion for truth has propelled this research and work. While you might not agree with everything in this book, I hope it will give you a serious and thoughtful look into the spreading theology of Calvinism.

Many of my close friends and family are advising me to "be careful" while writing this book. Though their counsel stems from a desire to prevent unnecessary division within the body of Christians, it does so at the neglect of carefully examining the claims of Calvinism. Such a book is personal to them, as they know many good people who consider themselves to be Calvinists and who could potentially be hurt by criticism of their doctrine. This is an understandable concern. Few Christians are attracted to the challenge that their core beliefs about God could be inconsistent with what the Bible says. But the desire to avoid conflict should never deter historical, scientific, or biblical scrutiny.

Anyone serious about defending his doctrines and beliefs in God must welcome outside inspection, for it is through these examinations that undefiled truth passes the test, while everything else is done away with. I know many good people who are atheists, Mormons, Buddhists, and everything else in the wide world of religion and philosophy. Yet, if my friend does not believe in God, should I not try and convince him? Should I not question the Mormon who believes that Jesus was the brother of Lucifer? Should I shy away from relaying the words of Jesus to a Buddhist simply to avoid a disagreement? From the Bible's point of view, unity among the multitude of world religions can only be acceptable in God's eyes when the truth separates those in Jesus Christ and those not.

The same can be said concerning the body of Christ. It is God's desire that His Body be united but never at the expense of His truth. Mormons, Jehovah's Witnesses, and Seventh-day Adventists all claim to be in the same body of Christ that evangelical, orthodox Christians claim to be in, but they, in fact, are not.[1]

One could counter that the differences in world religions consist of major, essential doctrines, whereas the difference between the doctrines of Calvinism and those of other Christian denominations is petty and insubstantial. One could also claim that although the core doctrines of orthodox Christianity might be applied as a rule to judge other religions, and more so, debates within Christian denominations, they cannot ultimately "know" all things and thus cannot compare all things to themselves.

---

[1] Further mention of "orthodoxy" will not refer to the Orthodox Church of the Byzantine Empire or the contemporary denominations by that name but to those doctrines that have been generally and traditionally accepted by evangelical Christians.

So, what can be said in my defense? First and most importantly, as we will discover in this book, the philosophy and theology of Calvinism are not, in fact, trivial diversities in belief and interpretation of God's Word but are monumental truth claims that pose a great threat to orthodox Christianity. This is not an argument concerning whether or not women should wear head coverings while they pray or what types of music Christians should listen to, or even what denomination is superior. This issue is much more important, having much graver consequences. Secondly, the core doctrines of Christian orthodoxy do not claim to be the standard of all things and thus should not be the standard in areas of the less important and arguable. Although I have always admired some old defenders of the faith, a wise believer once told me, "Some defenders' pursuits of orthodoxy go too far." He meant that there remain gray areas within the Christian faith that some scholars attempt to paint black or white. It is the gray area that I wish to stay away from. I hope to let the essential doctrines of biblical theology be clearly seen as black or white—leaving the gray open for discussion and honorable debate.

INTRODUCTION

If I had to label myself, I would say that I am a mainstream, Bible-believing, evangelical Christian. I actually do not belong to a Christian denomination. I only say this to make an interesting point that some devotees of Calvinism also label themselves as basically the same. In my experiences with Reformists, I have noticed that more often than not, though they tend to reject the label of "Calvinist," they nonetheless seem to desire to be distinguished from the "non-Calvinist." The Calvinist's desire to distinguish himself from the non-Calvinist makes sense, due to the large doctrinal differences that separate the two, amidst, I admit, the many similarities. I distinguish myself from the Calvinist, as well. I do not want to be considered Calvinist or reformed in theology any more than I want to be considered anything I am not. Such titles and labels are never completely accurate, especially when used as authoritative descriptions of one's Christian identity, but they do give us a basic structure for distinguishing among the variety of doctrines within the Christian faith.

I am a youth pastor at a nondenominational Bible-teaching church. Because of its name, many people associate my church with the well-known charismatic movement of "Vineyard" churches worldwide; yet I am careful to clarify the differences between those churches and mine.[2] Many times a month, people will call and ask for our gathering

---

[2] The Association of Vineyard Churches, or the Vineyard Movement, is a charismatic and evangelical Christian denomination founded by John Wimber in 1974. It has been associated with many charismatic events such as the 1994 Toronto blessing.

times, assuming this church to be a U.S. branch of the Vineyard Community Churches. When I inform the callers who we are, they usually respond by asking me to clarify the differences. I mention that the churches have differences in doctrine, church services, teachings, worship styles, and much more. I do this not to imply that John Wimber's Vineyard Churches are cultish, because they are not, but simply to clarify unique differences. Is this shameful? Is this being too divisive? Not at all. Would a Jehovah's Witness like to be labeled as a Latter-day Saint or attend Mormon services? Would you mind if you were associated as a Catholic or Jehovah's Witness, if you were neither of these? While the theologies of each of these groups includes beliefs in Jesus, sin, and Heaven, each goes by a different name for a reason: they have divergent beliefs. The same is true for evangelicals, nondenominationalists, Baptists, Lutherans, Presbyterians, Methodists, and Calvinists. While the differences that separate these groups and denominations seem inconsequential, they are quite the opposite.

Although some doctrinal beliefs are trivial, some are so significant that they can put one's eternal future at risk. Concerning Calvinistic doctrine, "What is at stake is nothing less than the question of how we are saved from our sins and granted eternal life—a question toward which no believer can rationally be indifferent."[3] In reality, "The doctrines of Calvinism, *if really believed and consistently practiced*, are detrimental to evangelism, personal soul winning, prayer, preaching, and practical Christianity in general."[4]

In light of the fact that some renowned Christians believe that the practicing of Calvinism can be detrimental to the Christian's calling, this book will hopefully reveal the polar differences between Calvinism

---

[3] Jerry L. Walls and Joseph R. Dongell, *Why I Am Not a Calvinist* (Downers Grove, IL: InterVarsity Press, 2004), 18.

[4] Laurence M. Vance, *The Other Side of Calvinism*, rev. ed. (Pensacola, FL: Vance Publications, 2002), x.

and orthodox Christianity and educate the Calvinist, the non-Calvinist, and everyone in the middle.

Recently, my uncle, who learned that I was writing about Calvinism, asked me what I had to say about Calvinism that others have not said yet. I simply replied that I thought I had some original thoughts. I purposely did not mention anything about Calvinism in relation to cults. He then asked what I wanted people to learn from the book. I responded that despite the fact that most Christians do not know what Calvinistic doctrine really is, Calvinism is rapidly spreading throughout Christendom. He agreed and stated that he had a number of friends in the Dutch Reformed Church who, he thought, had no idea of the core of Calvinistic doctrine. He then said, "It's like Mormonism . . . people don't know what they believe." If anyone could say such a thing, my uncle could. He was a Mormon for some time in his earlier years before being shown the truth of God's Word, the truth about what Mormonism teaches, and the discrepancies between the two.

Are there any similarities between Mormonism and Calvinism in regards to their relation to orthodox Christianity? Are there similarities between Jehovah's Witnesses' doctrine and Calvinism? Can similarities be found between their leaders and those of Calvinism? Is it possible to find legitimate connections between the world of cults and Calvinism? Due to the long history of Catholicism, most people in Christendom at large now know the stark differences between the practicing Catholic and the Protestant Christian. The clear and very notable doctrinal stances held by Mormons and Jehovah's Witnesses distinguish them from the orthodox Christian and are quite obvious to those who inquire. However, the same cannot be said of Calvinism. One might assume that this seemingly vagueness of doctrinal differences between the two is because Calvinism is itself orthodox. But, my research reveals otherwise. My purpose in writing this book is not only to show that Calvinism is unorthodox, but that it has a potential of sharing characteristics of a classic Christian cult.

If the possibility that Calvinism reveals cult-like characteristics sounds shocking or offensive, might I humbly say that the whole truth of

Calvinism and/or cults has not yet been addressed. Laurence M. Vance, in his definitive work on Calvinism's dark side, titled *The Other Side of Calvinism*, writes, "There exists a tremendous ignorance of the true nature of Calvinism" due to "its controversial nature."[5] And R. C. Sproul states in *Willing to Believe* that, "We live in an age that abhors controversy, and we are prone to avoid conflict."[6] We find within this "controversial nature" a challenge facing people in search of truth. In a brief conversation and prayer time with pastor and public apologist Cliffe Knechtle[7], I sensed that even he was reluctant to make a committed stance on the issues of Calvinism. In 2004, Calvinist pastor and author Robert Godfrey wrote, "Many Christians have no knowledge about Calvinism," despite the fact that he claims to "continue to see the fruit of Calvinism in various denominations and theologies."[8] In my study of Calvinism, the only people who seem to talk openly about it are those who believe and proclaim it. I admit that on the surface, differences between the Calvinist and non-Calvinist seem trivial. But leading Calvinists assert the great significance of their theology: "The issues involved . . . are indeed grave, for they vitally affect the Christian's concept of God, of sin, and of salvation."[9] Calvinism critics Walls and Dongell seem to agree, stating in their book, *Why I Am Not a Calvinist*:

---

[5] Vance, *The Other Side of Calvinism*, x.

[6] R. C. Sproul, *Willing to Believe: The Controversy over Free Will* (Grand Rapids: Baker Books, 1997), 19.

[7] Cliffe Knechtle's ministry is called "Give Me an Answer—real answers to tough questions about Christianity." It began as an outgrowth of his on campus dialogues about biblical truths within top universities in the United States.

[8] Robert Godfrey, *An Unexpected Journey—Discovering Reformed Christianity*, (Phillipsburg, NJ: P&R Publishing Company, 2004), 9.

[9] David N. Steele, Curtis C. Thomas, and S. Lance Quinn *The Five Points of Calvinism: Defined, Defended, and Documented*, 2nd ed. (Phillipsburg, NJ: P&R Publishing Company, 2004), 13.

To the casual observer, it may appear that there is little if any real difference between the two positions. But agreement at the level of broad claims about sovereignty, love, and freedom masks profound disagreements about how these matters are understood in detail . . . Arminianism and Calvinism represent starkly opposing theological visions, at the heart of which are *profoundly different views of God.*[10] [Italics mine]

Profoundly different views of God. This is what lies at the heart of the matter—not relatively nontheological issues like styles of music or liturgy but the grave position of holding onto *different views of God.* In the pursuit for truth, amid obstacles and rabbit trails, one should always remember that the heart of the matter is indeed different views of God. These are in fact *serious* theological differences that separate evangelical Christians from Mormons, Jehovah's Witnesses, and other cults. The biblical picture, knowledge, and revelation of God are at stake! Even R. C. Sproul, the popular Calvinist pastor, clearly states, "Reformed theology . . . is driven first and foremost by its understanding of the character of God."[11] This general assertion by Calvinists prompted the title to Dave Hunt's book, *What Love Is This? Calvinism's Misrepresentation of God.* Exposure of the biblical inconsistencies within Calvinistic doctrine reveals that Calvin's God differs from the orthodox, biblical God. Chuck Smith, founder of Calvary Chapel states, "The doctrinal distinctive of Reformed Theology cannot be reconciled with what we know about God from His holy word."[12] William MacDonald, author of over eighty books,

---

[10] Walls and Dongell, *Why I Am Not a Calvinist,* 216.

[11] R. C. Sproul, *What Is Reformed Theology? Understanding the Basics* (Grand Rapids: Baker Books, 1997), 20.

[12] George L. Bryson, *The Dark Side of Calvinism: The Calvinist Caste System* (Costa Mesa, CA: The Word for Today, Calvary Chapel Publishing, 2004) Foreword—Chuck Smith.

concludes that Calvinism portrays "God in a totally unscriptural manner."[13] Joseph R. Chambers says, "Calvinism makes our Heavenly Father look like the worst of despots."[14] It is this Calvinistic painting of God that moved Vance to conclude, "Calvinism is therefore, the greatest 'Christian' heresy that has ever plagued the Church."[15]

In April 2006, Campus Crusade for Christ International similarly sounded an alarm in a letter sent out nationwide. The letter read:

> *Dear friend in Christ,*
>
> *This spring, millions of people will be talking about Jesus—but not the Jesus you and I know.*

As I began reading, I had hoped this was a letter addressing the Jesus of Calvinism because "the Jesus you and I know" is not the Jesus of Calvinism. The letter continued:

> *This Jesus never claimed to be God, never resurrected from the dead, was married and had a child, and founded a church based on lies.*
>
> *This is the "Jesus" of The Da Vinci Code. Amazingly, Sony Pictures is marketing this film—with these claims—with the phrase "Seek the Truth."*
>
> *Obviously, this could be viewed as an assault on our faith. But it also opens up a tremendous opportunity to talk about Jesus while He is on the minds of millions. Now is a critical moment to rebut these lies about Jesus and show people that they can seek the truth—and find it—in the true Jesus Christ of the Bible!*[16]

---

[13] Dave Hunt, *What Love Is This? Calvinism's Misrepresentation of God* (Sisters, OR: Loyal Publishing, 2002).

[14] Hunt, *What Love Is This?* Exceptional Endorsements.

[15] Vance, *The Other Side of Calvinism*, x.

[16] *Campus Crusade for Christ International*, general mail.

Campus Crusade shed light on the god of *The Da Vinci Code* just as the cult authority, Walter Martin, shed light on the gods of Mormonism, Christian Science, and many others. Both Mormonism and Christian Science hold heretical beliefs about God, His personality, divinity, love, will, and character. If false dogmas of Jesus claim to have biblical support, they must be rectified. And if indeed the god of Calvinism is so far from the traditional and biblical understanding of God, why are so very few Christians acknowledging its unorthodoxy? Where is the rectification? If the letter from Campus Crusade were addressing the Jesus of Calvinism, it could have been written like this:

> *This spring, millions of people will be talking about Jesus—but not the Jesus you and I know. This Jesus, although supposedly an all-loving God, actually condemns billions to Hell without giving them the free will to believe in His salvific claims. Although the New Testament says that He "desires all mankind to be saved," the Jesus of Calvinism can be found a gross Liar by denying all mankind the liberty of free will.*

> *Obviously, this could be viewed as an assault on our faith. But it also opens up a tremendous opportunity to talk about Jesus while He is on the minds of millions of Calvin followers. Now is a critical moment to rebut these lies about Jesus and show people that they can seek the truth—and find it—in the true Jesus Christ of the Bible.*

The Campus Crusade letter got it right. The organization attempted to expose and correct a heretical view of God, one that is often held by unbelievers. In the aftermath of Dan Brown's *The Da Vinci Code*[17], Campus Crusade's actions were necessary and appropriate. How much more important is it to bring correction to Calvinism's misinterpretation of

---

[17] *The Da Vinci Code* is a 2003 mystery-fiction novel written by author, Dan Brown. It portrays many erroneous beliefs pertaining to the Christian faith as being factual. As of 2009, 80 million copies have been sold.

Scripture and of God? I know many evangelical pastors/teachers who attempt to protect their church against the heresies found in classic Christian cults such as Mormonism, Christian Science, and Jehovah's Witnesses. But what about Calvinism? If Calvinism's depiction of God is likewise marred, then why might this book's thesis seem implausible to some?

As early as the second century, heretical and twisted beliefs were being combated by church fathers and defenders of the faith. The constant assault on the gospel of Christ and the character and divinity of Jesus led the church to define its beliefs by the canonization of the Bible and by the proclamation of the *Apostles' Creed* and the *Nicene Creed*. By the early 1500s, the notion that the Catholic Church leaned more on tradition than on biblical doctrine was recognized by both Christian laymen and Catholic authorities. Martin Luther was the first successful crusader in publicly exposing the contradictions between Catholic and biblical practices. On Luther's heels, John Calvin led the Protestant/Reformed movement, taking with him millions of non-Catholic Christians.

Between Europe's religious reformation and the discovery of America with "freedom of religion" as its hallmark, deviations from the Christian faith grew rampant. Mormonism, Christian Science, and Jehovah's Witnesses were all birthed in a time of American revivalism. As historian George Marsden remarks, "Anti-intellectualism was a feature of American Revivalism."[18] Many Americans who converted to unorthodox and unbiblical sects of the Christian faith did so from a lack of knowledge and reason. The same happened with Calvinism during Europe's Reformation. Yet due to the overwhelming benefits that Protestants found by separating themselves from the Catholic Church, such as hearing the Bible in their own language and the priesthood of all believers, the unsound system of Calvinism and its founder have gone nearly unnoticed and is today considered simply an issue worth overlooking.

---

[18] George Marsden, *Fundamentalism and American Culture* (New York, Oxford, 1980), 186.

CHAPTER ONE

Christian Orthodoxy and Calvinism

Christian Orthodoxy

The task of winnowing Christian doctrine to determine what is orthodox and what is not is no easy challenge. There are many thoughts, opinions, and definitions as to what the rules are when defining doctrinal "wrongs" from "rights." As we examine the claims of Calvinism, we must develop a standard by which it is appraised in order to determine with some accuracy whether or not it measures up to what I call *historical Christian orthodoxy according to sound biblical exposition.*

The first step in separating the orthodox from the unorthodox is determining from where a certain theology stems. Every religion, sect, and cult holds to something—a book or leader—by which it extrapolates directions and guidelines for functioning both corporately and individually. For the orthodox Christian, the Bible alone is the only source of authority for doctrine and worship. Martin Luther's *sola scriptura* means "by Scripture alone," and this concept is the first step in distinguishing between what is orthodox and what is not. "The Reformation serves as a powerful historical reminder that Scripture itself, and not any particular school of theology that lays claim to it, is and must remain the rule of faith for the church."[19]Amazingly, this dogmatic

---

[19] www.apologeticswiki.com/index.php?title=Heresies: A_Survey_I-24k - accessed; January 18, 2010, Internet.

standard was not completely brought to the Catholic Church until the early 1500s. And although the Catholic Church does derive many of its essential doctrines from the Scriptures, it also yields to tradition as a source of authority. The Second Vatican Council states, "Both sacred tradition and Sacred Scripture are to be accepted and venerated with the same sense of loyalty and reverence."[20]

The concept of *sola scriptura*, though relatively simple, is paramount in determining if a religion is orthodox. It quickly separates from orthodoxy those sects of Christianity that hold to any source other than, in place of, or in addition to the Bible. Groups that would, therefore, be excluded from Christian orthodoxy include Roman Catholicism (which also draws doctrine from church tradition and papal infallibility), Mormonism (which draws doctrine from Joseph Smith's *Book of Mormon*), and Christian Science (which draws doctrine from Mary Baker Eddy's *Science and Health*), among many others. Through Martin Luther's sola scriptura principle, all religions that claim biblical orthodoxy while looking to any other source for spiritual direction are found to be unorthodox.

Yet, behind this first line in the sand, which excludes many religious sects from claiming orthodoxy, there lies a vast world of interpretational differences among those that do. Within the spectrum of sola scriptura—Bible-based theologies—we still meet the challenge of weeding out erroneous interpretations and beliefs from those that are biblically consistent. Although differences in interpretation have always tested churches throughout Christendom in the pursuit of reaching the most biblically accurate doctrines, these differences are for the most part marginal and nonessential. Denominations that differ in minor doctrines yet maintain the same essential beliefs about God (theology proper) include Baptists, Methodists, Lutherans, Anglicans, and Presbyterians.

---

[20] http://www.vatican.va/archive/hist. The Second Vatican Council, Dogmatic Constitution on Divine Revelation, II, 9. accessed; January 15, 2010, Internet.

Christian churches that differ in the nonessentials of the faith give rise to denominations, whereas churches that differ in the essentials give rise to entirely different theologies. Because Calvinism differed in the essentials of Catholic Christianity in the sixteenth century, it was and still is referred to as "Reformed Theology," with leading Calvinists proclaiming that its five points form nothing less than "the basic framework of God's plan for saving sinners."[21]

It is important to note that the essential doctrines are those recognized and required for salvation, while the others, although not unimportant, are debatable and secondary in significance. Nearly all Christian denominations agree on the essentials of their faith, thereby allowing the Christian Church to grow without division. Although small degrees of interpretation can still be found within Christianity, the foundation of the faith is solid and unalterable, despite heretical claims throughout the ages.

Those denominations that cling to the authority of the Bible are also united by allegiance to the essential tenets of the faith established in the early church creeds and confessions. Webster's dictionary defines Christian orthodoxy as, "the Christian faith as formulated in the early ecumenical creeds & confessions."[22] In evaluating evangelical orthodoxy, Jeffery K. Haden, writer for the Institute for the Study of American Religion, concludes that:

> Whatever the definition, evangelicals have followed a basic format in their consideration of the non-conventional religions. Each group is examined and judged according to its allegiance to doctrines and practices which deviate from those of orthodox Christian faith. The orthodox Christian tradition is expressed in the

---

[21] Steele, Thomas, and Quinn, *The Five Points of Calvinism*, "Preface to the First Edition," xxi.

[22] *Webster's Third International Dictionary*, 1986 ed. s.v. "Christian Orthodoxy."

ancient creeds of the church (such as the Apostles' and Nicene) and explicated in the writings of the early church fathers who defined and rejected the classic heresies . . . [23]

Because the essentials of the Christian faith are built from the ancient church creeds, we will now take a look at the two most frequently referenced. Both creeds were designed to unite the church under the essentials of Christianity, as well as to defend the faith from pagan and speculative philosophical beliefs.

The Apostles' Creed[24]

1. I believe in God almighty
2. And in Christ Jesus, his only son, our Lord
3. Who was born of the Holy Spirit and the Virgin Mary
4. Who was crucified under Pontius Pilate, and was buried
5. And the third day rose from the dead
6. Who ascended into heaven
7. And sitteth on the right hand of the Father
8. Whence he cometh to judge the living and the dead
9. And in the Holy Ghost
10. The holy church
11. The remission of sins
12. The resurrection of the flesh
13. The life everlasting [25]

---

[23] www.americanreligion.org. Haden, Jeffrey, Institute for the Study of American Religion, accessed; January 26, 2010, Internet.

[24] There are various versions of the creed with different dates. The one above is called the Creed of Marcellus and was given to Julius, the Bishop of Rome, c.340.

[25] Henry Bettenson and Chris Maunder, eds. *Documents of the Christian Faith*, 3rd ed. (New York: Oxford University Press, 1999), 26–27.

The 'Nicene' Creed[26]

We believe in one God the Father All-sovereign, maker of heaven and earth, and of all things visible and invisible;

And in one Lord Jesus Christ, the only-begotten Son of God, Begotten of the Father before all worlds, Light of Light, true God of true God, begotten not made, of one substance with the Father, through whom all things were made; who for us men and for our salvation came down from the heavens, and was made flesh of the Holy Spirit and the Virgin Mary, and became a man, and was crucified for us under Pontius Pilate, and suffered and was buried, and rose again on the third day according to the Scriptures, and ascended into the heavens, and sitteth on the right hand of the Father, and cometh again with glory to judge living and dead, of whose kingdom there shall be no end:

And in the Holy Spirit, the Lord and the Life-giver, that proceedeth from the Father, who with Father and Son, is worshipped together and glorified together, who spake through the prophets:

In one holy Catholic and Apostolic Church:

We acknowledge one baptism unto remission of sins. We look for a resurrection of the dead, and the life of the age to come. [27]

The common standard we must note in both the *Apostles' Creed* and the *Nicene Creed* is that they are both dependent solely upon the authority of the canon or soon-to-be canonized Scriptures (as opposed to personal experience and/or tradition). Today, biblically orthodox churches can be defined as those whose doctrines come solely from the Bible and whose doctrinal essentials agree with the historic church creeds and confessions. We now have a universal standard, which can serve as the criterion to measure the teachings of any other confessing sect.

---

[26] The dates range from c. AD 374 to 381.

[27] "(c) The 'Nicene' Creed," in *Documents*, ed. Bettenson and Maunder, 28, 29.

Calvinism

One of those confessing sects within Christendom is Calvinism, also known as "Reformed Theology" or "Covenant Theology." Although there are slight differences among the three, they are all based squarely on John Calvin's core teachings. *The Westminster Dictionary of Theological Terms* defines Calvinism as the "developed and systematized teachings of John Calvin (1509–1564), which spread throughout Europe and internationally from the 16th century to the present day. It is also called the Reformed tradition. Calvinism embraces both theological beliefs and a way of life." [28]

John Calvin was born in the wake of Martin Luther's (1483–1546) reformation of the Roman Catholic Church. Martin Luther was twenty-six years old when John Calvin was born; when Luther died at the age of sixty-three, Calvin was thirty-seven. In fact, Calvin was a mere eight years old when Martin Luther penned his *Ninety-Five Theses* in 1517. John Calvin was born into a radical time of church history. After he departed from the Catholic Church at a relatively young age and graduated with an education in law, he wrote the first edition of his *Institutes of the Christian Religion*, which was printed in 1536. Calvin was twenty-seven years old that year. In light of the fact that he spent the remainder of his life revising the *Institutes*, Dave Hunt writes that they:

> could not possibly have come from a deep and fully developed evangelical understanding of Scripture. Instead they came from the energetic enthusiasm of a recent law graduate and fervent student of philosophy and religion, a young zealot devoted to Augustine and a newly adopted cause.[29]

---

[28] Donald K. McKim, *Westminster Dictionary of Theological Terms* (Louisville, Kentucky: Westminster John Knox Press, 1996) s.v. "Calvinism."

[29] Hunt, *What Love Is This?*, 39.

Although undergoing many modifications until its final edition in 1559, it is from the *Institutes* that Calvinism draws its doctrine and interpretation of Scripture. Thus, Calvinists are those who adhere to the theological thoughts and dogmas of John Calvin. Calvinism is not a denomination or a philosophical system of theological thoughts; it is a way of life. Sproul dedicates his book *What Is Reformed Theology?* to Jim Seneff, who "*live[d] out* Reformed Theology."[30]

To help early followers understand Calvin's theology, leading Calvinists created an acronym of five letters that captured the essence of what he taught. The acronym is widely known as TULIP, and has been coined "The Five Points" of Calvinism. These famous five points were established by the Synod of Dort in 1618 and remain the pillars of Calvinist theology today. Adherence to and belief in TULIP is the defining mark of a Calvinist. TULIP's five points stand for: **T**otal Depravity, **U**nconditional Election, **L**imited **A**tonement, **I**rresistible **G**race, and **P**erseverance of the Saints.

Before we take a closer look at the five points of TULIP, I have found a very simple test for determining whether one is a true Calvinist or just a Calvinist by association.[31] The question to ask a potential Calvinist is this: "Do you believe that you will be saved or damned <u>for</u> all eternity because you were saved or damned <u>from</u> all eternity?"[32] If the person answers "no," one can assume that he knows little or nothing of the essential elements of Calvinistic doctrine. If he responds "yes," one can conclude that he understands what he believes. Almost everyone whom I have asked this question has responded with a "no." Some of

---

[30] Sproul, *What Is Reformed Theology?* 157. Italics added.

[31] I learned this test from George Bryson's primer on Calvinism, *The Five Points of Calvinism: "Weighed and Found Wanting,"* in the chapter called "An Even Lazier Man's Guide to Understanding Calvinism."

[32] George L. Bryson, *Calvinism, Weighed and Found Wanting*, (Costa Mesa, CA: The Word for Today, 1996, 2002), 50–52 [online]; accessed 27 September 2010; available from http://evangelicalarminians.org/files/Bryson..pdf; Internet.

those people, however, insist they are still Reformed. They justify this claim by calling themselves "four-point Calvinists." We will cover the fallacy of adhering to four-point Calvinism shortly.

This simple question is a fairly accurate method for determining one's stance on Calvinism. It cuts through the sometimes confusing theological terms and gets right to the point by reducing the five points to one. Again: "Do you believe that you will be saved or damned for all eternity because you were saved or damned from all eternity?" Because a true Calvinist believes in preordained eternal salvation or damnation of all individuals, the Calvinist also must believe in something called *reprobation*. Sproul calls reprobation the "flip side of election . . .the dark side."[33] He defines reprobation as "God's decreeing from all eternity that certain unfortunate people are destined for damnation."[34] However, "unfortunate" seems to be the wrong word. It is unfortunate when someone gets a flat tire on the way to work. It is something else when one is eternally punished in Hell for being born in a spiritual state that they could not change, or that God would not change.

If outspoken Calvinist R. C. Sproul wrote of something called the "dark side of election," can Laurence M. Vance's 788-page book titled *The Other Side of Calvinism* be dismissed as mere anti-Calvinism hatred? Or can George Bryson's 398-page book called *The Dark Side of Calvinism* be dismissed by the Calvinist? Because many Calvinists shy away from the "dark" or "other" side of Calvinism (reprobation), George Bryson makes clear that, "You cannot have an unconditional election without an unconditional reprobation any more than you can have one side of a coin without the other also."[35] It is, in fact, Bryson's *The Dark Side of Calvinism* that "focus[es] on his, [Calvin's] distinct

---

[33] R. C. Sproul, *Essential Truths of the Christian Faith* (Wheaton, IL: Tyndale Publishers, Inc., 1992), 165.

[34] Ibid., 166.

[35] Bryson, *The Dark Side of Calvinism*, 374.

doctrines of reprobation and damnation."[36]

Likewise, Norman Geisler opens the spectrum to all Calvinists, stating. ". . . we must not shrink from the necessary inference that there are two sides to predestination," and that "All Calvinists, like it or not, must hold some form of double-predestination—the logic of their position demands it." [37]

To be sure that the doctrines concerning salvation, reprobation, and damnation are essential to the Calvinistic faith, R. C. Sproul writes, like Bryson, "Every coin has a flip side. There is also a flip side to the doctrine of election. Election refers to only one aspect of the broader question of predestination. The other side of the coin is the question of reprobation."[38] He also points out that the "reprobate, who are passed over by God, are ultimately doomed, and their damnation is as certain and sure as the ultimate salvation of the elect."[39] If anyone believes that the differences between orthodox Christianity and Calvinism are petty, please note that Sproul made these statements in his book titled **Essential** *Truths of the Christian Faith* [boldface mine].

Although not a Calvinist, G. K. Chesterton cynically wrote that, "The essence of Calvinism was certainty about salvation."[40] He could have written instead that the essence of Calvinism was certainty about damnation and been just as accurate. But, very few Calvinists are that honest about this essential truth of their theology. To be clear, Calvinism can be summed up in one Calvinist's profession that, "Some people have no

---

[36] Ibid., 22.

[37] Geisler, Norman L., *Chosen but Free*, (Minneapolis: Bethany House Publishers, 2001), 215.

[38] Sproul, *Essential Truths*, 173.

[39] Ibid., 174.

[40] G. K. Chesterton, *Irish Impressions* (New York: John Lane Company, 1919), 204.

chance at all."[41] In describing the Reformation era, *World History of KMLA* recounts that "the essence of Calvinism" is man being unable to "achieve salvation by merit; his fate (salvation or damnation) is predestined."[42] Vance more accurately states that the "essence of Calvinism" is the belief that "God, by a sovereign, eternal decree, has determined before the foundation of the world who shall be saved and who shall be lost."[43] George Bryson agrees, saying, "You will be saved or damned for all eternity because you were saved or damned from all eternity."[44] Because every point in Calvinism denies that mankind has free will, a final way to sum up the five teachings of TULIP is to memorize the title of the second chapter in the second volume of John Calvin's *Institutes of the Christian Religion*: "Man Now Deprived of Freedom of Will and Miserably Enslaved."

It should be noted that the non-Calvinist's definitions of Calvinism are far more accurate than those of the Calvinist. As we have seen, leading Calvinists have been in the practice of revealing only the "good" parts of their doctrine while downplaying the parts that are not. On the other hand, non-Calvinists, without fear or guilt, can rightly relay both the salvific and damning doctrines of Calvinistic theology.

The critical claims of Calvin's theology should be setting in as we begin to understand how the famous five points of Calvinism can be boiled down to one radical point, which can potentially devastate one's biblical knowledge of the character and love of God, His Son Jesus' work on the cross, and the present mission of the Holy Spirit. This is the issue: the character and love of God based on a man's interpretation of the

---

[41] Allen, Jim, "Blessed Hope Ministries" website, 2002 accessed 29 September 2008; available from http://www.Blessedhope.ws /bibl.html, Internet.

[42] World History at KLMA, Era of Reformation part C (1.). accessed 27 September 2008; available from http://www.zum.de/ whkmla/, Internet.

[43] Vance, *The Other Side of Calvinism*, 245.

[44] Bryson, *The Five Points of Calvinism*, 4, 52.

Bible. Calvin's interpretation has serious consequences regarding biblical orthodoxy. George Bryson writes:

> My contention is that Calvinism is not simply a protest or correction of the errors of the Roman Catholic Church, as so many mistakenly believe. Instead, it is a challenge to all Christians everywhere who believe God has a saving love for and saving interest in all of mankind, as expressed in **John 3:16, 1 Timothy 2:4, 2 Peter 3:9**, and elsewhere throughout the pages of Scripture. [45]

Despite Calvinist vaunts of sound hermeneutics, the Calvinistic doctrine reveals otherwise. Although R. C. Sproul claims that Calvinists "are not therefore, to set one part of Scripture against another,"[46] the very heart and soul of the Reformed faith does just that. The one "part of Scripture"—**God's sovereignty** in election—is held so highly that the other "part of Scripture"—**man's free will** in election—is simply buried. Philip Schaff, in his *History of the Christian Church*, accurately writes, "If one important truth is pressed to the exclusion of another truth of equal importance, it becomes an error and loses its hold upon the conscience."[47] Thus, it is not the doctrines of the elect or God's sovereign power that are in error, but those who persist to press them to the exclusion of man's free will and choice.

From the Bible I can believe wholeheartedly that while God is completely sovereign, He has given man a *universal* offer of salvation and the free will to choose it. This seeming contradiction in the

---

[45] Bryson, *The Dark Side of Calvinism*, 25.

[46] Sproul, *What Is Reformed Theology?* 56.

[47] Philip Schaff, *History of the Christian Church, vol. 8, History of the Reformation*, "The Swiss Reformation," [online at Christian Classics Ethereal Library (Dallas, TX: Electronic Bible Society, 2002), 477; accessed 27 September 2010; available from http://www.ccel.org/s/schaff/history/8_toc.htm; Internet.

relationship between man and God can be weakly hypothesized and illustrated, but I believe it through nothing less than faith in God's written and holy Word. Spurgeon writes honestly about balancing the two scriptural truths:

> The system of truth revealed in the Scriptures is not simply one straight line, but two; and no man will ever get a right view of the gospel until he knows how to look at the two lines at once. For instance, I read in one Book of the Bible, "The Spirit and the bride say, Come. And let him that heareth say, Come. And let him that is athirst come. And whosoever will, let him take the water of life freely." Yet I am taught, in another part of the same inspired Word that "it is not of him that willeth, nor of him that runneth, but of God that sheweth mercy." I see, in one place, God in providence presiding over all, and yet I see, and I cannot help seeing, that man acts as he pleases, and that God has left his actions, in a great measure, to his own free-will. Now, if I were to declare that man was so free to act that there was no control of God over his actions, I should be driven very near to atheism; and if, on the other hand, I should declare that God so over-rules all things that man is not free enough to be responsible, I should be driven at once into Antinomianism or fatalism. That God predestines, and yet that man is responsible, are two facts that few can see clearly. They are believed to be inconsistent and contradictory to each other. If, then, I find taught in one part of the Bible that everything is fore-ordained, that is true; and if I find, in another Scripture, that man is responsible for all his actions, that is true; and it is only my folly that leads me to imagine that these two truths can ever contradict each other. I do not believe they can

ever be welded into one upon any earthly anvil, but they certainly shall be one in eternity. They are two lines that are so nearly parallel, that the human mind which pursues them farthest will never discover that they converge, but they do converge, and they will meet somewhere in eternity, close to the throne of God, whence all truth doth spring.[48]

I agree that the question of how God's sovereignty and man's free will work together can hardly find an adequate answer this side of eternity. But the central issue of God's intent to save all or some is black-and-white. One either believes the simple historical message of the Bible through Jesus or the points of John Calvin (all or none). The following poem simply and accurately describes the main point of Calvinism:

> Jesus loves me! This I know
> Predestination tells me so
> Sovereign God loves me so well,
> But He may want you in hell!
>
> Yes, Jesus loves me
> Well, maybe He loves me
> I sure hope He loves me
> I guess I'll never know!
>
> Jesus loves me, I will win!
> Cannot fall away by sin.
> Can't resist His grace, it's true,
> Died for me but not for you.

---

[48] Charles Haddon Spurgeon, "A Defense of Calvinism," The Spurgeon Archive [online]; accessed 15January 2010; available from http://www.spurgeon.org/calvinis.htm; Internet.

Yes, Jesus loves me
Well, maybe He loves me
I sure hope He loves me
I guess I'll never know!

Jesus gives just bread and wine,
Spiritualizing is just fine.
His body's trapped at God's right hand,
Way far off Christ takes His stand.

Yes, Jesus loves me
Well, maybe He loves me
I sure hope He loves me
I guess I'll never know!

Jesus loves me! Where is He?
Up in heaven, can't you see?
Can't be sure where I will go
Jesus' little lamb, or no?

Yes, Jesus loves me
Well, maybe He loves me
I sure hope He loves me
I guess I'll never know!

Never pictures will I see,
No vain images for me!
Tear the paintings off the wall,
Trash them, kick them down the hall.

Yes, Jesus loves me
Well, maybe He loves me
I sure hope He loves me
I guess I'll never know!

Principles that regulate,
All our worship, ain't they great?
Even if we aren't too sure,
Which points really are secure.

Yes, Jesus loves me
Well, maybe He loves me
I sure hope He loves me
I guess I'll never know![49]

This poem illustrates the "flip side of election" better than any Calvinist writings I have read. Yet, despite the astounding differences between TULIP theology and Christian orthodoxy, Calvinism still claims not only to be biblically accurate but to have a ". . . system of pure Biblical belief which stands firmly on the word of God."[50]

Christian Orthodoxy and Calvinism Compared

Some Calvinists have declared:

"It has been correctly said that Calvinism is pure Biblical Christianity in its clearest and purest expression."[51]

"Calvinism is the gospel. Its outstanding doctrines are simply the truth that makes up the gospel."[52]

---

[49] Author unknown: McCain, Paul, (a Lutheran Reverend posted it on his blog) http://cyberbrethren.com/. July 2, 2008. Also see discussion at http://www.aomin.org/aoblog/index.php?itemid=1073; Internet.

[50] W. J. Seaton, *The Five Points of Calvinism* (Edinburgh: The Banner of Truth Trust, 1970), 17–18.

[51] Leonard J. Coppes, *Are the Five Points Enough? The Ten Points of Calvinism* (Denver: Leonard J. Coppes, 1980), 5.

[52] David J. Engelsma, *A Defense of Calvinism as the Gospel* (South Holland, IL: The Evangelism Committee, Protestant Reformed Church, n.d.), 4

As the truth claims of Calvinism are tested by the biblically orthodox standard, we will notice glaring inconsistencies between the two. To do this, we must come back to consider whether or not the claims of Calvinism have any part in the historic roots of biblical orthodoxy.

Is Calvinism's authority from Scripture alone?

1. While Calvinism claims to adhere to the Scripture alone, its allegiance to TULIP makes such a claim ultimately untrue.

Are Calvinism's interpretations of essential doctrines radically different from the traditionally orthodox?

2. As we delve into the pillars of Calvinistic doctrine, we will see that Calvinism's interpretation of fundamental doctrines of salvation greatly diverges from the traditionally orthodox.

Are Calvinism's central doctrines presented in the early creeds and confessions?

3. Calvinism's fundamental doctrines are not mentioned in the historic and essential creeds or confessions of the faith and were evidently not assumed by the early church fathers.

The fact that Christianity's most prominent early church creeds do not mention the core doctrines of Calvinism (predestination, reprobation, limited atonement, etc.) indicates that there was no question or argument about identifying those for whom Christ died. It is of utmost significance to note that the doctrine of Jesus dying for the sins of the world was universally agreed upon by Catholic and non-Catholic Christians far before the time of Calvin or the creation of TULIP doctrine. Indeed, even before the rise of Catholicism, there was no

---

[online]; accessed 27 September 2010; available from
http://www.prca.org/pamphlets/ pamphlet_31.html; Internet.

legitimate debate having to do with the ideas found within Calvinistic doctrine. Otherwise, the Nicene Creed would probably have been more specific in mentioning such important doctrines of salvation as predestination and reprobation. While it is true that Calvinism does not *directly* oppose the essentials of the Apostles' and Nicene Creeds, what it dogmatically assumes about Christ's *limited* atonement and God's will is completely antithetical to the Christian faith.

Although some Christian thinkers such as Augustine (AD 354–430) did, in fact, express thoughts concerning the mystery of God's predestination and man's free will, it was not until Calvin's doctrines that the teaching of predestination was brought to the erroneous conclusion that man has no ability to exercise free will. Reformed Theology/Calvinism did not play a key role in any creed written before the Westminster Confession of Faith (1646). To say that Calvinism is an orthodox theology based upon "the early ecumenical creeds and confessions"[53] may have a hint of truthfulness, but ultimately it is a false assertion.

Norman Geisler has authored or co-authored nearly seventy respected books and hundreds of articles. He has taught at top seminaries throughout the nation and has spoken or debated in nearly thirty countries around the world. In his book, *Chosen but Free: A Balanced View of Divine Election*, first published in 1999, he utterly dismantles the claim that Calvinism's core belief—that man lacks freewill in regards to salvation—has a stake in church history before Calvin himself. He states:

> With the exception of the later writings of St. Augustine . . . virtually all of the great thinkers up to the Reformation affirmed that human beings possess power of contrary free choice, even in a fallen state. None believed that a coerced act is a free act. In short, all would have rejected the extreme

---

[53] *Webster's Third International Dictionary* (1986 ed.), s.v. "Calvinism".

Calvinists' view that God acts irresistibly on the unwilling.[54]

Geisler then quotes twenty examples of early to late church fathers and their confirmations that man can indeed exercise free will. His list includes Justin Martyr (AD 100–165), Ireneus (AD 130–200), Athenagoras of Athens (second century), Theophilus of Antioch (second century), Tatian of Syria (late second century), Bardaisan of Syria (c. 154–222), Clement of Alexandria (c. 150–215), Tertullian (AD 155–225), Novatian of Rome (c. 200–258), Origen (c. 185–254), Methodius (c. 260–311), Archellaus (c. 277), Arnobius of Sicca (c. 253–327), Cyril of Jerusalem (c. 312–386), Gregory of Nyssa (c. 335–395), Jerome (c. 347–420), John Chrysostom (AD 347–407), early Augustine (AD 354–430), Anselm (AD 1033–1109), and Thomas Aquinas (AD 1224–1274).[55]

Yet, Calvinist author, Loraine Boettner, disagrees. In his book, *The Reformed Doctrine of Predestination*, he attempts to show that the doctrines of Calvinism were held before John Calvin or the Westminster Confession of Faith. One should note that only one out of the book's twenty-eight chapters is entitled "Calvinism in History." The first section of this chapter is titled "Before the Reformation," which is only two pages long. Boettner claims that the gospel as intended by Paul is Calvinistic in nature. He accuses the early church fathers of blatantly ignoring Paul's true meaning by "assum[ing] that man had full power to accept or reject the gospel." Boettner further cites that, "Some of their writings contain passages in which the sovereignty of God is recognized; yet along side of those are others which teach the absolute freedom of the human will."[56] Boettner claims that the concept of free will was not taught in the gospel but that the church leaders merely "assumed" its existence. Boettner's argument is

---

[54] Geisler, *Chosen but Free*, 150.

[55] Ibid., 150–59.

[56] Loraine Boettner, *The Reformed Doctrine of Predestination* (Phillipsburg, NJ: P&R Publishing, 1991), 365.

an attempt to say that although the doctrine of predestination "received . . . little attention" both prior to "Augustine's day"[57] and after, the ideas of Calvinism did not begin with Calvin but underlay the gospel. According to Boettner, Paul himself was a "Calvinist," and any other interpretation of man's free will versus predestination in the early church came from the ignorance of the early church fathers.

Boettner's argument is weak. His only hope in demonstrating that true Calvinism existed in some form before John Calvin was making mention of the Christian theologian, Augustine, whom Boettner believed to be "the first true interpreter of Paul."[58] Is Boettner's audience supposed to believe that all apostolic fathers, apologists, and polemicists before Augustine's day had incorrectly interpreted the Scriptures? Boettner's assertion that of all the early church fathers and defenders of the faith, only Augustine was able to interpret correctly the Scriptures should be evidence that Calvinistic doctrine is opposed to the historically orthodox doctrines. Such a statement by Boettner reveals a heavily biased attempt to defend the theology of Calvinism more than biblical and historical truth. Boettner ends his argument by inaccurately linking some forerunners of the Reformation with Calvinistic beliefs:

> Wycliffe was a reformer of the Calvinistic type, proclaiming the absolute sovereignty of God and the foreordination of all things. His system of belief was very similar to that which was later taught by Luther and Calvin. The Waldensians also might be mentioned for they were in a sense "Calvinists" before the Reformation, one of their tenets being that of Predestination.[59]

---

[57] Ibid., 366.

[58] Ibid.

[59] Ibid., 367.

Boettner's argument is so feeble that it fails to stand up to even a mild investigation. A Christian who believes in the absolute sovereignty of God is not necessarily a Calvinist. Yet Boettner writes that some pre-Reformers who believed such were "in a sense Calvinists." In an additional attempt to add substance to his argument, Boettner claims that Martin Luther and John Calvin taught the same doctrine of predestination. But this, too, is simply false. Christian author and apologist Don Matzat sheds light on Boettner's claim:

> In dealing with the issue of election or predestination, Luther understood the impasse at which one arrives by retaining the total depravity of man, universal grace, and God's election of individuals, but he never tried to harmonize the teachings. He feared that he would be forced to make concessions that would violate biblical truth.[60]

As will later be made clear, it was Calvin who, in trying to harmonize the sovereignty of God with the free will of man, fulfilled Luther's fear of "violat[ing] biblical truth." Those acquainted with Martin Luther's teachings will find Boettner's notion that predestination is "in a sense" Calvinist to be inaccurate. Although Luther did believe in predestination, he knew when to stop making logical conclusions that would stray from biblical truth and Christian unity. Luther writes:

> A dispute about predestination should be avoided entirely . . . I forget everything about Christ and God when I come upon these thoughts and actually get to the point to imagining that God is a rogue. We must stay in the word, in which God is revealed to us and salvation is offered, if

---

[60] Don Matzat, "Martin Luther and the Doctrine of Predestination," *Issues, Etc. Journal*, vol. 1, no. 8 (October 1996) [online]; accessed 28 September 2010; available from http://www.issuesetcarchive.org/issues_site/resource/journals/v1n8.htm. Internet.

we believe him. But in thinking about predestination, we forget God. However, in Christ are hid all the treasures (Col. 2:3); outside him all are locked up. Therefore, we should simply refuse to argue about election.[61]

Luther also writes:

Such a disputation is so very displeasing to God that he has instituted Baptism, the spoken Word, and the Lord's Supper to counteract the temptation to engage in it. In these, let us persist and constantly say, I am baptized. I believe in Jesus. I care nothing about the disputation concerning predestination. [62]

To bolster their theological position, many Calvinists assert that because some Reformers and theologians believed in the doctrine of predestination they were aligned with Calvin's interpretation of it. Calvinist and Reformation historian Robert Godfrey does just this in his book, *An Unexpected Journey*. He writes, "We must remember that in the history of the church great theologians from Augustine to Thomas Aquinas to Martin Luther as well as many Reformed theologians have believed in predestination."[63] Godfrey also acknowledges, however, that Calvin and Luther held to differences concerning "sacraments, the church, and the Christian life." More importantly, where "Reformed and Lutherans parted company" was not only on the issue of predestination but on election too. While "Lutheran theology confessed a doctrine of election" it maintained that "it was part of the hidden will of God and not a revealed part of the Christian [life]." [64] Calvin took the doctrine of election many steps further.

---

[61] Martin Luther, cited in *What Luther Says* by Plass, Ewald, "Election."

[62] Luther, Martin, cited by Plass, Ewald, "Election."

[63] Godfrey, 70.

[64] Godfrey, 63.

Boettner's comments ultimately reveal themselves to be unable to support the premise that Calvinist doctrine existed in church history before the time of John Calvin. Calvinism's doctrines within TULIP are not found in any creed or confession of the early church and therefore lie outside the basic definition of Christian orthodoxy. Historical and biblically balanced Christian orthodoxy simply do not align with Calvinism.

Calvinist Craig Brown, in his book *The Five Dilemmas of Calvinism*, fails to answer his own question: "What is the historical basis for Reformed theology?"[65] In nine short pages, Brown mentions Augustine as one who taught the depravity of man and then nonchalantly passes over twelve hundred years of church history to the time of Martin Luther and John Calvin. It is not surprising that neither Boettner nor Brown can find evidence of Calvinism before John Calvin, even in light of Brown's attests to having "spent a lot of time studying church history."[66]

Let us remember that the doctrines of Calvinism were officially created nearly 1,600 years after the rise of Christianity at the Synod of Dort held at Dordrecht in the years 1618 and 1619. Fifty-four years after John Calvin died in Geneva on May 27, 1564, at the age of fifty-five, the Synod of Dort conceived the famous TULIP doctrines. Although (very) few Christians who believed in Calvin-like doctrines wrote on predestination before the 1500s, it was Calvin who solidified any prior notion or beliefs into the theology that is presently called by his name. As time passed, an even more detailed confession of Calvinism was birthed.

Eighty-two years after his death and twenty-eight years after the Synod of Dort, the Anglican Westminster Confession of Faith was written (1646–1647). While the Synod of Dort is famed for establishing the five main points (TULIP), the *Westminster Confession* is a more

---

[65] Craig R. Brown, *The Five Dilemmas of Calvinism* (Orlando: Ligonier Ministries, 2008), 13.

[66] Ibid., 21.

exhaustive look into the tenets of Calvinism. The Westminster Confession of Faith is commonly quoted in the writings of Calvinists as being the "rule of thumb" for Christian orthodoxy. The fact that a majority of Calvinists look to the Westminster Confession instead of the Bible as being the rule of orthodoxy confirms that their doctrine is at odds with the vast majority of historical Christianity.

We should also be aware that the Westminster Confession of Faith "is a Reformed confession of faith, in the Calvinist theological tradition."[67] It was drafted by 121 Puritan Calvinists in order to define the doctrines that sprang from the Reformation. Within it we read of double predestination (reprobation) and "the Puritan doctrine that assurance of salvation is different or separable from saving faith."[68] Though there are some biblically sound doctrines within the *Westminster Confession*, it also contains many ideas that are far more systematic. While this confession remains the standard for defining Calvinistic orthodoxy, it should not have authoritative power for defining Christian orthodoxy.

In conclusion, we must emphasize that the history of Calvinism began at the time of Calvin himself. It is impossible for history to record Calvinism before John Calvin lived. Although Calvinism has played a large part in church history from 1600 to present, its doctrines have played little, if any, part in early church history. Or, as Norman Geisler states, "Plainly, then, belief is our responsibility and is rooted in our ability to respond. This view has overwhelming support by virtually all the great church fathers up to the sixteenth century."[69] He later states, "This means that virtually the whole of the Christian tradition up to the

---

[67] Westminster Confession of Faith, accessed, January 15, 2010. http://en.wikipedia .org/wiki/ > Westminster_ Confession _of Faith, http://www.feedbooks.com/book/4154, Internet.

[68] Westminster Confession of Faith, accessed, January 15, 2010. http://en.wikipedia .org/wiki/ > "Westminster_ Confession _of Faith". Internet.

[69] Geisler, *Chosen but Free*, 35.

Reformation stands against the characteristic views of what we have called extreme Calvinism in this book."[70]

Note: It should be understood that Geisler's view of "extreme Calvinism" is equivalent to what I define as a regular Calvinist who is consistent with the doctrinal beliefs of Calvinism. Geisler is of the opinion that an "extreme Calvinist" is one who believes in limited atonement and, thus, is one who is more Calvinistic than Calvin himself. He states:

> "An extreme Calvinist is defined here as someone who is more Calvinistic than John Calvin (1509–1564), the founder of Calvinism. Since it can be argued that John Calvin did not believe in limited atonement (that Christ died only for the elect), then it would follow that those who do are extreme Calvinists."[71]

> ". . .it seems clear that Calvin was not a Calvinist, at least at one crucial point: limited atonement. This is why we have preferred to call this view extreme Calvinism throughout this book; it goes beyond what Calvin himself taught on the matter."[72]

A Calvin Comeback

In this section, we will begin to explore why Calvinism is making a comeback. We will also try to answer the question as to why fervent and young Christians are specifically being converted to Calvinism and how it seems to appeal to the intellectual.

I was first introduced to Calvinism when I was in high school. It was a Saturday morning. I was at a Carl's Jr. grabbing a bite to eat when a

---

[70] Ibid., 167.

[71] Ibid., 56.

[72] Ibid., 160.

youth pastor approached me to talk about his youth group. They were having a car wash in the parking lot. When I told him of my own faith, hoping to receive some sort of encouragement, I was instead asked sharply if I was a Calvinist. My mind backpedaled. I was confused. I didn't know what a Calvinist was. As I slowly mumbled out that I really didn't know, the man pressed the question harder, and I struggled to make sense of the cartoon images of *Calvin and Hobbes* running through my head. In my defense, all I could say was that we were both Christians—we believed the Bible.

I am not the only one to have had a less than enjoyable introduction to Calvinism. Joshua Harris, the Calvinist and famed young author of *I Kissed Dating Goodbye*, now pastoring at Covenant Life Church in Gaithersburg, Maryland, shares his distasteful first-time encounter with Calvinism:

> I'm sorry to say that they represented the doctrines of grace with a total lack of grace. They were spiteful, cliquish, and arrogant. I didn't even stick around to understand what they were teaching. I took one look at them and knew I didn't want any part of it.[73]

To be honest, my experience with the Calvinist made me feel a bit stupid. I didn't even know what a Calvinist was, let alone the doctrinal stances of Calvinism. On top of that, the young pastor seemed obsessed with making sure that I knew he was a Calvinist and that I was not. If people can "get high" on Jesus, he seemed pretty high on Calvin—and I, like Joshua Harris, didn't want what he had to offer. Yet even with some unpleasant first impressions, Calvinism has now become a popular expression of the Christian faith.

---

[73] Joshua Harris, quoted by Collin Hansen in "Young, Restless, Reformed: Calvinism is Making a Comeback—And Shaking Up the Church," Christianity Today vol. 50, no. 9 (September 2006): 1 [online]; accessed 27 September 2010; available from http://www.christianitytoday.com/ct/2006/ september/42.32.html; Internet.

On February 24, 1947, *Time* magazine featured an article titled "Religion: Calvinist Comeback?"[74] Sixty-four years later, Calvinism is no longer making a comeback, but is on center stage, and many Christians are noticing. On March 12, 2009, *Time* magazine wrote that this new zeal for Calvinism was one of "Ten Ideas Changing the World Right Now."[75] Hunt writes, "With the recent upsurge of Calvinism, a number of leading Calvinists have begun to take a far more aggressive stance in its public promotion."[76] Calvinist and author of, *Letters to a Young Calvinist—An Invitation to the Reformed Tradition*, James Smith writes:

> Who would have guessed that in our postmodern culture something as austere as Calvinism would be both hip and hot? Quite apart from the five-hundredth anniversary of John Calvin's birth in 2009, over the past several years what has been described as the "new Calvinism" has generated increasing interest and devotees.[77]

Walls and Dongell, likewise, note that "Calvinism seems to be staging a remarkable comeback":[78]

> We have observed an intense and growing interest in this issue among Christians of all ages. Not long ago, we took part in a debate on Calvinism hosted by a local church. It

---

[74] Online; accessed 27 September 2010; available from http://www.time.com/ time/magazine/article/0,9171,801853,00.html; Internet.

[75] Online; accessed 15 December 2010; available from http://www.time.com/time/specials/packages/article/0,28804,1884779_1884782_1884760,00.html; Internet.

[76] Hunt, *What Love Is This?* 21.

[77] James K. A. Smith, *Letters to a Young Calvinist—An Invitation to the Reformed Tradition*, (Grand Rapids: Brazos Press, 2010), ix.

[78] Walls and Dongell, *Why I Am Not a Calvinist*, 13–15.

was attended by nearly a thousand people—most of whom looked to be high school, college, or seminary students.[5] Most stayed for the entire three-hour debate, and many remained afterward to continue questioning the participants. . . . For the past several years, however, several influential Baptist leaders, many of them young, have been calling for a revival of Calvinism. They have observed that segments of their denomination, like much of American evangelicalism, have become theologically thin, spiritually superficial, and morally confused.[79]

Christian writer, Paul L. Freeman, has also felt the waves of Calvinism's effects:

There is a system of teaching abroad today which is infecting our fundamental churches, Bible institutes, Christian colleges, and seminaries. It is known as Five-Point Calvinism and originated with John Calvin's interpretation of the Word of God. The fearsome thing about it is its spread into fundamental churches and schools with little opposition. [80]

Vance writes that there has been a "resurgence of Calvinism in the Southern Baptist Convention."[81] This is confirmed by Tom Ascol, the Executive Director of Founders Ministries, whose Reformed Web site notes that at the Southern Baptist Convention (SBC), "Several

---

[79] Ibid. (Footnote 5, "This debate was held at Southland Christian Church in Lexington, Kentucky, on April 12, 2002. The Calvinist representatives in the debate were Thomas R. Schreiner and Bruce A. Ware of Southern Baptist Seminary).

[80] Paul L. Freeman, "What's Wrong with Five -Point Calvinism?" [online]; accessed 18 January 2010; available from http://www.gnbcbible.com/ 5points.htm; Internet.

[81] Vance, *The Other Side of Calvinism*, 25.

speakers felt the need to mention Calvinism or some aspect of the doctrines of grace."[82] It continues:

> "Regardless of the negative attitude that was displayed toward reformed theology, the fact that so many brought it up and felt compelled to speak to it is a good indication that more and more people are considering it. This can only be healthy for the denomination as it will inevitably move us toward more and more theological dialogue."[83]

Although the Christian Reformed Church is a denomination that has only about 300,000 members in 1,000 congregations across the United States and Canada, its theology can be found in nearly every conceivable Christian denomination. In 1999, a survey concluded that there were 746 Reformed denominations worldwide.[84] Within America's thirty-five largest denominations, the Christian Reformed Church is ranked 30th with the Dutch Reformed Church ranking as 25th with 289,000 members. However, these relatively low numbers are not accurate in determining the current growth of Calvinism. In the *Handbook of Denominations in the United States*, Calvinism itself is counted as a denomination. However, Calvinism is not limited to its own "denomination." Its theology has spread and is hidden within many denominations. For instance, in some Baptists churches (mostly Southern Baptists, which ranked the second largest denomination in America next to Catholicism with 33,830,000 members) there has been huge growth in the number of adherents to Calvinistic ideas. One can only wonder at the

---

[82] Tom Ascol, "More Thoughts on the SBC in Greensboro," Founders Ministries Blog, entry posted 15 June 2006; accessed 18 January 2010; available from http://blog.founders.org/2006_06_01_archive.html; Internet.

[83] Ibid.

[84] Wikipedia, [online]; accessed 18 January 2010; available from http://en.wikipedia. org/wiki/, "Reformed_ churches", Internet.

growing numbers of Calvinistic/Reformed followers within all denominations.[85] Reformed organizations all over the world are advancing and promoting the theology of Calvinism, including:

Alliance for Confessing Evangelicals

(ACE)—Formerly Christians United for Reformation (CURE)[86]

Center for Reformed Theology and Apologetics

The Center for Reformed Theology and Apologetics is a nonprofit organization established for the purpose of promoting Reformed Theology and Apologetics on the World Wide Web.[87]

Genevan Institute for Reformed Studies

"The Genevan Institute was founded to provide a center where committed reformed scholars and students can work together to study and do research in areas related to the historic reformed faith and its application to contemporary situations. The Institute will also explore ways to better define, explain, and propagate biblical methods of study and the principles those methods yield, and to encourage a broad and humble submission to the sovereign and merciful God of Scripture." The GIRS is considered "a world-wide ministry." Claiming that in March, 2005, they "had visits from over 103 countries and delivered an average

---

[85] *Handbook of Denominations in the United States*, 12th Edition.

[86] Summary appears on web site; accessed 16 June 2007; available from, http://www.alliancenet.org; Internet.

[87] Summary appears on web site of Woodruff Road Presbyterian Church; accessed 18 January 2010; available from http://www.woodruffroad.com/page. asp?p_key=9563DB4DA236463DA27EDC85D86ED351; Internet. Also see the organization's web site: The Genevan Institute for Reformed Studies [GIRS] at http://www.girs.com/; Internet.

of 888 pages to visitors each day. We provide a ministry of education from God's word which is active 24 hours every day."[88]

Ligonier Ministries

Features the teaching of Dr. R. C. Sproul, Distinguished Visiting Professor of Theology and Apologetics at Knox Theological Seminary in Ft. Lauderdale, Florida. "Ligonier Ministries' purpose is to awaken as many people as possible to the holiness of God by proclaiming, teaching, and defending God's holiness in all its fullness." Many . . . individuals subscribe to Ligonier's *Tabletalk* journal.[89]

Because of the current wave of Calvinistic thought, Christianity is now finding many college-bound students attending Calvinist and Reformed institutes. Walls and Dongell point out Calvinism's effect upon the popular Christian music group, Caedmon's Call, quoting the band's lead singer, Derek Webb, as taking comfort in his apparent inability to choose salvation. In an interview, Webb said:

> We just try to be as true as we can to what we believe to be the Biblical angle of salvation. . . . spiritual death is like a physical corpse—what can a corpse do to help itself rise from the dead? If the language of Genesis, Romans, and Ephesians is true (that the day we ate of the fruit, we died and have to be made alive in Christ) what kind of choice does that give us?[90]

---

[88] GIRS [online]; accessed 16 June 2007; available from http://www.girs.com; Internet.

[89] See web site for Ligonier Ministries: http://www.ligonier.org/; accessed 16 June 2007. The purpose statement appears at http://www.ligonier.org/events/2011-national-conference/schedule/. *Tabletalk* is billed as daily Bible study or a devotional magazine: http://www.ligonier.org/tabletalk; Internet.

[90] "The Call of Caedmon," interview by Dan Ewald, *All Access* (November 2000), cited by Walls and Dongell, *Why I Am Not a Calvinist*, 27.

Not only is Calvinism generally becoming widespread, it is specifically gaining popularity among the young. On June 14, 2006, on *Spero News*, an international information Web site, Reverend Brian Giaquinto titled his article, "Calvinism Debated at Southern Baptist Convention: Reformed Theology Is a Rapidly Growing Movement in the SBC." In the report from the floor of the convention, Giaquinto notes that:

> The breakout session most widely-attended was "Differing Views of Election." Attendance was predicted to be so staggering that it was offered on three separate occasions in the largest ballroom of the hotel where the convention was held. The predictions were accurate. Reformed theology, or Calvinism, is a rapidly growing movement in the SBC, especially among younger pastors.

> Consequently, the fervor of this theological debate has been growing steadily over the past few years.[91]

Collin Hansen's article, "Young, Restless, and Reformed," published in the September 2006 issue of *Christianity Today*, sums up the claim that Calvinism is growing among the new generation of Christians. Collin also claims that Calvinism's growing popularity has a negative effect on the church: "Already, this latest surge of Reformed theology has divided Southern Baptist churches and raised questions about the future of missions." He also notices how this new surge of Calvinism may steal the public spotlight: "While the Emergent 'conversation' gets a lot of press for its appeal to the young, the new Reformed movement may be a larger and more pervasive phenomenon."[92]

---

[91] Online: accessed 14 June 2006; available from http://www.speroforum.com/a/4013/Calvinism-debated-at-Southern-Baptist-Convention; Internet.

[92] Collin Hansen, "Young Restless Reformed," *Christianity Today* vol. 50, no. 9 (September 2006)33 [online]; accessed 27 September 2010; available from http://www.christianitytoday.com/ct/2006/ september/42.32.html; Internet.

On January 9, 2009, the *New York Times* published an article about the controversial and popular evangelical pastor, Mark Driscoll, and his influence among the young:

> With his taste for vintage baseball caps and omnipresence on Facebook and iTunes, Driscoll, who is 38, is on the cutting edge of American pop culture. Yet his message seems radically unfashionable, even un-American: you are not captain of your soul or master of your fate but a depraved worm whose hard work and good deeds will get you nowhere, because God marked you for heaven or condemned you to hell before the beginning of time. Yet a significant number of young people in Seattle — and nationwide — say this is exactly what they want to hear. Calvinism has somehow become cool, and just as startling, this generally bookish creed has fused with a macho ethos. At Mars Hill, members say their favorite movie isn't "Amazing Grace" or "The Chronicles of Narnia" — it's "Fight Club."[93]

More evidence of the spread of Calvinism is cited in the recently published book, *Calvinism in the Las Vegas Airport: Making Connections in Today's World*, by Richard J. Mouw[94] Although its intent is not to defend Calvinistic doctrine, the new book is much needed for Calvinists. The back cover says, "If you are a Calvinist, Richard Mouw 'shows how to live gently and respectfully with others.'"[95] In making Calvinism appeal

---

[93] Molly Worthen, "Who Would Jesus Smack Down?" *The New York Times* 6 January 2009 [online] accessed 28 September 2010]; available from http://www.nytimes. com/2009/01/11/magazine/11punk-t.html; Internet.

[94] Richard Mouw, *Calvinism in the Las Vegas Airport* (Grand Rapids: Zondervan, 2004), back cover.

[95] Ibid.

more to a younger generation, Mouw admits the view that the TULIP doctrines, "when stated bluntly,. . . have a harsh feel about them." He continues to say that "to articulate them with gentleness and respect takes some effort." And he asks himself, "How do I as a TULIP-lover speak gently and respectfully to non-Christians about what I believe?"[96] A great question! When the doctrines of Calvinism are rightly understood, one cannot imagine how a Calvinist might "gently" and "respectfully" explain to an unbeliever that if they were not one of God's elect, their inescapable destiny is to be eternally reserved in the fires of Hell. And again, how would a Calvinist say peacefully that his "God of love" chooses to condemn billions of souls to Hell without the offer or chance to be forgiven and saved? The key question raised for me about the writing of Mouw's book is: Why would a Calvinist want to tell others about what they believe, and why would anyone want to hear it? If God's elect can do nothing to resist entering into His love, mercy, and grace, just as the nonelect can do nothing to enter into it, what are the motives for wanting to share such a message with the world?

The tone of Mouw's book seems to be a sort of diluted Calvinism, which I believe is just another way that this old theology is infiltrating a younger generation. Mouw considers himself to be a "four-point Calvinist"—a position that usually appeals to the masses of those who find trouble with the conclusions of Calvinism but that is, in reality, a myth.

David Cloud of "Way of Life Literature," recently reported on the Calvinistic growth he had observed among "Fundamentalists." He responds to *Christianity Today*'s September 2006 article by saying that:

> It documents the rapid spread of Calvinism in Evangelical circles, and I am seeing the same thing among Fundamentalists. The report cites John Piper, R. C. Sproul, R. Albert Mohler, Louie Giglio, Joshua Harris, J. I. Packer, and the Puritans as among the chief influences

---

[96] Ibid., 14–15.

responsible for the upsurge in Calvinism. Piper's book *Desiring God* has sold more than 275,000 copies. The trend toward the acceptance of Calvinism is evident at leading evangelical seminaries such as Trinity Evangelical Divinity School, Gordon-Conwell Theological Seminary, and Southern Baptist Theological Seminary. Under the direction of Al Mohler, Southern Seminary has become "a Reformed hotbed" and is turning out "a steady flow of young Reformed pastors."[97]

In the September 2009 issue of *Christianity Today* Timothy George writes:

> There is evidence . . . that Calvin is making a comeback. This past year has seen numerous conferences, lectures, and publications evaluating Calvin and his role as one of the most consequential thinkers of the last millennium. A few months ago, *Time* magazine published a story on the top ten forces that are currently changing the world. In addition to expected trends like the increasing role of the Internet and the global financial crisis, the renaissance of Calvinism in America came in as number three on the list. The evangelical blogs are abuzz, and Twitter is atweet, with comments on free will and predestination, original sin and sovereign grace.[98]

George continues, stating that in "a recent survey, some 30 percent of recent graduates from seminaries affiliated with the Southern

---

[97] David, Cloud, "Calvinism On The March Among Evangelicals" Fundamental Baptist Information Service. [online]. Accessed 18 October 2010; http://www.wayoflife.org/files/category-calvinism.html; Internet.

[98] Timothy, "John Calvin: Comeback Kid," *Christianity Today* vol. 53, no. 9 (September 2009): 1 [online]; accessed 28 September 2010; available from http://www.christianitytoday.com/ct/2009/september/14.27.html; Internet.

Baptist Convention, America's largest Protestant denomination, identify themselves as Calvinists."[99]

We end this chapter not by citing an impersonal statistic or by quoting a theological buff but by viewing the personal statements of pastors who confirm the growth of Calvinism. These excerpts were written in response to an article written by David Cloud. Cloud writes:

> In response to an article I posted to the Fundamental Baptist Information Service on September 25, 2006, I got many e-mails from pastors who confirmed my view that Calvinism is growing among fundamental Baptists. Following are a few excerpts from these e-mails:
>
> I would have to say that from what I have seen your concern about Calvinism growing in our circles is not unfounded. The Bible college from which I graduated took a stand against Calvinism (and still does officially), but during some recent turmoil there, they have brought back to head the Bible department a man who just a few years ago was pressured to leave because of his calvinistic beliefs. . . . it is disappointing to see how few preachers even recognize the calvinistic nature of his teachings, or are willing to look into them. He and the school deny any calvinism, but I have seen his class notes, and talked to students in his classes, and the calvinism is plain to see for anyone looking for it.
>
> I see Calvinism as becoming a greater and greater problem as time progresses and I have stated the same to my own church family as well. Not only are many of the independent Baptist churches leaning towards Calvinism,

---

[99] Ibid.

but the one IFCA church in town is also infiltrated by Calvinism. At the very least, much of what I have seen amongst Independent Baptist Churches around here is a softness regarding Calvinism—a refusal to address the false teachings that John Calvin and his followers propagated.

I think that Calvinism has long been in Independent Baptist churches. I left Tennessee Temple Seminary in 1978 because I was discouraged by the Calvinism there. Dr. Wingate was the main culprit but there were others. Dr. Preston Philips was a 5 pointer.

I have also noticed a Calvinistic trend among 'young fundamentalists' who blog a lot online. The typical 'young fundamentalist' blogger, from what I've seen, is one reared in a Hyles type church, who may have even attended H.A.C., and who later rejects the 'hysterical' elements of that kind of fundamentalism, including the shallow soul-winning techniques. By the by, they drop a lot of what they formerly stood for, including the KJV, etc. Once they get past the 'A B C repeat after me' salvation formula, their soteriology often seems to come full swing into the realm of Calvinism. I view it as a matter of backlash against the methods they were trained with. They begin to question the shallow side, and rightly so, but while still in that questioning phase they are ripe for the pickings to false teachers of every sort on the subject. Their natural inclination is to run as far away as they can from the false no-repentance salvation, and they run right past the Biblical position straight into the arms of Calvin. They also tend to get mixed up on exactly what is and what is not properly to be labeled 'Lordship Salvation.' . . . You have to figure for so many that are out there blogging, there must be hundreds that are not. It makes you wonder how pervasive and common it really is, especially among the younger set, and especially among those who leave Hyles-ism behind them.

You are absolutely correct in your assumption that Calvinism is growing among fundamentalism. I've been a fundamentalist all my life, and I was at one point a 5-point Calvinist. I am NOT any longer, but I do believe I can look at this particular subject from an 'inside' view. I knew at my college (Pensacola Christian College) there was (and I believe still is) a large Calvinist 'underground.' In fact, there is at least one Bible faculty member there who is rumored to be one. The most obvious place to look is on the Sharper Iron blog (www.sharperiron.org). You can see it there in the forums. I think this may also be attributed to the growing influence of John MacArthur, John Piper and Mike Dever among fundamentalists.

I believe Calvinism is rapidly spreading through fundamental Baptist circles fueled mainly by the theological inclusivism of many of our Bible Colleges and seminaries.

Simply said, I know of several young graduates who have come out of Bob Jones who have this Calvinistic mentality who did not enter with it.

I hear that Calvinism is being promoted in many fundamental Bible colleges and seminaries. I notice more and more Calvinistic and Banner of Truth books each time I visit the BJU campus bookstore. . . . I think many younger preachers start reading Calvinists and eventually become 'Five-Pointers.'

Most of the 'conservative' pastors in the upstate South Carolina area align themselves with the idea that they are a 2 to 3 point Calvinist. However, when I first became a pastor in the area over 11 years ago the men that were 2 to 3 points are now full 5 point Calvinists and 9 out of 10 are in the purpose driven/Rick Warren influence. It may also be noted that all the Baptist Churches that are dropping the Baptist name and becoming a purpose driven church are pastored by 5 point Calvinists. One even is named Five Point Fellowship.

I have personally witnessed Calvinism on the rise in Fundamental Baptist circles ever since the 1960's. I am from upstate NY, and my family attended a Dutch Reformed church where Calvinism is essential to the belief system which includes both Covenant and Reformed Theology. Both independent Baptist churches in our area were heavily influenced by Calvinistic teachings in the 1970's from BBC Clarks Summit. . . . Here in Illinois, I have engaged a new pastor who adopted Calvinism while a missionary with BWM. . . . He claims to be leading his people into the views of amillenialism, while he is feeding them a weekly diet of calvinistic and covenant theology.

I am deeply concerned with the spread of Calvinism in fundamental schools today. I'm afraid many young preachers are accepting the Calvin Philosophy as an easy way out to avoid the work of soulwinning. Sadly, we have a lot of 'professional pastors' but very few 'soulwinning pastors' today. I know all the theological problems with Calvinism, but how about addressing the practical problems like churches not growing, souls not being saved, drawing people from other churches but seeing very few salvations.

Our churches are in trouble and we had better get back to some old-fashioned evangelism!

A very good friend of mine said to me, 'Bob, what changes have you seen here in American churches since you've been back?' I quickly noted the rise in reformed theology in some of my supporting churches, as well as just talk along those lines that pastors have alluded to or directly spoken in support of getting back to reformed thinking. He said he had not noticed that but would pay more attention. About a month later, he phoned me and said that I was right. He is seeing it more and more, and reviewing some past occasions, he remembers more talk in that area. So, there truly is a trend developing here in this area. [100]

Calvinists: Present and Past

. . . It is Calvinism, accurately understood and fairly represented, that poses the greatest intellectual, emotional, spiritual, theological, and scriptural challenge, even and perhaps especially to those who call themselves Calvinists. [101]

—George Bryson

Now that we can see that Calvinism is gaining popularity, the question we must answer is why. But first, we must make a distinction between those who were *raised* with a Calvinistic background and those who have *converted* to it. We will first look at those young people who are converting to Calvinism and attempt to understand why Calvinism bewitches the fervent and intellectual believer specifically.

---

[100] Cloud, David, Fundamental Baptist Information Service, (Port Huron, MI), http://www.wayoflife.org/, [online] accessed October 18 2006; Internet.

[101] Bryson, *The Dark Side of Calvinism*, 17–18.

Remember Giaquinto's observation that, "Reformed Theology, or Calvinism, is rapidly growing . . . especially among younger pastors."[102] Walls and Dongell explain the phenomenon:

> Part of Calvinism's attraction is that it represents a stark alternative to the superficial, seeker-sensitive theology that predominates in many churches in America. In such churches, God is often reduced to a "cosmic bellhop" whose only concern is to meet whatever needs contemporary people feel in their lives. Doctrine is dismissed as irrelevant, Scripture is used as a self-help manual, and worship is replaced by various forms of entertainment. Well, the God of Calvinism is far from a cosmic bellhop. He is not obliged to do anything for you except send you to hell, and, if he chooses to do so, he is glorified by your damnation. Calvinism is, if anything, serious about doctrine, passionate about the Bible, and zealous for the glory of God. As such, it appears to be the perfect antidote to the trivialities prevalent in the contemporary church."[103]

In her recent (2009) article in *The New York Times*, Molly Worthen reports how and why Calvinism is growing among theologically dissatisfied evangelicals:

> According to Ed Stetzer, the director of LifeWay Research, a Southern Baptist religious polling organization, Mars Hill is "a reaction to the atheological, consumer-driven nature of the modern evangelical machine."

---

[102] Giaquinto, "Calvinism Debated at Southern Baptist Convention."

[103] Walls and Dongell, 17.

Over the past two decades, preachers in places as far-flung as Minneapolis and Washington, D.C., in denominations ranging from Baptist to Pentecostal, are pushing "this new, aggressive, mission-minded Calvinism that really believes Calvinism is a transcript of the Gospel," according to Roger Olson, a professor of theology at Baylor University. They have harnessed the Internet to recruit new believers, especially young people. Any curious seeker can find his way into a world of sermon podcasts and treatises by the Protestant Reformers and English Puritans, whose abstruse writings, though far from best-selling, are enjoying something of a renaissance. New converts stay in touch via blogs and Facebook groups with names like "John Calvin Is My Homeboy" and "Calvinism: The Group That Chooses You."

New Calvinists are still relatively few in number, but that doesn't bother them: being a persecuted minority proves you are among the elect. They are not "the next big thing" but a protest movement, defying an evangelical mainstream that, they believe, has gone soft on sin and has watered down the Gospel into a glorified self-help program. In part, Calvinism appeals because — like Mars Hill's music and Driscoll's frank sermons — the message is raw and disconcerting: seeker insensitive.

They call the preaching "authentic" and "true to life." Traditional evangelical theology falls apart in the face of real tragedy, says the 20-year-old Brett Harris, who runs an evangelical teen blog with his twin brother, Alex. Reducing God to a projection of our own wishes trivializes divine sovereignty and fails to explain how both good and evil have a place in the divine plan.[104]

In teaching a young adult group in a Pentecostal Church in Hawthorne, California, as well as teaching at a Catholic university over in Marina del Rey, James Smith writes:

> This was certainly not the most likely seedbed for Calvinism to take root. And yet these young people, hungry for theological depth and an intellectual tradition, welcomed the Reformed tradition as a breath of fresh air."[105]

In a confession that Calvinism needs to be "kinder" and "gentler," Calvinist pastor James McGuire confirms the words of Walls and Dongell about "trivialities being prevalent in the contemporary church" when he states, "The mood of many in the Reformed camp is anything but kinder and gentler as they wrestle with the seeming mudslide of lukewarm evangelicalism which, they contend, has lost the holiness of God in a man-centered gospel."[106] Likewise, Hansen also writes about the newfound theology and "its exuberant young advocates." He states that they "reject generic evangelicalism and tout the benefits of in-depth biblical doctrine."[107]

I have taken close note of some of the characteristics shared by those who adhere to Calvinism. Generally, they are very serious about their faith. Like the people described by Walls and Dongell, they are "serious about doctrine, passionate about the Bible, and zealous for the

---

[104] Worthen, Molly, "Who Would Jesus Smack Down?"

[105] Smith, James, *Letters to a Young Calvinist*, 126.

[106] James N. McGuire, "A Kinder, Gentler Calvinism," *RTS Reformed Quarterly*, vol. 19, no. 2 (Summer 2000) [online]; accessed 30 September 2010; available from http://rq.rts.edu/summer00/mcguire.html; Internet.

[107] Hansen, "Young, Restless, and Reformed," 33.

glory of God."[108] They are a model to me in having a passion for pursuing God—a passion specifically rooted in their thirst for biblical knowledge. They share a hunger for the truth. George Bryson notes similarly as he explains why he wrote his book against Calvinism: "One reason I go after Calvinism as I do in this book is precisely because those who embrace it (or may be tempted to take a turn down the theologically-Reformed road) are sincere and devout believers."[109]

I am of the opinion that this commonality among converts to Calvinism is more than a mere coincidence. Despite their passion and seemingly discerning minds, I believe that my fellow believers have been hoodwinked by spiritual intellectualism. In their passionate and zealous pursuit of truth, they have abandoned the simple childlike faith in the Good News of Jesus for a complex and systematic theology of a fervent sixteenth-century lawyer. Vance writes:

> The stumbling block for the Calvinist is the simplicity of salvation, so upon rejecting this, a system has to be constructed whereby salvation is made a mysterious, arcane, incomprehensible, decree of God. Thus, the basic error of Calvinism is confounding election and predestination with salvation, which they never are in the Bible, but only in the philosophical speculations and theological implications of Calvinism. [110]

Before a number of my colleagues became Reformed in their theology, they shared yet another characteristic: they were unsettled in what they were being taught and, thus, in what they believed. They wanted truth and apparently did not think they were receiving it—

---

[108] Walls and Dongell, 17.

[109] Bryson, *The Dark Side of Calvinism*, 16.

[110] Vance, *The Other Side of Calvinism*, 35.

whether from their Bible colleges or their churches. Rod Benson, author in *John Mark Ministries*, points out that those who get pulled into cults often have "unfulfilled expectations of traditional churches: an impersonal atmosphere, a perception of irrelevance, inadequate teaching, or irresponsible leadership." When this happens, "cults move in, offering what seems superior."[111]

Norman Geisler and Ron Rhodes agree that:

> The church has failed to doctrinally train its members; it has failed to make a real moral difference in the lives of its members; it has failed to meet people's deepest needs; and it has failed to provide people with a sense of belonging. The failure of the church is wide and deep, and this has made it easy for cults to flourish.[112]

W. Robert Godfrey's book, *An Unexpected Journey: Discovering Reformed Christianity*, further illuminates this point. In nearly every chapter of this book, Godfrey tells of his frustrations with contemporary churches, and how he eventually found both spiritual and intellectual fulfillment through Reformed Theology. The passage below represents an accurate example of Godfrey's criticism of non-Reformed churches:

> In many places today, worship has become a spectacle or entertainment whose focus is more on human performance than on God. The response to such worship is not so much faith and repentance, but amazement, appreciation, and applause. Many contemporary churches have become like ancient Greek theaters where the aim of

---

[111] Rod Benson, "Why Do People Join Religious Cults?"John Mark Ministries [online]; accessed 16 June 2006; available from http://www.jmm.aaa.net.au/articles/9498.htm; Internet.

[112] Norman L. Geisler, and Rhodes Ron, *Correcting the Cults: Expert Responses to Their Scripture Twisting* (Grand Rapids: Baker Books, 1977), 14.

the gathering was catharsis—a heightening of emotions with a healing effect.[113]

Besides being disappointed with the church at large, cult members usually share a love and excitement for their newfound theology. Kristina Jones, an ex-member of the Christian cult "Children of God," explains the typical appeal of a cult: "Their [the cult leader's] message was alive, exciting and unique, totally unlike the normal churches which at that time seemed dead, mediocre and boring."[114] Likewise, two young seminary students in *Christianity Today* echo this idea, claiming to have experienced a new sense of freedom and excitement from Calvinism and admitting that, "Accepting predestination into our lives was the most freeing thing that has ever happened to us spiritually."[115] Walls and Dongell have noticed that people can easily misunderstand the theology of Calvinism by assuming that it is "a liberating doctrine that breathes new life into sterile and legalistic devotional life."[116] As we will understand later, admitting one's allegiance to Reformed Theology in an attempt to reinvigorate one's supposed mundane religion could threaten sound biblical doctrine. The temptation to leave sound doctrine and theology at the expense of something that seems alive, exciting, and unique can at times entice anyone. This is especially true when the temptation comes disguised as being the true orthodox theology of the apostle Paul, Augustine, Calvin, Spurgeon, or Sproul. Oddly, those who fall victim to such a ploy desire to be "serious about doctrine, passionate about the Bible, and zealous for the glory of God."[117]

---

[113] Godfrey, *An Unexpected Journey*, 29.

[114] Kristina Jones, Eyewitness: Why people join cults BBC News, http://news.bbc.co.uk/2/hi/africa/688317.stm, Internet.

[115] Christianity Today, October 23, 2003, p. 44.

[116] Walls and Dongell, *Why I Am Not a Calvinist*, 9.

[117] Walls and Dongell, *Why I Am Not a Calvinist*, 17.

Once an adherent of the Reformed Theology is faithful to hearing the messages and reading the literature of its founding fathers, a deep sense of academic pride will most likely take root. Although this picture does not describe every Calvinist, it is typical. Again, we refer to the ex-cultist, Kristina Jones, who "was deeply impressed by the way they [the cult members] knew the Bible, the Lord, and above all their radical approach to the gospel."[118] Anyone familiar with cults knows that the members are almost always awestruck by their leaders' knowledge and interpretations of God's Word and are united in admiration of their leaders' radical approach to the gospel. If anything, Calvinism has a radical approach to the gospel. Even the mild mannered and nonconfrontational Chuck Smith, Calvary Chapel founder, has referred to Calvinism as "unscriptural and radical."[119] Under Calvinism, salvation is not made available to all people, and in the words of John Calvin, God receives pleasure[120] not only to admit people to Heaven, but also to damn them to Hell. Calvin writes:

> Scripture clearly proves . . . that God by his eternal and immutable counsel determined once for all those whom it was his pleasure one day to admit to salvation, and those whom, on the other hand, it was his pleasure to doom to destruction.[121]

---

[118] Jones, Eyewitness: Why people join cults BBC News, http://news.bbc.co.uk/2/hi/africa/688317.stm, Internet.

[119] Chuck Smith, "Foreword" to *The Dark Side of Calvinism: The Calvinist Caste System*, by George Bryson (Santa Ana, CA: Calvary Chapel, 2004).

[120] The word "pleasure" has various usages and might convey one's "choice or will" as much as it can mean "satisfaction and enjoyment."

[121] John Calvin, Institutes of the Christian Religion, 3.21[online]; accessed 27 January 2010; available from http://www.reformed.org/books/institutes/books/book3/bk3ch21.html; Internet.

According to Calvinism, the word "world" means "select few" and there is no such thing as free will in regard to salvation. As Robert Godfrey has come to believe, "Nowhere in the Bible is the phrase 'free will' to be found. The idea of free will is never used as a factor in the salvation of sinners."[122] In this radical but biblically inaccurate approach to the gospel, cultists are deeply impressed by "how well" their leaders know the Bible.

As noted before, Calvinists tend to be intellectually passionate about the Bible. Calvinist Curt Daniel admits that a common pitfall among his brethren is "Calvinist intellectualism."[123] This is apparent when we know the scholarly credentials of leading Calvinists, not only of today but of history. Unlike average cult leaders, who possess an illegitimate education at best, Calvinists pride themselves in their learning. A self-proclaimed *Kuyperian* (a specific type of Calvinist),[124] Richard Mouw, explains that he grew up in an "anti-intellectualism sort of evangelism." Wanting to abandon this, he found himself attracted to the Synod of Dordt Calvinism, calling it "Heady stuff!" In college, he took a "growing interest in intellectual matters" as he became increasingly disappointed by the teachings of his church. He flirted "with both liberal Protestantism's social gospel teachings and Roman Catholic social thought" but quickly discovered "that neither of those perspectives could satisfy" him.[125]

---

[122] Godfrey, *An Unexpected Journey*, 66.

[123] Daniel Curt, Appendix E: "The Practical Applications of Calvinism," in *The Five Points of Calvinism: Defined, Defended, Documented*, ed. David N. Steele, Curtis C. Thomas, S. Lance Quinn, 194.

[124] Abraham Kuyper (1837–1920) was a politician and theologian. He served as the prime minister of the Netherlands from 1901–1905. He was thought to have started Neo-Calvinism and coined "common grace," a term frequently used in Reformed Theology.

[125] Mouw, *Calvinism in the Las Vegas Airport*, 22, 70, 71.

Calvinism gives the newly recruited a false sense that one's intellect is satisfied. Calvinists take pride in many aspects of their faith, but especially their knowledge of God's Word. Ben Witherington states:

> It must be said from the outset to their eternal credit that scholars who look to Calvin and Luther and their legacy pride themselves on being biblical and giving meticulous attention to the biblical text. This is not a surprise since both Calvin and Luther were formidable exegetes and theologians, and they set examples that many have sought to follow ever since. [126]

Writing of popular pastor, Mark Driscoll and his New Calvinism, Molly Worthen states that although its "teachings do not jibe with Enlightenment ideas about human capacity . . . they have appealed to a wide range of modern intellectuals."[127]

Calvinists desire to stand out among complacent Christians who might not be as educated in biblical studies as they are. At face value, being intellectual about the Bible is not an error in itself. That is, until intellectualism takes over. Dr. Ron Comfort, president and founder of Ambassador Baptist College in Lattimore, North Carolina, has noticed this. He observes the similarities between the ancient heresy of Gnosticism and present day Calvinism. He notes what the *International Standard Bible Encyclopedia* writes about Gnosticism:

> Gnosticism is Christianity perverted by a learning and speculation. The intellectual pride of the Gnostics refined away the gospel into a philosophy making salvation

---

[126] Ben Witherington, III, *The Problems with Evangelical Theology: Testing the Exegetical Foundations of Calvinism, Dispensationalism, and Wesleyanism* (Waco, TX: Baylor University Press, 2005), 4.

[127] Worthen, "Who Would Smack Jesus Down?"

exclusive and not universal. They lived under the conviction that they possessed a mysterious knowledge that could only be understood by them.[128]

Comfort concludes with the question, "Now, I wonder, does that sound like something that is prevalent in our land today?"[129] The parallels between Calvinism and Gnosticism are stunning. By speculative and intellectual assumptions, both Gnosticism and Calvinism deviate from orthodox Christianity in concluding that salvation is exclusive.

The place of intellectualism within Calvinism stems from the roots of its academic fathers. Starting with Augustine (354–430), and continuing to Spurgeon (1834–1892), the appeal to biblical scholasticism has encouraged intellectuals such as A. W. Pink, R. C. Sproul, John Piper, and James White. All these men are serious about their faith, serious about truth, and serious about being Reformed. In fact, A. W. Pink might have been my favorite expositor of the Bible except for his allegiance to Reformed Theology, which I believe has tainted his otherwise sound expository skills. We will see examples later. One reason Robert Godfrey came to Calvinism was because of its "rich history and . . . great intellectual heritage."[130] He also wrote that the "intellectual side of the faith was very important" to him.[131] "My confidence in the intellectual viability and respectability of

---

[128] John Rutherford, "Gnosticism," in *International Standard Bible Encyclopedia* [online]; accessed 20 January 2010; available from http://www.bibletools.org/index.cfm/fuseaction/Def.show/RTD/ISBE/ID/3837/Gnosticism.htm; Internet.

[129] Ron Comfort, "Fruits of Calvinism" [online]; accessed 18 January 2010; available from http://www.ambassadors.edu/resources/Fruits_of_Calvinism.pdf; Internet.

[130] Godfrey, *An Unexpected Journey*, 74.

[131] Ibid., 76.

Calvinism was greatly helped by my acquaintance with the work of Cornelius Van Til."[132]

L. L. Brown Publishing recently boasted its offer to make Calvinism's *Geneva Bible* available "to Christians serious about understanding the Bible."[133] The advertisement implies that anyone who does not have the Reformed version of the Bible cannot be too serious about understanding God's Word.

Although knowing the Bible well can indeed be a sign of spiritual maturity, it is by no means the rule in determining if one's theology is orthodox. Statistics have repeatedly shown that Mormons and Jehovah's Witnesses "know the Bible" and are "better versed" than the average orthodox Christian, which is another distinguishing mark of those who join cults. It makes sense that Calvinism urges an intellectual approach to the Bible, since R. C. Sproul claims sola scriptura as a "foundational stone."[134]

Sola scriptura is translated "by Scripture alone"—meaning that the Bible is the only authoritative source to withdraw doctrine, beliefs, and practices for the Christian. On the surface, it may seem that Calvinism's claim of sola scriptura makes it an orthodox theology. Yet this claim can also be seen in the case of the Catholic Church. While the Catholic Church does not rely on other holy books (apocrypha excluded) it rests on tradition equally or more heavily than on the Scriptures. The same can be said of Mormonism, which holds to doctrines based more on the *Book of Mormon (The Pearl of Great Price and Doctrine and Covenants)* than from the Scriptures. Jehovah's Witnesses have also circumvented the true meaning of sola scriptura by inventing their own translation of the Scriptures (New World Translation). And while Reformed followers boast of biblical

---

[132] Ibid.

[133] L. L. Brown Publishing, *Introduction to the Geneva Bible* [online]; accessed 18 January 2010; available from http://www.reformedreader.org/gbn/en.htm; Internet.

[134] Sproul, *What Is Reformed Theology?* 42.

academia and scholarly study of Scripture, we cannot help but see that Calvinism rests on the works of John Calvin just as much as it does on Scripture. Obviously, Calvinists are held to a high standard when it comes to knowing God's Word, but their doctrinal beliefs are, in fact, incompatible with their claim of sola scriptura. Despite a scholarly approach to God's Word, Calvinists come up short-handed in orthodox biblical doctrine, because their theology is pulled mainly from Calvin's *interpretation* of Scripture. Consider the following question: When one thinks of Calvinism, does he think sola scriptura or of John Calvin's five points?

Within this duet of *"sola calvina"* and sola scriptura, young Calvinists are dancing to a dangerous and unorthodox beat. Calvinism's radical approach to the gospel, along with its historical academia (1600–present), is paving the way for many young and zealous Christians to unknowingly find themselves adhering to a cultish side of Calvinism.

But what about those Calvinists who were born into the faith, and who were therefore not drawn into it by intellectualism or spiritual unrest? Due to Calvin's strong influence throughout the last four centuries, many Christians today claim to be Calvinists merely by religious heritage. Most of them are "complacent" Calvinists and ultimately are unfamiliar with the true meanings and implications of their religious doctrines. Many Christians today would probably consider themselves Calvinists without any knowledge of why. As time passes, the desire to know the why's and what's of their faith seems to fade. This would mean that the current resurgence of Calvinism might be partially buttressed by uninformed adherents, a characteristic shared by many cults. If indeed Calvinism has a cultish side, then we must ask how it has found such a supportive foundation on which to stand. To do this we must recall its origins.

Shortly after Martin Luther had broken from the Catholic Church, Calvin's *Institutes* were written. Many European countries were in the midst of a theological revolution. People who joined the bandwagon of religious separation were grabbing at anything other than the questionably works-based salvation of Catholicism. Many clung to

Calvin's misinterpreted election-based salvation. Despite all the good Calvin might have added to the Reformation, he brought enough wrong to necessitate another one. But how would uneducated laymen know that? How would the population know that the five points of Calvinism represented a Jesus who did not love the world but found "pleasure" in condemning the majority of mankind to Hell for causing them to sin?

Why masses of Protestants in the mid-1500s would call themselves Calvinistic in doctrine is understandable when viewed historically. In light of some abuses such as simony—selling indulgences and burdensome sacraments found within the Roman Catholic Church—Calvin's theology of salvation apart from any sacrament was not merely an appealing option, but was probably welcomed with open arms and hearts. We must remember that four hundred years ago, there was not a galaxy of denominations from which to choose. In general, there were really only two main options: Protestant (which encompassed Lutherans and Calvinists) or Catholic. I realize that if I had lived four hundred years ago, knowing what I know now, I, too, would call myself a Reformist in order to separate myself from the corruption that had sadly crept its way into the Catholic Church. But nearly half a millennium has passed since the Reformation and many claims to orthodoxy have been staked within the Christian faith. While some of these assertions are doctrinally sound, others are not. Yet, the Christian is called to discern the good from the bad, or the biblical from the unbiblical. Not only can time expose imperfect theologies but it can also reveal misguided doctrine. Today, while Calvinism's doctrines are growing in popularity, the Christian must either see the biblical discrepancies or choose to gloss over them. I believe that many older believers today consider themselves Reformed out of a desire to remain faithful to their heritage.

In closing, Calvinism is making a comeback today not only because its claims of representing solid biblical intellectualism appeal to modern youth, but because these claims rest on a four hundred-year history that has been built by many famous Christian intellectuals. The rich history of Calvinism indeed has the power to entice people and hold onto them for generations. As a result, Calvinism is able to remain in the picture despite its unbiblical underbelly.

Calvinism's Permeating Influence

I was discussing the claims of this book with a relative of mine. She is not a Calvinist but has friends who are. She thinks this book's title is absurd and unrealistic. After some of her initial objections were dismantled, she resorted to a plea that its thesis must be wrong because so many historical Christian figures and present-day Christian leaders are considered Calvinists. If I contradict what *they* say, either I am wrong or *they* are wrong.

In trying to understand the present surge of Calvinism, we must know some of its history, its evolution, and its followers. We must know that the current popularity of Calvinism is not random but has been nurtured by influential Christian leaders. Because of this history, it is easy to see why today's Calvinist giants like John Piper, R. C. Sproul, and James White are bold in their proclamation of Calvinism as being true biblical gospel. If Calvinism is indeed an unorthodox theology, how can some of today's leading church leaders remain outspoken about its veracity? These are educated, intelligent, and godly men placed in the Christian spotlight. As the problem may not lie within individual character, it could lie with the collective sources of misinterpreted doctrine.

Laurence M. Vance lists some of the more well-known Calvinists who have helped prepare the way for the present-day Calvinistic movement: Herman Bavinck (1854–1921); G. C. Berkouwer (1903–1996); Louis Berkhof (1873–1957); J. Oliver Buswell (1895–1977); Gordon H. Clark (1902–1985); William Cunningham (1805–1861); Robert L. Dabney (1820–1898); John Dick (1764–1833); Jonathan Edwards (1703–1758); Archibald A. Hodge (1823–1886); and Charles Hodge (1797–1878), to name a few.[135] Vance deduces:

---

[135] Vance, *The Other Side of Calvinism*, 33.

> Because [historical Calvinist leaders] are for the most part
> conservative and orthodox, Calvinism has been equated
> with orthodoxy and therefore established a foothold on
> theology. And because they have written a majority of the
> theology books, it is very difficult to find a work on
> systematic theology that is not Calvinistic.[136]

In fact, a leading voice in Calvinism today is Wayne Grudem. His
Systematic Theology, first printed in 1994, continues to be a best seller with
over 250,000 copies in print as of 2000. We can guess that these books
are filling seminary bookshelves—seminaries like Al Mohler's. Just in
October 2010, *Christianity Today* contributor, Molly Worthen wrote, *"The
Reformer—How Al Mohler transformed a seminary, helped change a denomination,
and challenges a secular culture."* Mohler serves as the current president of the
Southern Baptist Theological Seminary in Louisville, one of the Southern
Baptist Convention's leading seminaries. Worthen writes that upon
Mohler's arrival in the SBC, "his intention to steer Southern seminary in
a Reformed direction became clear."[137]

> "It was like John Grisham's *The Firm*," says Carey
> Newman, director of Baylor University Press, who joined
> Southern's faculty in 1993 but left after five tense years.
> "Al recruited young lieutenants, students who were spies
> in the classes who would report back to him what was
> being said in every classroom."[138]

---

[136] Ibid.

[137] Molly Worthen, "The Reformer—How Al Mohler transformed a
seminary, helped change a denomination, and challenges a secular culture."
Christianity Today 1 October 2010 [online]. Accessed 15 December 2010].
Available from http://www.christianitytoday.com/ct/2010/october/3.18.html.

[138] Ibid.

Worthen continues to record that the SBC was systematically penetrated with Calvinism:

> Through a combination of forced resignations and "golden parachute" retirement packages, Mohler purged the School of Theology, closed the School of Social Work, and replaced moderates with inerrantist faculty who agreed with him on abortion, homosexuality, women's ordination, and his brand of Reformed theology. (As proof of the seminary's current "diversity," some faculty protest that they are only four-point Calvinists.)[139]

It is very important to know, and worth repeating Vance's words that this new Calvinistic takeover occurs in part because "Calvinism has been equated with orthodoxy and [has] therefore established a foothold on theology."[140] This should lead us to ask: Were the Christian leaders listed above five-, four-, or three-point Calvinists? Were they actually promoting Calvinistic doctrine or did they simply consider themselves Calvinistic rather than Catholic? Was being Reformed forefront in their minds, or was it not really an important matter? Was promoting Calvinism more of a priority than promoting Jesus? Regardless of their personal convictions or to what extent they believed in Calvin's five points, they were regarded as Calvinists. We must understand this when following the history of Calvinism.

It is not always easy to know who is a Calvinist and who is not since there is no outward mark to distinguish them. A Calvinist is not necessarily a member of a certain church or affiliated with a certain denomination. R. C. Sproul assures his readers that Reformed Theology is much more than "a comprehensive exposition of each and every article

---

[139] Ibid.

[140] Vance, *The Other Side of Calvinism*, 33.

of Reformation doctrine."[141] The theology of Calvinism is "all inclusive"—meaning that any Christian from any denomination can claim to be Calvinistic in belief. Vance identifies the effect that this "all-inclusive" theology of God has had on the last four hundred years of church history by noting that,

> the Presbyterian and Reformed groups are inherently Calvinistic. The differences in doctrine between Presbyterian and Reformed individuals and churches are rather insignificant, especially in relation to the doctrines of Calvinism. Therefore, their theologians are without exception all Calvinistic.

Among the theologians described, Vance lists, along with the others previously noted : Herman Hoeksema (1886–1965); Abraham Kuyper (1837–1920); J. Gresham Machen (1881–1937); John Murray (1898–1975); William G. T. Shedd (1820–1894); Henry B. Smith (1815–1877); James H, Thornwell (1812–1862); Francis Turretin (1623–1687); Cornelius Van Til (1895–1987); Geerhardus Vos (1862–1947); and Benjamin B. Warfield (1851–1921).[142]

Vance concludes that although Calvinistic theologians belonging to different denominations share their disagreements on a number of less important aspects of faith, it is "nevertheless, their Calvinism [that] is the one common bond which unites them."[143] The "Reformation Theology" Web site, http:// www. reformation theology.com[144] agrees that despite

---

[141] Sproul, *What Is Reformed Theology?* 9.

[142] Vance, *The Other Side of Calvinism*, 33.

[143] Ibid., 34.

[144] See, www.reformationtheology.com, [online] accessed on 21 December 2010; Internet.

the trivial differences in denominations, it is the essential Calvinist theology that unites. It states:

> We are a community of confessing believers from various backgrounds with solidarity in Reformed Theology. Our contributors include a wide diversity of traditions: Baptists, Presbyterians, Charismatic, Non-denominational and Independent. Even though we may have differences on non-essential matters, we are all committed to the Biblical and Christ-exalting truths of the Reformation such as the five solas, the doctrines of grace, monergistic regeneration, and the redemptive historical approach to interpreting the Scriptures.[145]

Vance continues to help explain the all-inclusive theology of Calvinism:

> All Calvinists, whether they be Presbyterian or Reformed, Primitive Baptist or Sovereign Grace Baptist; all Calvinists, whether they be premillennial or amillennial, dispensational or covenant theologist; all Calvinists, whether they go by the name or not; all Calvinists have one thing in common: God, by a sovereign, eternal decree, has determined before the foundation of the world who shall be saved and who shall be lost. To obscure the real issue, a vocabulary has been invented to confuse and confound the Christian. The arguments about supralapsarianism and infralapsarianism, total depravity and total inability, reprobation and preterition,

---

[145] Timmy Brister, http://provocationsandpantings.blogspot.com/2005/10/random-stuff-for-week-of-1021-1027.html; monday, october 24, 2005, accessed on 21 December 2010; Internet.

synergism and monergism, free will and free agency, common grace and special grace, general calling and effectual calling, perseverance and preservation, and the sovereignty of God are all immaterial. [146]

Calvinism has crept into every denomination and almost every school of theological thought for the last four hundred years, having established a powerful grip on theology. We will now take a look at its five major points and their boiled-down essential meanings.

---

[146] Vance, *The Other Side of Calvinism*, 35.

CHAPTER TWO

A Tulip Explained and Uprooted in Laymen's Terms

> If you really understand Reformed Theology, we should just sit around shaking our heads going, "It's unbelievable. Why would God choose any of us?" You are so amazed, you're not picking a fight with anyone, you're just crying tears of amazement that should lead to a heart for lost people, that God does indeed save, when He doesn't have to save anybody.[147]
>
> —Joshua Harris

Joshua Harris does not give a thoughtful or accurate definition of Calvinism. But with little doubt, this seemingly humble explanation, typical of Calvinists, is often nothing more than a façade that understandably sidesteps the reality of the Calvinists' portrayal of God electing people to Hell. Indeed, the Calvinistic doctrine of reprobation is a crucial part of Calvinism that cannot be dismissed by anyone who, as Joshua Harris puts it, desires to "really understand Reformed Theology."

Because TULIP is the hallmark of Reformed Theology, hopefully we can develop a better understanding of this doctrine than what Mr. Harris offers. This will be a very concise and logical interpretation of the five points of Calvinism, or as Sproul writes, (possibly attempting to make Calvinism seem less Calvinistic) "the Five Points of Reformed Theology."[148]

---

[147] Quoted by Collin Hansen in "Young, Restless, Reformed."

[148] Sproul, *What Is Reformed Theology?* 115.

Exhaustive books have been written by both Calvinists and non-Calvinists about the five points. One could go on and on about the biblical and philosophical details that can be argued regarding each point. For a comprehensive look at the tenets of Calvinism, read John Calvin's *Institutes of the Christian Religion*, R. C. Sproul's *What Is Reformed Theology?* and George L. Bryson's *The Five Points of Calvinism*. In this book, we will cut to the heart of each point, looking at both its absolute meaning and what it means in light of each of the other points.

When I was young in the faith, my first consideration of the five points caused little trouble for me. I considered them to be generally accurate. Not until years later, when I took the time to read them with care did I began to see how all the points were built upon each other, asserting the same principle that mankind has not, cannot, and will not practice free will in regard to salvation. We must remember that the essential meaning of the five points—individually and as a whole—portrays a God who elects people to both Heaven and Hell while being the author of both saving faith and condemning sin.

The five points of Calvinism cling to one another in an ongoing circle. If one of the links is proven false, not only is the circle broken but *all* points are dismantled. To avoid being repetitive in uprooting Calvin's TULIP, we will address the essential truth that each point denies: the truth that God has given all of mankind a free will and that Christ's atonement was for all because He desires all to be saved. We must note, however, that even within deception, there almost always exists some sort of truth. Each point of Calvinism is rooted in biblical truth. In *The Other Side of Calvinism*, Vance shows this to be true:

> The depravity of man is a biblical doctrine, but as we
> have seen, the Calvinistic doctrine of Total Depravity is
> not. Likewise, although the doctrine of election is also
> scriptural, the Calvinistic doctrine of Unconditional
> Election is certainly not. The third point of Calvinism,
> Limited Atonement, is so controversial and difficult to

defend that many Calvinists reject it. Although salvation is unquestionably by grace, the Calvinistic doctrine of Irresistible Grace, as proved in the previous chapter, teaches salvation by another Gospel.[149]

As should any student of God's Word, we must rightly distinguish between the divine and the carnal to expose and hopefully eradicate theological errors—whether New Age mysticism, Scientology, Mormonism, or Catholic dogma, the essential doctrines of Christianity must be scripturally examined and logically judged. If the theology of Calvinism is found to be biblically flawed, that should at least be acknowledged by anyone claiming to be a Christian. As we look at each point of Calvinism, we must not forget that although all five points are based upon scriptural truths, they are taken to radical extremes, which end up being more systematic than biblical and more cultish than orthodox.

Tulip

Total Depravity Explained

The "T" in TULIP stands for *Total Depravity*. The Calvinist's concept of Total Depravity is not the basic doctrine that man is born in a total and corrupt state of sin, upon which all Christians fundamentally agree. Orthodox Christianity has always maintained the biblical truth that "nothing good dwells . . . in [the] flesh."[150] Orthodox Christianity asserts that mankind is fallen and that we are all in serious need of salvation from the effects and judgment of sin (both the state we were born in and the sin we ourselves commit). That man apart from God is corrupt and in need of divine help is a biblical truth backed by a multitude of verses. Mankind has no hope, except for the work of Jesus, to be delivered from sin and cannot perform enough good works to please God, except

---

[149] Vance, *The Other Side of Calvinism*, 187.

[150] Romans 7:18, NKJV.

through His Son Jesus Christ. But this is not what Calvinism means by the definition of Total Depravity.

As Calvinism's terminology can be ambiguous, the term "Total Depravity" is misleading. When Calvinists speak of Total Depravity, they are in fact referring to something completely different—something called *Total Inability*. Total Inability is a doctrine invented by Calvinists meaning that man is *unable* to believe the gospel. Though Calvinists claim that Total Inability and Total Depravity are not the same thing, they usually use the two terms synonymously. Vance points this out, writing that the Calvinist doctrine of Total Depravity is "unpretentiously stated by Calvinists as referring to man's *inability* to freely believe on Jesus Christ for salvation."[151] It is paramount then, to know that when Calvinists speak of Total Depravity, they are almost always referring to their particular doctrine of Total Inability.

Concerning the depravity of man, John Calvin wrote:

> . . . our nature is not only utterly devoid of goodness, but so prolific in all kinds of evil, that it can never be idle. Those who term it concupiscence use a word not very inappropriate, provided it were added (this, however, many will by no means concede) that everything which is in man, from the intellect to the will, from the soul even to the flesh, is defiled and pervaded with this concupiscence; or, to express it more briefly, that the whole man is in himself nothing else than concupiscence.[152]

The Canons of Dort likewise states:

> . . . all people are conceived in sin and are born children

---

[151] Vance, *The Other Side of Calvinism*, 187.

[152] Calvin, *Institutes*, 2.1.8 [online]; accessed 28 January 2010; available from http://www.reformed.org/master/index.html?mainframe=/books/institutes/books/indxb k3.html; Internet.

of wrath, unfit for any saving good, inclined to evil, dead in their sins, and slaves to sin; without the grace of the regenerating Holy Spirit they are neither willing nor able to return to God, to reform their distorted nature, or even to dispose themselves to such reform.[153]

The Westminster Confession states:

Man, by his fall into a state of sin, has wholly lost all ability of will to any spiritual good accompanying salvation: so as, a natural man, being altogether averse from that good, and dead in sin, is not able, by his own strength, to convert himself, or to prepare himself thereunto.[154]

A. W. Pink puts it bluntly, ". . . the sinner, of himself, cannot repent and believe." [155]

A number of classic verses used by Calvinists to support the doctrine of Total Depravity are as follows:

Genesis 6:5: "Then the LORD saw that the wickedness of man was great in the earth, and that every intent of the thoughts of his heart was only evil continually."

Psalms 51:5: "Behold, I was brought forth in iniquity, and in sin my mother conceived me."

---

[153] "Canons of Dort, III & IV, Article 3" [online]; accessed 20 January 2010; available from http://www. reformed. org/documents/wcf_with_proofs/; Internet.

[154] "Westminster Confession of Faith," 7.3 [online]; accessed 20 January 2010; available from http://www. reformed.org/documents/wcf_with_proofs/; Internet.

[155] A. W. Pink, *The Sovereignty of God*, [online]; accessed 20 January 2010; available from http://www.reformed.org/books/pink/index.html?mainframe=/books/pink/pink_sov_08.html; Internet.

Ecclesiastes 7:20: "For there is not a just man on earth who does good and does not sin."

Ecclesiastes 9:3: "This is an evil in all that is done under the sun: that one thing happens to all. Truly the hearts of the sons of men are full of evil; madness is in their hearts while they live, and after that they go to the dead."

Jeremiah 17:9: "The heart is deceitful above all things, and desperately wicked; who can know it?"

Jeremiah 13:23: "Can the Ethiopian change his skin or the leopard its spots? Then may you also do good who are accustomed to do evil."

Mark 7:21–23: "For from within, out of the heart of men, proceed evil thoughts, adulteries, fornications, murders, thefts, covetousness, wickedness, deceit, lewdness, an evil eye, blasphemy, pride, foolishness. All these evil things come from within and defile a man."

John 3:19: "And this is the condemnation, that the light has come into the world, and men loved darkness rather than light, because their deeds were evil."

John 8:34: "Jesus answered them, 'Most assuredly, I say to you, whoever commits sin is a slave of sin.'"

Romans 3:10–11: "As it is written: 'There is none righteous, no, not one; There is none who understands; There is none who seeks after God.'"

Romans 8:7–8: "Because the carnal mind is enmity against God; for it is not subject to the law of God, nor indeed can be. So then, those who are in the flesh cannot please God."

1 Corinthians 2:14: "But the natural man does not receive the things of the Spirit of God, for they are foolishness to him; nor can he know them, because they are spiritually discerned."

Ephesians 2:1–3: "And you He made alive, who were dead in trespasses and sins, in which you once walked according to the course of this world, according to the prince of the power of the air, the spirit who now works in the sons of disobedience, among whom also we all once conducted ourselves in the lusts of our flesh, fulfilling the desires of the flesh and of the mind, and were by nature children of wrath, just as the others."

Titus 3:3: "For we ourselves were also once foolish, disobedient, deceived, serving various lusts and pleasures, living in malice and envy, hateful and hating one another."

After reading these verses at first consideration, a Christian (especially a Calvinist) may be tempted to think that a rejection of Total Depravity would deny the biblical truth that all men are confined under sin. But this is not necessarily the case. When Vance concluded his chapter on Total Depravity in *The Other Side of Calvinism*, he accurately wrote, "A denial of the Calvinistic doctrine of Total Depravity does not entail in any way a rejection or toning down of the Biblical doctrine of man's fall into sin and subsequent depravity."[156] Yet, the Calvinist would have you believe otherwise. It must be clearly stated that this author contends (as any non-Calvinist) that although all men are exceedingly sinful, the world is pursued and convicted by God and is indeed able to respond to His offer of salvation.

In dealing with Total Depravity and/or Total Inability, we must also know what the convicting of the Holy Spirit is and what it is not. Scripture is clear that the Holy Spirit convicts the world of sin (**John 16:8**). If it were not for the convicting work of the Holy Spirit, how then would a sinner be convicted of something called sin and his need for God? Just as Calvinist theology equates Total Depravity with Total Inability, so it also equates conviction with regeneration. A

---

[156] Vance, *The Other Side of Calvinism*, 239.

Calvinist believes that God does not merely convict a sinner in order to believe, but that God must save the sinner in order to believe. As we have seen, Calvinist theology teaches that a sinner must be spiritually regenerated in order to be convicted of sin. To be spiritually regenerated means to be born again, made alive, to be saved. Calvinist theology teaches that salvation or regeneration precedes faith. John Piper states:

> We believe that the new birth is a miraculous creation of God that enables a formerly "dead" person to receive Christ and so be saved. We do not think that faith precedes . . . the new birth. Faith is the evidence that God has begotten us anew. [157]

By this doctrine, God alone elects those for salvation and denies any free will to mankind.

Total Depravity means that God gives His chosen elect the faith in order to be regenerated. Total Depravity (Total Inability) boils down to the unorthodox belief that God only chooses to save some, or, in other words, that God desires the vast majority of mankind to suffer in Hell. Remember this in thinking of the "T" in TULIP. The Bible teaches that regeneration is the result of faith. Calvinism teaches the opposite— that faith is a result of regeneration.

The doctrine of Total Depravity gives the illusion that man is unable to believe because he has a sinful nature. Calvinists believe that none of mankind, neither the damned nor the elect, can practice free will in regard to salvation. Only those to whom God grants faith are saved and will consequently believe. Calvinism has taken the orthodox belief of man's sinfulness and need for God to an unorthodox conclusion that He only desires some to be saved. The importance of Total Depravity in dismantling TULIP cannot be underestimated. As

---

[157] John Piper, "Irresistible Grace" [online]; accessed 20 January 2010; available from http://www.monergism.com/thethreshold/articles/piper/ irresistible.html; Internet.

it is the first of the points, it is the foundation upon which all the others are built. The rest of the doctrines can only be understood in the light of Total Depravity.

Tulip

Total Depravity Uprooted

The biblical truth in which Total Depravity is rooted is that man is born a sinner, is totally depraved regarding the things of God, and is totally unable to save himself. Indeed, we can agree with the Calvinist that, "There is none that seek after God."[158] Yet, Total Depravity according to Calvinism means that one must be regenerated by God before he can place saving faith in Jesus. Again, the Calvinist believes that because man is totally depraved (TRUE), he lacks the good sense or capability to place faith in Christ apart from God's regenerating work (FALSE). Is this a contradiction? If man is depraved, as the Bible teaches, how can he become saved apart from God's intervention? Indeed, the Bible teaches that God must intervene in the lives of the depraved. God has pursued the world. The world has not pursued God. "While we were still sinners Christ died for us" (**Romans 5:8**). Jesus taught that it is the work of the Holy Spirit that will convict men to turn to God: "When He [the Holy Spirit] comes He will convict the world of sin and of righteousness and of judgment" (**John 16:8**). Although the Lord reaches out to us in many different ways (through His Word, preaching, teaching, evangelizing), all human efforts ultimately rely on the power of God to see the fruit of salvation.

Orthodox and historical Christianity has always maintained that once this act of conviction happens by the grace of God, the sinner is responsible either to believe or not. That is why Paul says in **Romans 1:14–16**:

---

[158] Romans 3:10–11, NKJV.

I am a debtor both to Greeks and to barbarians, both to wise and to unwise. So, as much as is in me, I am ready to preach the gospel to you who are in Rome also. For I am not ashamed of the gospel of Christ, for it is the power of God to salvation for everyone who believes, for the Jew first and also for the Greek.

Yet, if Paul believed in TULIP theology, why would he "be under obligation" to anyone to do anything if it is God alone who chooses those for salvation apart from anything anyone does? Historical orthodox Christianity by sound biblical exposition has always taught that once faith (by common sense and the conviction of the Holy Spirit) is placed in Christ as Lord God, regeneration leading to salvation can then take place. As Dave Hunt remarks, "The Bible always presents faith as the condition of salvation."[159]

Through the doctrine of Total Depravity, the Calvinist erroneously believes that God's intervention not only convicts the depraved but actually *regenerates* the depraved. Therein lies the heretical difference. When God convicts someone of sin, as taught in John 16, that person has the free will either to respond to the conviction or deny it. If this is not so, the Calvinist must answer many questions. One example is from **John 11**. Why, after proclaiming, "He who believes in Me, though he may die, he shall live," and, "whoever lives and believes in Me shall never die," did Jesus ask Mary, "Do you believe this?" How absurd it would be for Jesus to tell Mary the knowledge of everlasting life and then ask for her answer if, according to Calvinism, she had absolutely no choice to respond?

To put it in other words, the Bible teaches that God *convicts all men* for the purpose of *saving all*, whereas Calvinists teach that God only enables a few to believe for the purpose of saving only a few. The underlying meaning of Total Depravity is opposed to **1 Timothy 2:3–6**, which reads:

---

[159] Hunt, *What Love Is This?*, 99.

For this is good and acceptable in the sight of God our Savior, who desires all men to be saved and to come to the knowledge of the truth. For there is one God and one Mediator between God and men, the man Christ Jesus, who gave himself a ransom for all.

Calvinistic doctrine also takes away the free will of man by teaching that regeneration comes before faith. The Bible teaches that man has the ability to respond to the conviction of the Holy Spirit, resulting in regeneration. The Bible blatantly shows that the sinful man has a responsibility to come to God—to repent, to believe, to confess, and to be born again. To believe otherwise reveals a disturbing misunderstanding of Scripture. Yet Calvinism completely does away with the responsibility of man in its attempt to show that God saves people before they have the ability to respond to Him.

James White argues that anyone who is not a Calvinist holds to a belief called *synergism*, which is defined as "the belief that God's grace cannot save unless joined in the effort by the will of the man."[160] Synergism is opposed to *monergism*, which is the belief that God's grace is able to save man apart from his free will. James White further defines synergism as the belief that God's creatures actually give Him "aid" in the salvation process. He writes that synergism gives the *"fallen* creature . . . ability to control God's free and sovereign work of salvation." Then he audaciously associates all Christians who are not Calvinists with belief in this doctrine. White believes that the act of *receiving* (as in receiving God's grace) is a type of "work" that takes away from the sovereignty of God. He therefore concludes that a man's free will to receive the gospel somehow "controls God's work of salvation."[161] Dave Hunt applies practical reality to the argument by asking White, "Does a woman 'control'

---

[160] Dave Hunt and James White, *Debating Calvinism* (Sisters, OR: Multnomah Publishers, 2004), 63.

[161] White, in *Debating Calvinism*, 68-69.

a man because she can either accept or reject his proposal of marriage?"[162] Not only is James White's argument for synergism seriously flawed, but so too is his assumption that all non-Calvinists hold to this belief.

Despite Calvinism's highly acclaimed standard of quality exegesis, the account of Jesus raising Lazarus from the dead is often used as a textual illustration supporting Calvin's doctrine of Total Depravity. This is a hermeneutical mistake. The student of the Bible should beware when any doctrine, let alone essential doctrine, is supported from a narrative story that lacks any instruction, especially when a particular belief is set against a number of other clear teachings. This reading of Scripture is comparable to the practice of Jehovah's Witnesses, who pull a number of erroneous doctrines from the poetic books of Proverbs and Ecclesiastes. This way of using Scripture is one of the characteristics of a cult. Josh McDowell writes that cults often claim that:

> . . . the Scriptures are their final source of authority; [however,] we find they [cults] consistently misuse the Scriptures to establish their own peculiar beliefs. This is accomplished chiefly by quoting texts out of context while omitting other passages relevant to the subject.[163]

Calvinist R. C. Sproul actually validates McDowell's statement, in his book *What Is Reformed Theology?* In the chapter "Monergistic Regeneration," Sproul fails to cite a single verse showing that the Bible supports this belief. Instead, Sproul gives the reader a class in Latin and Greek terminology with such words as *monergism, synergism, operative grace, and cooperative grace.*[164] Instead of making a sound case for monergistic regeneration, all Sproul does is pull a heretical doctrine of salvation from

---

[162] Dave Hunt, in *Debating Calvinism*, 80.

[163] Josh McDowell, *Handbook of Today's Religions* (Nashville: Thomas Nelson Publishers, 1983), 46.

[164] Sproul, *What Is Reformed Theology?*, 184.

the simple story of Lazarus, saying, "Perhaps a good illustration of Monergistic, life-giving power is the raising of Lazarus from the dead."[165] Sproul tries to provide a biblical foundation for his peculiar belief at the expense of "quoting texts out of context while omitting other passages relevant to the subject."[166] Because of this hermeneutical mistake, his example and thoughts on the monergistic resurrection are incorrect.

The usual argument given in defense of Total Depravity lies in a question: Because the Bible depicts man as being dead apart from God, how can he choose to have faith in the Gospel of Jesus on his own? Although many Calvinist authors pose this question as a foundation for their doctrine, it is not logically or biblically sound. By pulling doctrine from the Lazarus account, Calvinists have dug themselves into a mess of unanswerable theological questions.

First, if the Bible depicts man as being spiritually dead before God brings life, then how can a corpse do anything that opposes God's will? As mentioned before, Lazarus did nothing to "aid" Jesus in bringing him back from the dead. Yet, in contradicting Calvin's doctrine that the unregenerate nature is "so prolific in all kinds of evil, that it can never be idle,"[167] Lazarus did nothing to oppose God's will. As the story of Lazarus might paint a good picture of how God does not need help from His creatures to bring about life, it fails to support other Calvinistic doctrines, which insist that the spiritually dead person can only displease God. If we were to base doctrine on the Lazarus account as some Calvinists do, we would conclude that the spiritual "corpse" can neither please nor displease God. This leads us to the next point.

Secondly, if Calvinism maintains the belief that man is spiritually dead before God's regenerating work and is unable to do any good, but only evil, how do we explain that unregenerate men not only do good

---

[165] Ibid.

[166] McDowell, *Handbook of Today's Religions*, 46.

[167] Calvin, *Institutes*, 2.1.8.

acts but are capable of living morally good lives? Jesus said in Matthew 7:11, "If you then, being evil, know how to give good gifts to your children . . ." In this verse, Jesus refers to the condition of man apart from God as being "evil." Orthodox Christianity holds to this truth, as does the Calvinist. Yet Jesus also acknowledged the fact that even "evil" men can still do good works. He indicated that "sinners" do have the common sense to differentiate between good and evil. In **Luke 6:33**, Jesus says, "If you do good to them which do good to you, what credit is that to you? For even sinners do the same." If Jesus taught that "evil" people have the ability to do good, how can Calvinism reasonably defend its claim that the unregenerate cannot choose to believe in the goodness of the gospel of Jesus?

Yet, Calvinists try to find a way around this by claiming that although the unregenerate can generically do good, on a human level they can do nothing of spiritual importance and cannot truly discern between right and wrong. Calvinism further claims that only the elect can understand the things (knowledge, truth, will, etc.) of God. This is contrasted to the unregenerate, who are spiritually dead. But again, the Bible speaks differently concerning the matter. In **Romans 1**, Paul explains how God reveals Himself to those whom we would deem unregenerate. He writes:

> [18] For the wrath of God is revealed from heaven against all ungodliness and unrighteousness of men, who suppress the truth in unrighteousness, [19] because what may be known of God is manifest in them, for God has shown *it* to them. [20]For since the creation of the world His invisible *attributes* are clearly seen, being understood by the things that are made, *even* His eternal power and Godhead, so that they are without excuse, [21]because, although they knew God, they did not glorify *Him* as God, nor were thankful, but became futile in their thoughts, and their foolish hearts were darkened.

²²Professing to be wise, they became fools, ²³and changed the glory of the incorruptible God into an image made like corruptible man—and birds and four-footed animals and creeping things. ²⁴Therefore God also gave them up to uncleanness, in the lusts of their hearts, to dishonor their bodies among themselves, ²⁵who exchanged the truth of God for the lie, and worshiped and served the creature rather than the Creator, who is blessed forever. Amen. ²⁶For this reason God gave them up to vile passions. For even their women exchanged the natural use for what is against nature. ²⁷Likewise also the men, leaving the natural use of the woman, burned in their lust for one another, men with men committing what is shameful, and receiving in themselves the penalty of their error which was due. ²⁸And even as they did not like to retain God in *their* knowledge, God gave them over to a debased mind, to do those things which are not fitting; ²⁹being filled with all unrighteousness, sexual immorality, wickedness, covetousness, maliciousness; full of envy, murder, strife, deceit, evil-mindedness; *they are* whisperers, ³⁰backbiters, haters of God, violent, proud, boasters, inventors of evil things, disobedient to parents, ³¹undiscerning, untrustworthy, unloving, unforgiving, unmerciful; ³²who, knowing the righteous judgment of God, that those who practice such things are deserving of death, not only do the same but also approve of those who practice them.

We must highlight seven parts of Paul's letter and keep in mind God is revealing Himself to the unregenerate.

1. The unregenerate hold God's truth in unrighteousness (v.18).
2. That which is known of God is manifest in them, for He has revealed it to them (v.19).

3. God's invisible attributes are clearly seen by His creation, making all accountable (v.20).
4. The unregenerate knew God but chose not to glorify Him (v.21).
5. They exchanged the truth of God for a lie (v. 25).
6. They did not like to retain God in their knowledge (v. 28).
7. They knew the judgment of God (v. 32).

After describing how God has revealed Himself to sinners, Paul then concludes, "Therefore you are inexcusable, O man, whoever you are . . ." (**Romans 2:1**) The question then remains: How can the unregenerate, hold back, suppress, and exchange the knowledge of God and His truth when, as Calvinists claim, they are spiritually dead and unable to do so? **Romans 1** makes quite clear that sinners know of God, see the evidence of His existence and even understand His judgments (**John 16:8**), and yet still choose to reject Him. This sad reality indeed reiterates the extent of man's depravity but is far from Calvinism's distortion of it. Rather, **Romans 1** points out that sinners not only have the ability to understand God but have the ability (freewill) to respond to Him.

For Calvinism to maintain that unregenerate people lack the ability or common sense to differentiate between good and evil and that they are incapable of accepting the gospel and grace of God apart from being regenerated is incompatible with both Scripture and reason. If sinners repay those who do good to them, and if unregenerate fathers give good gifts to their children, then such people are indeed able to see and accept the good grace of God through Jesus' sacrifice without first being regenerated by God. Yet, as James Smith maintains, "the Reformed formula [is] that 'regeneration precedes faith.'"[168]

Geisler also sees the fallacy of believing "that regeneration is logically prior to faith." While calling it a "fundamental pillar" of Calvinism, he concludes that "nothing could be more contrary to the clear statements

---

[168] Smith, *Letters to a Young Calvinist*, 19.

of Scripture." [169] He points out:

> Even after Adam sinned and became spiritually "dead" (**Genesis 2:17**; cf. **Ephesians 2:1**) and a sinner "by nature" (**Ephesians 2:3**), he was not so completely depraved that he could neither hear the voice of God nor make a free response.[170]

Geisler further states: "God's image in Adam was *effaced* by the Fall but not *erased*. It was marred but not destroyed. . . . Even those under the power of Satan are there by a free act of 'disobedience' (**Ephesians 2:2**)."[171] Geisler also explains that,

> even though they are spiritually "dead," the unsaved persons can perceive the truth of God. In Romans, Paul declares emphatically that God's truth is "clearly seen" by them so that they are "without excuse" (1:20). Adam and Eve were spiritually "dead" after they ate the forbidden fruit. Yet they could hear the voice of God and responded to Him (**Genesis 3:10**). And this was not merely a hearing of the tangible sounds. Their reaction reveals that they understood the meaning of the words.
>
> Third, "dead" is only one of the many figures of speech used to describe the fallen state. It is also depicted as "sickness," which does not imply the person had no ability to hear and respond to God (**Matthew 9:12**). In short, depravity involves

---

[169] Geisler, *Chosen but Free*, 235.

[170] Ibid., 32.

[171] Ibid., 33.

the *corruption* of life but not its *destruction*.[172]

As Geisler affirms, "However, contrary to strong Calvinism, in regard to the freedom of *accepting* God's gift of salvation the Bible is clear: Fallen beings are free." [173]

Another point is that if man were totally deprived of any common sense and knowledge of good and bad, then evil would run the world. If man could do nothing right or good, he must do everything wrong and evil. As John Calvin stated, man's nature is "so prolific in all kinds of evil, that it can never be idle."[174] If this were true, evil would completely take over. Even with a few elect in the world, humankind would cease to exist. Yet, Calvinists get around this by believing that God restrains mankind's will to do complete evil. What is peculiar to Calvinism is not that they believe God holds mankind back from being completely overtaken by evil but their assertion that God also withholds mankind's ability to do good; namely, to respond positively to the gospel.

Before the rest of the TULIP doctrines are even addressed, one must recognize that the Calvinist doctrine of Total Depravity concludes that salvation was not intended for all people. To back up the claims that salvation is exclusive to the elect, Calvinists usually refer to two verses:

> *John 6:44:* "*No one can come to Me unless the Father who sent Me draws him; and I will raise him up at the last day.*"

> *John 6:64–65:* "*But there are some of you who do not believe.' For Jesus knew from the beginning who they were who did not believe, and who would betray Him. And He said, 'Therefore I have said to you that no one can come to Me unless it has been granted to him by My Father.'*"

---

[172] Ibid., 59.

[173] Ibid., 33.

[174] Calvin, *Institutes of Christian Religion*, 2.1.8.

Do these verses point out that regeneration precedes faith and that the Father only desires for some to be saved? They do not. They simply establish the points that were already made. First, it is the Father who pursues man, and secondly, apart from the conviction of the Holy Spirit, man is hopelessly lost. The above verses give no hint that faith is the result of regeneration; nor do they determine the number of people the Father draws. In the verses below, we will see that both the conviction of the Holy Spirit that may lead to salvation is intended for all and that faith results in salvation, not the other way around.

John 16:8: "And when He [the Holy Spirit] has come He will convict the world of sin, and of righteousness, and of judgment."

1 Timothy 2:1–6: " First of all, then, I urge that entreaties and prayers, petitions and thanksgivings, be made on behalf of all men, for kings and all who are in authority, so that we may lead a tranquil and quiet life in all godliness and dignity. This is good and acceptable in the sight of God our Savior, who desires all men to be saved and to come to the knowledge of the truth. For there is one God, and one mediator also between God and men, the man Christ Jesus, who gave Himself as a ransom for all, the testimony given at the proper time."

1 Timothy 4:10: "For it is for this we labor and strive, because we have fixed our hope on the living God, who is the Savior of all men, especially of believers."

Hebrews 2:9: "But we do see Him who was made for a little while lower than the angels, namely, Jesus, because of the suffering of death crowned with glory and honor, so that by the grace of God He might taste death for everyone."

2 Peter 3:9: "The Lord is not slow about His promise, as some count slowness, but is patient toward you, not wishing for any to perish but for all to come to repentance."

Revelation 3:20: "'Behold, I stand at the door and knock; if anyone hears My voice and opens the door, I will come in to him and will dine with him, and he with Me.'"

Revelation 22:17: "The Spirit and the bride say, 'Come.' And let the one who hears say, 'Come.' And let the one who is thirsty come; let the one who wishes take the water of life without cost."

John 7:37–38: "Now on the last day, the great day of the feast, Jesus stood and cried out, saying, 'If anyone is thirsty, let him come to Me and drink. He who believes in Me, as the Scripture said, "From his innermost being will flow rivers of living water."'"

John 11:25–26: "Jesus said to her, 'I am the resurrection and the life; he who believes in Me will live even if he dies, and everyone who lives and believes in Me will never die. Do you believe this?'"

John 20:30–31: "Therefore many other signs Jesus also performed in the presence of the disciples, which are not written in this book; but these have been written so that you may believe that Jesus is the Christ, the Son of God; and that believing you may have life in His name."

Romans 1:14–16: "I am under obligation both to Greeks and to barbarians, both to the wise and to the foolish. So, for my part, I am eager to preach the gospel to you also who are in Rome. For I am not ashamed of the gospel, for it is the power of God for salvation to everyone who believes, to the Jew first and also to the Greek."

Romans 5:6–8: "For while we were still helpless, at the right time Christ died for the ungodly. For one will hardly die for a righteous man; though perhaps for the good man someone would dare even to die. But God demonstrates His own love toward us, in that while we were yet sinners, Christ died for us."

Romans 10:8–13: "But what does it say? 'The word is near you, in your mouth and in your heart'—that is, the word of faith which we are preaching, that if you confess with your mouth Jesus as Lord, and believe in your heart that God raised Him from the dead, you will be saved; for with the heart a person believes, resulting in righteousness, and with the mouth he confesses, resulting in salvation. For the Scripture says, 'WHOEVER BELIEVES IN HIM WILL NOT BE DISAPPOINTED.' For there is no distinction between Jew and Greek; for the same Lord is Lord of all, abounding in riches for all who call on Him; for 'WHOEVER WILL CALL ON THE NAME OF THE LORD WILL BE SAVED.'"[175]

To conclude, while Total Depravity teaches the biblical truth that man was born in a sinful state and is consequently inclined toward doing evil, its addenda remains inconsistent with both human nature and biblically orthodox interpretation. The doctrine's first addition is that faith in God is possible only after one is born again. The second is that unregenerate people lack the common sense and ability to choose and accept the grace of God. Total Depravity implies that it is by both God's work and will that all of mankind is denied the ability to choose in the saving work of Jesus. In essence, the elect are forced to believe while the rest are denied the chance. Therefore, from the start Calvinism robs mankind of free will in the name of Total Depravity only to do it again in the name of Unconditional Election.

---

[175] From 1 Timothy 2:1–6 to Romans 10:8–3, the NASB was used in place of the NKJV.

Tulip

Unconditional Election Explained

The "U" in TULIP stands for *Unconditional Election*. This point is based upon the biblical premise that God has elected His children. This, in and of itself, is true. The Bible is clear that God has chosen His people. So what does this mean? It simply means that God has a chosen group of children He refers to as His "elect." The word "elect" is used four times in the Old Testament and twenty times in the New Testament. But Calvinism adds that the process of election is performed without regard for the free will of man. In a systematic theology, the issue of election is much easier to comprehend if people are denied free will. Unfortunately, not every theological concept can be systematically reduced to logical explanations. Another problem with the Calvinist doctrine of unconditional election is that while Scripture is clear about God's elect, it is also clear that all men have free will and can choose to believe or disbelieve the claims of the gospel. To avoid this mystery, Calvinists have removed the idea of man's free will by adding an unbiblical doctrine that the elect have *unconditionally* been chosen. Yet the word "unconditional" is not found in Scripture. As Vance states, "The term Unconditional Election suffers from the addition of a contrived prefix to an otherwise biblical doctrine."[176]

To interpret Unconditional Election correctly, we must understand its connection to Total Depravity. Because mankind is denied the ability to choose salvation (T), the election of the saved is completely unconditional (U) upon man's will, desire, or response to the gospel. The only hope of being one of God's unconditionally elect lies in God's predestined plan. As we will see, God's predestined plan or "decree," as explained in the doctrine of Unconditional Election, makes Christianity a fatalistic religion and God the author, reason, and cause for sin.

---

[176] Vance, *The Other Side of Calvinism*, 241.

John Calvin clarifies:

By predestination we mean the eternal decree of God, by which he determined with himself whatever he wished to happen with regard to every man. All are not created on equal terms, but some are preordained to eternal life, others to eternal damnation; and, accordingly, as each has been created for one or other of these ends, we say that he has been predestinated to life or to death.[177]

Again, Calvin writes:

We say, then, that Scripture clearly proves this much, that God by his eternal and immutable counsel determined once for all those whom it was his pleasure one day to admit to salvation, and those whom, on the other hand, it was his pleasure to doom to destruction. We maintain that this counsel, as regards the elect, is founded on his free mercy, without any respect to human worth, while those whom he dooms to destruction are excluded from access to life by a just and blameless, but at the same time incomprehensible judgment. [178]

On the Doctrine of Election, Article 16 of the Belgic Confession (1561) states:

We believe that—all Adam's descendants having thus fallen into perdition and ruin by the sin of the first man— God showed himself to be as he is: merciful and just. He is merciful in withdrawing and saving from this perdition those whom he, in his eternal and unchangeable counsel,

---

[177] Calvin, *Institutes*, 3.21.5.

[178] Ibid., 3.21.7.

has elected and chosen in Jesus Christ our Lord by his pure goodness, without any consideration of their works. He is just in leaving the others in their ruin and fall into which they plunged themselves.[179]

The Canons of Dordrecht (1619) define Unconditional Election as:

. . . the unchangeable purpose of God whereby, before the foundation of the world, out of the whole human race, which had fallen by its own fault out of its original integrity into sin and perdition, He has, according to the sovereign good pleasure of His will, out of mere grace, chosen in Christ to salvation a definite number of specific persons, neither better nor more worthy than others, but involved together with them in a common misery. He has also from eternity appointed Christ to be the Mediator and Head of all the elect and the foundation of salvation and thus He decreed to give to Christ those who were to be saved, and effectually to call and draw them into His communion through His Word and Spirit. He decreed to give them true faith in Him, to justify them, to sanctify them, and, after having powerfully kept them in the fellowship of His Son, finally to glorify them, for the demonstration of His mercy and the praise of the riches of His glorious grace.[180]

---

[179] "The Belgic Confession," Article 16: "The Doctrine of Election," [online]; accessed 20 January 2010; available from http://www.reformed.org/ documents/index.html?mainframe=http://www.reformed.org/documents/BelgicConf ession.html; Internet.

[180] "The Canons of Dordrecht," Article 7: "Election" [online]; accessed 20 January 2010; available from http://www. reformed.org/documents/index.html? mainframe=http://www.reformed.org/documents/canons_of_dordt.html; Internet.

The Westminster Confession (1646) reads as follows:

God from all eternity did by the most wise and holy counsel of his own will freely and unchangeably ordain whatsoever comes to pass: . . . By the decree of God, for the manifestation of his glory, some men and angels are predestinated unto everlasting life, and others foreordained to everlasting death. These angels and men, thus predestinated and foreordained, are particularly and unchangeably designed: and their number is so certain and definite that it cannot be either increased or diminished. Those of mankind that are predestinated unto life, God, before the foundation of the world was laid, according to his eternal and immutable purpose, and the secret counsel and good pleasure of his will, hath chosen in Christ, unto everlasting glory, out of his free grace and love alone, without any foresight of faith or good works, or perseverance in either of them, or any other thing in the creature, as conditions, or causes moving him thereunto . . . The rest of mankind God was pleased . . . to ordain them to dishonor and wrath for their sin . . .[181]

All those whom God hath predestinated unto life, and those only, he is pleased, in his appointed and accepted time, effectually to call, by his Word and Spirit, out of that state of sin and death, in which they are by nature, to grace and salvation by Jesus Christ . . . This effectual call is of God's free and special grace alone, not from anything at all foreseen in man, who is altogether passive therein . . . Others, not elected, although they may be

---

[181] "The Westminster Confession of Faith," 3.1-7.

called by the ministry of the Word, . . . yet they never truly come to Christ, and therefore cannot be saved . . .[182]

While many Christians would like to wrap their minds around the working of God's sovereignty and how it operates with the will of man, Calvinists appear not to struggle with the question at all simply by eliminating completely the idea that man has a free will. Calvinism uses verses that refer to the elect to show that the elect are "unconditionally" chosen. This conclusion is neither stated nor supported by the Bible. The following verses are typically used by Calvinists to support the doctrine of Unconditional Election.

John 15:16: "You did not choose Me, but I chose you and appointed you that you should go and bear fruit, and that your fruit should remain, that whatever you ask the Father in My name He may give you."

Acts 13:48: "Now when the Gentiles heard this, they were glad and glorified the word of the Lord. And as many as had been appointed to eternal life believed."

Romans 9:15–16: "For He says to Moses, 'I will have mercy on whomever I will have mercy, and I will have compassion on whomever I will have compassion.' So then it is not of him who wills, nor of him who runs, but of God who shows mercy."

Ephesians 1:4–5: "just as He chose us in Him before the foundation of the world, that we should be holy and without blame before Him in love, having predestined us to adoption as sons by Jesus Christ to Himself, according to the good pleasure of His will."

---

[182] Ibid., 10.1-4.

Ephesians 1:11: "In Him also we have obtained an inheritance, being predestined according to the purpose of Him who works all things according to the counsel of His will."

Philippians 1:29: "For to you it has been granted on behalf of Christ, not only to believe in Him, but also to suffer for His sake."

1 Thessalonians 1:4–5: "knowing, beloved brethren, your election by God. For our gospel did not come to you in word only, but also in power, and in the Holy Spirit and in much assurance, as you know what kind of men we were among you for your sake."

2 Thessalonians 2:13: "But we are bound to give thanks to God always for you, brethren beloved by the Lord, because God from the beginning chose you for salvation through sanctification by the Spirit and belief in the truth."

2 Timothy 1:8–9: "Therefore do not be ashamed of the testimony of our Lord, nor of me His prisoner, but share with me in the sufferings for the gospel according to the power of God, who has saved us and called us with a holy calling, not according to our works, but according to His own purpose and grace which was given to us in Christ Jesus before time began."

Though these verses reveal the truth that God indeed has an elect, they fail to support the meaning of Unconditional Election. While they highlight the "election" part of Unconditional Election, they fail in supporting its "unconditional" part.

Progressing in their logical interpretation of God's predestining power, Calvinists have concluded that His decree has not only predetermined each person to eternal life or eternal damnation, but has ordained all of each one's prior actions too. Because Calvinists attribute Unconditional Election to God's eternal decree, they must come to the systematic conclusion that nothing happens by chance or by the will of man, but that all things, both holy and sinful, come from God's will.

The Westminster Confession of Faith states, "God from all eternity, did, by the most wise and holy counsel of His own will, freely, and unchangeably ordain whatsoever comes to pass."[183]

Again, John Calvin writes, "By predestination we mean the eternal decree of God, by which he determined with himself whatever he wished to happen with regard to every man."[184]

Calvinist theologian William G. T. Shedd writes, "Nothing comes to pass contrary to His decree. Nothing happens by chance. Even moral evil, which he abhors and forbids, occurs by the determinate counsel and foreknowledge of God."[185]

Gresham Machen states that even the "wicked actions of wicked men and devils are brought to pass in accordance with God's eternal purpose."[186]

Edwin Palmer blatantly states that, "It is even biblical to say that God has foreordained sin. If sin was outside the plan of God, then not a single important affair of life would be ruled by God."[187]

Yet in light of these claims, Calvinists still maintain, as the Westminster Confession states, that "God is neither the author of sin" and that in His predestined plan, "the liberty or contingency of second causes" is not "taken away, but rather established."[188]

---

[183] Ibid., 3.1.

[184] Calvin, *Institutes*, 3.21.5.

[185] William G. T. Shedd, *Calvinism, Pure and Mixed* (Edinburgh: The Banner of Truth Trust, 1986), 37.

[186] Gresham Machen, *The Christian View of Man* (Edinburgh: the Banner of Trust, 1965), 46.

[187] Edwin Palmer, *The Five Points of Calvinism* (Grand Rapids: Baker Book House, 1980), 82.

[188] "The Westminster Confession of Faith," 3.1-3.

How one's actions and eternal destiny are predetermined by God with no detriment to man's free will has yet to be answered. As our study continues, the sophistry of Calvinist double talk will become more apparent. Once again, as with the first doctrine of Total Depravity, the effort given by the Calvinist to uphold the second petal of TULIP is done so at the expense of quoting verses out of context and presuming something that is not there. This distortion is severe. It has made God the author of sin and Christianity nothing less than a fatalistic theology.

The doctrine of Unconditional Election teaches that one is elected by God through His sovereign decree rather than by placing faith in Jesus Christ. Consequently, faith in Christ is essentially meaningless because God's choice of election is unconditional. By the nature of His unalterable decree, God unconditionally denies free will to all of mankind, both the elect and the nonelect.

Tulip

Unconditional Election Uprooted

Although the doctrine of Unconditional Election asserts that God's children are the elect, this view changes the orthodox understanding of the process of how one becomes elect. The orthodox view is plain in **1 Peter 1:2** when Peter refers to his fellow Christians as "elect." The word "elect" is found in the New Testament about twenty times, five of which come from Jesus' own mouth. It specifically refers to the spiritual sons and daughters in God's family. However, the word "unconditional" does not occur anywhere in the Bible, let alone in connection with the word "elect." Oddly enough, Sproul boasts that the word *"unconditional distinguishes the Reformed doctrine of predestination from that of other theologies."*[189] However, throughout his book, *What Is Reformed*

---

[189] Sproul, *What Is Reformed Theology?*, 142.

Theology? Sproul dodges the question of how the elect are unconditionally saved. He derails on tangents, explaining words that make inferences to the concept, but he remains unable to explain the concept itself with biblical support. All the while he makes statements that the novice Christian may easily fall for. For example, he says, "Theology also speaks of the inward call of God, which is not given to everyone."[190] Yet, he cites no verses to support this claim. First, it must be known that historical and biblically balanced theology does not speak of "the inward call." Even the *Westminster Dictionary of Theological Terms* fails to list the word or idea of an "inward call." That is because it is invented by Calvinism.

Although the Bible teaches that God's children are the elect, it also teaches that the mandate to be among the elect is conditioned upon one's placement of faith in Jesus. Because this understanding seems to compromise God's sovereignty, Calvinists conclude that the roster of the elect must be unconditional—unaffected by man's will, act, desire, or even faith. Yet the Bible shows this idea to be false. Salvation and election are offered universally to everyone who believes and confesses in Jesus as their Savior. The following passages, spoken by Jesus Himself, convey this truth.

> *John 3:14–18: "As Moses lifted up the serpent in the wilderness, even so must the Son of Man be lifted up; so that whoever believes will in Him have eternal life. For God so loved the world, that He gave His only begotten Son, that whoever believes in Him shall not perish, but have eternal life. For God did not send the Son into the world to judge the world, but that the world might be saved through Him. He who believes in Him is not judged; he who does not believe has been judged already, because he has not believed in the name of the only begotten Son of God."*

---

[190] Ibid., 144.

John 7:37–38: "*. . . 'If anyone is thirsty, let him come to Me and drink. He who believes in Me, as the Scripture said, 'From his innermost being will flow rivers of living water.'"*

John 11:25–26: "*. . . 'I am the resurrection and the life; he who believes in Me will live even if he dies, and everyone who lives and believes in Me will never die. Do you believe this?'"*

Matthew 10:32–33: "*'Therefore everyone who confesses Me before men, I will also confess him before My Father who is in heaven. But whoever denies Me before men, I will also deny him before My Father who is in heaven.'"*

Matthew 11:28: "*'Come to Me, all who are weary and heavy-laden, and I will give you rest.'"*

Matthew 16:24–25: "*'If anyone wishes to come after Me, he must deny himself, and take up his cross and follow Me. For whoever wishes to save his life will lose it; but whoever loses his life for My sake will find it.'"*

The apostle John echoes the claims of Jesus:

John 20:30–31: "*'Therefore many other signs Jesus also performed in the presence of the disciples, which are not written in this book; but these have been written so that you may believe that Jesus is the Christ, the Son of God; and that believing you may have life in His name.'"*

Revelation 3:20: "*'Behold, I stand at the door and knock; if anyone hears My voice and opens the door, I will come in to him and will dine with him, and he with Me.'"*[191]

---

[191] From John 3:14–18 to Revelation 3:20 the NASB was used.

> *Revelation 22:17: "And the Spirit and the bride say, 'Come!' And let him who hears say, 'Come!' And let him who thirsts come. Whoever desires, let him take the water of life freely."*

Paul the apostle also testifies of the open invitation of salvation in Jesus:

> *Romans 1:14–16: "I am a debtor both to Greeks and to barbarians, both to wise and to unwise. So, as much as is in me, I am ready to preach the gospel to you who are in Rome also. For I am not ashamed of the gospel of Christ, for it is the power of God to salvation for everyone who believes, for the Jew first and also for the Greek."*

> *Romans 5:6–8: "For when we were still without strength, in due time Christ died for the ungodly. For scarcely for a righteous man will one die; yet perhaps for a good man someone would even dare to die. But God demonstrates His own love toward us, in that while we were still sinners, Christ died for us."*

> *Romans 10:8–13: "But what does it say? 'The word is near you, in your mouth and in your heart' (that is, the word of faith which we preach): that if you confess with your mouth the Lord Jesus and believe in your heart that God has raised Him from the dead, you will be saved. For with the heart one believes unto righteousness, and with the mouth confession is made unto salvation. For the Scripture says, 'Whoever believes on Him will not be put to shame.' For there is no distinction between Jew and Greek, for the same Lord over all is rich to all who call upon Him. For 'whoever calls on the name of the LORD shall be saved.'"*

God desires all men to come to salvation, but His offer of salvation is conditional upon each person's response to the gospel. This truth is evident in the following verses:

1 Timothy 2:1–6: "Therefore I exhort first of all that supplications, prayers, intercessions, and giving of thanks be made for all men, for kings and all who are in authority, that we may lead a quiet and peaceable life in all godliness and reverence. For this is good and acceptable in the sight of God our Savior, who desires all men to be saved and to come to the knowledge of the truth. For there is one God and one Mediator between God and men, the Man Christ Jesus, who gave Himself a ransom for all, to be testified in due time."

1 Timothy 4:10: "For to this end we both labor and suffer reproach, because we trust in the living God, who is the Savior of all men, especially of those who believe."

2 Peter 3:9: "The Lord is not slack concerning His promise, as some count slackness, but is longsuffering toward us, not willing that any should perish but that all should come to repentance."

The biblical view of election is that salvation is offered to all but is dependent or conditional upon an individual's response to it. However, because Calvinism takes God's sovereign decrees to unbiblical extremes, it makes Him out to be the cause of sin. We cannot forget that some Calvinists believe "God has preordained sin" [192] and that "even moral evil, which He abhors and forbids, occurs by [His] determinate counsel and foreknowledge."[193] Such a doctrine cannot stand. As John Milton in his *Doctrina Christiana* says, "There are some people . . . who . . . assert that God is, in Himself, the cause and author of sin. . . . If I should attempt to refute them, it would be like inventing a long argument to

---

[192] Palmer, *The Five Points of Calvinism*, 82.

[193] Shedd, *Calvinism, Pure and Mixed*, 37.

prove that God is not the Devil."[194] How Calvinism gets around the following verses remains a mystery:

> *James 1:13–14, 17: "Let no one say when he is tempted, 'I am tempted by God'; for God cannot be tempted by evil, nor does He Himself tempt anyone. But each one is tempted when he is drawn away by his own desires and enticed. Every good gift and every perfect gift is from above, and comes down from the Father of lights, with whom there is no variation or shadow of turning."*

> *1 John 5:17: "All unrighteousness is sin . . ."*

> *1 John 3:8: "He who sins is of the devil . . ."*

> *Romans 9:14: "What shall we say then? Is there unrighteousness with God? Certainly not!"*

> *Deuteronomy 32:3–4: ". . .His work is perfect; For all His ways are justice, a God of truth and without injustice; Righteous and upright is He."*

> *2 Chronicles 19:7: ". . .there is no iniquity with the Lord our God."*

> *Job 34:10, 12: "Therefore listen to me, you men of understanding: Far be it from God to do wickedness, and from the Almighty to commit iniquity. Surely God will never do wickedly, nor will the Almighty pervert justice."*

> *Psalm 92:15: ". . .the Lord is upright; He is my rock, and there is no unrighteousness in Him."*

Contradicting the belief that God "desires all men to be saved" and that "God cannot tempt any man," the doctrine of Unconditional

---

[194] John Milton, "From *Christian Doctrine*," in *Milton—The Major Works* (Oxford: Oxford University Press, 2003), 723.

Election seems to make God out to be a fatalistic author of sin. Norman Geisler even writes that Calvinism "logically lays the blame squarely on God for the origin of evil."[195] As Vance states:

> Although Calvinists go out of their way to distance themselves from fatalism, they are in essence teaching the same thing. When a philosopher believes "what is to be will be" it is called determinism. When a stoic believes "what is to be will be" it is called fate. When a Muslim believes "what is to be will be" it is called fatalism. But when a Calvinist believes "what is to be will be" it is called predestination.[196]

Calvinism's doctrine of predestination is unbiblical and unorthodox. Historic and orthodox Christianity by sound biblical exposition have always taught that man is elected by God in accordance with faith in Jesus. That indeed anyone who confesses that Jesus is Lord will be saved. Becoming the elect of God is conditional on that basis.

Tulip

Limited Atonement Explained

The "L" in TULIP stands for *Limited Atonement*. Once again, we come to another biblical doctrine that is altered by a Calvinistic and fabricated prefix. The belief that Christ atoned for sinners in order to allow them to enter into a relationship with Him is shared by all Christians. Calvinists, however, take this belief a step further by claiming that the atoning work of Jesus was "limited," or in other words, not applicable to all people.

---

[195] Geisler, *Chosen but Free*, 137–38.

[196] Vance, *The Other Side of Calvinism*, 278.

The implications of this point in TULIP are quite clear: Limited Atonement means that Christ did not die for everyone, but only for the elect. This blatantly contradicts the historical and orthodox view that the atonement was made for all and is effective to all those who believe. James White explains the Calvinist position:

> God the Father decreed the salvation of an elect people, Christ died with the intention of redeeming those people through their union with Him and accomplished that task, and without fail the Holy Spirit brings that accomplished work to fruition in the life of the elect at the time and in the manner determined by God. [197]

Even though the teaching of Limited Atonement makes logical sense following the first two points of TULIP, many Calvinists have found themselves struggling to believe this one. The cause of the particular offense of this doctrine, given acceptance of the previous two (Total Depravity and Unconditional Election), both of which deny any free will of man, remains a mystery. The two doctrines that, in "TULIP," stand before and after the doctrine of Limited Atonement point to the belief that God denies mankind the free will to choose salvation. As Vance points out, the doctrine of Limited Atonement should not be:

> . . . cause for alarm, due to the fact of its non-essentiality. Limited Atonement is simply adding insult to injury, the injury being Unconditional Election. For if certain men are not of those elected to salvation, then what does it matter whether Christ died for them or not?[198]

---

[197] White, in *Debating Calvinism*, 170.

[198] Vance, *The Other Side of Calvinism*, 405.

Yet, many Calvinists diverge from their own systematic theology at this point, creating a sub-group of Calvinism: four-point Calvinism. This will be covered in the next chapter.

The Bible's silence concerning any limitation on the atonement of Jesus' sacrifice places Calvinists in a very difficult position when defending Limited Atonement. This third doctrine of TULIP theology stands solely on the preceding two points, having nothing but systematic logic in its defense, or as Vance states, "philosophical speculations." Because of the complete lack of Scripture to validate such a claim, we can only understand what John Calvin believed about a Limited Atonement by his misinterpretation of those verses that ironically negate the doctrine. An example is Calvin's commentary on **2 Peter 3:9**. The verse states, "The Lord is . . . longsuffering toward us, not willing that any should perish but that all should come to repentance." In his commentary on this verse, Calvin understands that God only "lays hold" of certain people. Calvin avoids justifying his interpretation by claiming it is part of God's "hidden purpose." Because of this, Calvin's interpretation cannot be scrutinized. He writes:

> But it may be asked, If God wishes none to perish, why is it that so many do perish? To this my answer is, that no mention is here made of the hidden purpose of God, according to which the reprobate are doomed to their own ruin, but only of his will as made known to us in the gospel. For God there stretches forth his hand without a difference to all, but lays hold only of those, to lead them to himself, whom he has chosen before the foundation of the world. [199]

How Calvin himself understood the doctrine of Limited Atonement is also evident in his commentary on **John 3:16**. This well-known verse

---

[199] John Calvin, *Calvin's Commentaries*, trans. William Pringle (Grand Rapids: Baker Books, 2005), 419–20.

proclaims, "God so loved the world that He gave His only begotten Son, that whoever believes in Him should not perish but have everlasting life." Yet Calvin writes, "For Christ is made known and held out to the view of all, but the elect alone are they whose eyes God opens, that they may seek him by faith."[200] Although the verse says nothing of the "elect" or about God opening up their "eyes," Calvin's unbalanced doctrines of predestination seem to control his otherwise sound expository skills.

When the Canons of Dort ratified the theology of Limited Atonement as expressed in TULIP, it stated that the doctrine:

> . . . was the entirely free plan and very gracious will and intention of God the Father that the enlivening and saving effectiveness of his Son's costly death should work itself out in all his chosen ones, in order that he might grant justifying faith to them only and thereby lead them without fail to salvation. In other words, it was God's will that Christ through the blood of the cross (by which he confirmed the new covenant) should effectively redeem from every people, tribe, nation, and language all those and only those who were chosen from eternity to salvation and given to him by the Father; that he should grant them faith (which, like the Holy Spirit's other saving gifts, he acquired for them by his death); that he should cleanse them by his blood from all their sins, both original and actual, whether committed before or after their coming to faith; that he should faithfully preserve them to the very end; and that he should finally present them to himself, a glorious people, without spot or wrinkle.[201]

---

[200] *Calvin Commentaries*, 642.

[201] "Canons of Dordt," 2.8 [online]; accessed 21 January 2010; available from http://www.creeds net/dordt/mp2.htm; Internet.

Calvinist historian W. Robert Godfrey confirms, "All the Calvinists at Dort agreed that the Bible . . . taught that Christ had died only for the elect."[202]

The Westminster confession also states that it was only for "those whom the Father hath given unto him" that "the Lord Jesus, by His perfect obedience and sacrifice of himself, which He through the eternal Spirit once offered up unto God, hath fully satisfied the justice of His Father."[203]

A contemporary expression of the same position has been written by retired Protestant Reformed minister G. Van Baren:

> But even more important, this truth of Scripture that Jesus dies only for the sins of His own people, is the only truth which exalts the power and glory of the Name of God. Any other divergent view detracts from the glory of His Name. Any view of the atonement which suggests that the ultimate decision concerning one's salvation rests with man, detracts from the power and glory of God. God does not share His power and glory with any! He is God alone! He has absolute power. He determines the beginning from the end. He determines the final destiny of every creature—and He does so in harmony with His perfect righteousness.[204]

It is important to understand that the previous statements and Confessions are based more upon logical progression than on plain Scripture. Many Calvinists believe that if God is sovereign and wills that all would be saved, then all would be saved. The unbiblical doctrine of

---

[202] Godfrey, *An Unexpected Journey*, 100.

[203] "The Westminster Confession of Faith," 8.5.

[204] G. Van Baren, "Limited Atonement" [online]; accessed 28 January 2010; http://www.prca.org/pamphlets/pamphlet_46.html; Internet.

universalism (or *universal atonement* or *universal redemption*) means that at the end of time, no one will be confined in Hell for the penalty of sins; all are redeemed regardless of their faith or lack of faith in Jesus. Because the Bible does not teach any sort of universal redemption, Calvinists conclude that God did not desire to save all. Leading Calvinists feel as if they are defending the sovereignty of God when they proclaim the veracity of Limited Atonement. Calvinists often argue that anyone who does not believe in their doctrine of Limited Atonement must therefore believe in the unbiblical doctrine of universal redemption. In his commentary on the Westminster Confession's description of Limited Atonement, G. I. Williamson shows us this logic:

> This section of the Confession [8.5] teaches us (1) that Christ made satisfaction to God for those whom He represented, (2) that this satisfaction was by active and passive obedience, and (3) that by this satisfaction Christ secured complete redemption for those whom He represented.

> Here we consider the doctrine of "particular" or "definite atonement." It has sometimes been called the doctrine of "limited atonement," because the Reformed Confessions acknowledge that Christ was a substitute for some men rather than all men. It is most unfortunate, however, that this term has given rise to the misconception that it is the Reformed churches that "limit" the atonement, whereas the Arminian groups do not. The truth is really the exact opposite. It is the Arminian system that "limits" the atonement while the Reformed system does not.

> In order to show this we need only to ponder the following fact: the Arminian (and likewise, the Lutheran and Roman Catholic) is compelled (by the plain teaching of Scripture) to admit that only some men actually will be

saved. Only those who subscribe to the totally unscriptural idea of a universal salvation deny this. All who maintain the historic Christian faith in even the broadest sense agree that only some shall be saved. Therefore, there is no disagreement as to whether or not the work of Christ ultimately terminates in the salvation of only a limited portion of the human race. If all who accept the scriptural dictum thus "limit" the ultimate number that shall be saved to merely a part of the human race, it is quite unjust when Reformed Christians alone are held in disrepute for "limiting" the atonement.[205]

Williamson's complaint is easy to counter. Although both Calvinists and non-Calvinists can agree on the belief that in the end only "some men actually will be saved," it is the Calvinist who teaches that salvation is only offered to a limited number (the elect). Non-Calvinists, on the other hand, believe that Jesus has made the offer of salvation to everyone. This radical and crucial difference in understanding Scripture—as well as the heart and mind of God—is made apparent through every point of Calvinist theology, thus giving a reasonable foothold for non-Calvinists to hold the Reformed Christian in "disrepute."

James White also believes that it is the non-Calvinist who actually "limits" the atonement of Christ by placing an emphasis on the person's freedom to choose everlasting life. He states:

> Of course, it should be noted in passing that everyone who is not a Universalist limits the atonement. The evangelical who thinks he is honoring the atonement by making it universal in scope needs to realize the cost of

---

[205] G. I. Williamson, *The Westminster Confession of Faith: For Study Classes* (Philadelphia: P&R Publishing Co., 1964, 2004), 103–04.

his position. If Christ died in the place of every man and woman in all of history (universal scope and intention), the atonement must be limited in its power and efficacy, for it does not actually result in the salvation of many of those God intended it to save.[206]

In the light of what some Calvinists have stated about their doctrine of Limited Atonement, a non-Calvinist's contempt for Calvinism can be understood. Calvinist Herman Hanko goes as far as saying, "For if Christ died for all men and all men are not saved, the cross of Christ is of no effect. Calvary is a sham."[207] To have such assurance in Limited Atonement to say that "Calvary is a sham" if it is found false is a clear indicator of the radically unorthodox conclusions found within Calvinism.

In order to understand Limited Atonement correctly we must pull our interpretation of it from the first two letters in TULIP. If man is totally unable to believe in Jesus (Total Depravity) and God's election is unconditional (Unconditional Election) then Limited Atonement means that Jesus' sacrifice to atone for sins was not a universal offer to mankind but a limited offer only to the elect. Once again, historical and orthodox Christianity by sound biblical exposition teaches that Christ died for the sins of all men—a universal offer of forgiveness dependent upon one's faith. On the spectrum of biblical salvation with man's freewill on one end and God's sovereignty on the other, this traditionally orthodox and balanced doctrine is a far cry from the radical and flawed views of both Universal Atonement and Limited Atonement.

---

[206] White, in *Debating Calvinism*, 170.

[207] Herman Hanko, *God's Everlasting Covenant of Grace* (Grand Rapids: Reformed Free Publishing Association, 1988), 15.

Tulip

Limited Atonement Uprooted

Limited Atonement is special in that it is the first point in TULIP that stands exclusively on the preceding two points without extrapolating upon any Scripture. While the first two points of TULIP twist Scripture to mean something clearly not intended, Limited Atonement has no Scripture behind it to misinterpret. Limited Atonement simply means that Jesus died only for the sins of the elect; His death on the cross and resurrection from the grave was intended only for the select few, thus making it "limited." It is this very teaching that evangelist and apologist John R. Rice considers to be the "heart of . . . Calvinist doctrine . . . that Christ did not die for all men."[208]

1 John 2:2 strikes to the heart of Limited Atonement. I am of the opinion that the Holy Spirit led the apostle John to write specifically to those in the kingdom who might be tempted to take their election to a prideful, heretical, or Calvinistic level. Calvinists take their election to this dangerous place by believing they are the only ones for whom Jesus died. They seem justified by asking, Why would Jesus die for those who would not believe? They argue that the blood of Jesus is nothing to be wasted, especially for unregenerate sinners. They believe that if Jesus' blood was shed for people who would not respond, it would be a waste and, therefore, that God would be less than sovereign. They conclude that if God is sovereign as He claims to be, and if He desires all mankind to be saved, and if all men do not end up being saved, then God is not absolutely sovereign. This is an error of logic, equating God's sovereignty with fatalism and man's will with control.

1 John 2:2 says, "And He [Jesus] Himself is the propitiation for our sins." Note that John, as one of the "elect" of God, said, *"our sins"*

---

[208] John R. Rice, *Some Serious, Popular False Doctrines Answered from the Scriptures* (Murfreesboro, TN: Sword of the Lord Publishers, 1970), 279.

(emphasis mine). The point in the beginning of the verse is that Jesus died for the sins of the elect. But the verse continues, "And He [Jesus] Himself is the propitiation for our sins; and not for ours only but also for the whole world."

Calvinists explain this verse and others like it by changing the definitions of words while using systematic logic to bring about their radically different interpretation. For now, it should be sufficient simply to know that **1 John 2:2** poses a clear and monumental threat to the TULIP theology of Limited Atonement.

With a lack of any plain scriptural support, the case given by leading Calvinists to support the doctrine of Limited Atonement is feebler than the arguments used to defend the other four points of TULIP. Many Calvinists find solace in the sermon "A Defense of Calvinism," by the great Charles Haddon Spurgeon. However, Spurgeon does not defend Calvinism as much as he defends the truth that the church is God's elect and that they are saved by grace, truths which non-Calvinists do not deny. Although Spurgeon has written thoughtfully on the two seemingly contradictory biblical truths of God's sovereignty and man's free will, he seems somewhat confused when addressing the doctrine of Limited Atonement. He writes:

> I know there are some who think it necessary to their system of theology to limit the merit of the blood of Jesus: if my theological system needed such a limitation, I would cast it to the winds. I cannot, I dare not allow the thought to find lodging in my mind, it seems so near akin to blasphemy. In Christ's finished work I see an ocean of merit; my plummet finds no bottom, my eye discovers no shore. There must be sufficient efficacy in the blood of Christ, if God had so willed it, to have saved not only all in this world, but all in ten thousand worlds, had they transgressed their Maker's law. Once admit infinity into the matter, and limit is out of the question. Having a

Divine Person for an offering, it is not consistent to conceive of limited value.[209]

Furthermore, Spurgeon seems to equate denial of Limited Atonement to acceptance of universal redemption:

> If Christ on His cross intended to save every man, then He intended to save those who were lost before He died. If the doctrine be true, that He died for all men, then He died for some who were in hell before He came into this world, for doubtless there were even then myriads there who had been cast away because of their sins. Once again, if it was Christ's intention to save all men, how deplorably has He been disappointed, for we have His own testimony that there is a lake which burneth with fire and brimstone, and into that pit of woe have been cast some of the very persons who, according to the theory of universal redemption, were bought with His blood. That seems to me a conception a thousand times more repulsive than any of those consequences which are said to be associated with the Calvinistic and Christian doctrine of special and particular redemption. To think that my Savior died for men who were or are in hell, seems a supposition too horrible for me to entertain.[210]

There is no scriptural support offered in Spurgeon's argument. His case is based purely on personal thoughts that are apparently "too horrible . . . to entertain." I disagree with Spurgeon's logic. The thought that Christ died only for those whom He would later force to believe is too horrible to entertain. Life's experiences have always taught us that

---

[209] Spurgeon, "A Defense of Calvinism."

[210] Spurgeon, "A Defense of Calvinism."

whenever we choose to love, we take the risk of not being loved in return. Paul relates this experience in **2 Corinthians 12:15**: "The more abundantly I love you, the less I am loved." But the Jesus of Calvinism could not say this. Because Calvinism's Jesus was guaranteed to be loved by those for whom He died, there would be no risk. Ben Witherington III rightly states that Calvinists "have a hard time understanding that holy love does not involve determinism, however subtle. Indeed love, if it is real love, must be freely given and freely received, for God has chosen to relate to us as persons, not as automata."[211]

If there was no offer for all to be forgiven, why, then, would Jesus lament over a people who could not respond to His love? (**Matthew 23:37**). Why would He cry out to those who were either forced to respond or to those who were incapable of responding? Paul writes that love "does not seek its own" and "bears all things" (**1 Corinthians 13:5, 7**). If, in fact, Jesus did die only for those who would return His love, Calvinism's portrayal of Jesus may have been accurate. But the fact that many people, whom Jesus has saved through the resurrection, deny Him is what makes His sacrifice so amazing. He willingly died, knowing that His offer would be rejected by some. The Bible says, "For God so loved the world . . . that whoever believes in Him . . ." The traditional belief that Jesus actually died for the sins of the world (meaning that Jesus made a sacrifice for those who would not accept it) seems better to explain the burden that Jesus continually bore for the lost.

Spurgeon writes:

> To imagine for a moment that He was the Substitute for all
> the sons of men, and that God, having first punished the
> Substitute, afterwards punished the sinners themselves,
> seems to conflict with all my ideas of Divine justice. That

---

[211] Witherington, *The Problem with Evangelical Theology*, 5.

Christ should offer an atonement and satisfaction for the sins of all men, and that afterwards some of those very men should be punished for the sins for which Christ had already atoned, appears to me to be the most monstrous iniquity that could ever have been imputed to Saturn, to Janus, to the goddess of the Thugs, or to the most diabolical heathen deities. God forbid that we should ever think thus of Jehovah, the just and wise and good![212]

Confusing, isn't it? First Spurgeon says, "Having a Divine Person for an offering it is not consistent to conceive of limited value," only to state later that "if it was Christ's intention to save all men, how deplorably has He been disappointed." Yet, the question at hand is whether or not Jesus' atonement was limited to the elect. To bring in the doctrine of universal redemption as a means of resolving this question is confusing and unnecessary. If I were a Calvinist, I would not put such great confidence in Spurgeon's "Defense of Calvinism." George Bryson seems to agree, concluding that Spurgeon, "the great evangelist . . . was at best an inconsistent Calvinist. He was a soul winner despite Reformed Theology and not because of Reformed Theology."[213]

Josh McDowell unknowingly acknowledges that Calvinism shares some similarities with other cults. In his book *Handbook of Today's Religions* he writes, "Within all branches of Christianity there is agreement that the deity of Christ was a perfect satisfaction to God as just and substitutionary punishment for the sins of the world."[214] Even though "all branches" of Christianity and denominations of both liberal and conservative persuasion could agree with this statement (granted that the word "world" is all-inclusive in representing every soul of man and

[212] Spurgeon, "A Defense of Calvinism."

[213] Bryson, *The Dark Side of Calvinism*, 331.

[214] McDowell, *Handbook of Today's Religions*, 38.

woman), Calvinists cannot. Thus, Calvinism, by its doctrine of Limited Atonement alone, disagrees with "all branches of Christianity," placing it outside the camp of orthodox Christianity.

Despite the arguments Calvinists use to support the idea of Limited Atonement, the doctrine is ultimately useless without scriptural support. In fact, Limited Atonement is an insult to one's natural intellect. I agree with Vance when he says, "To make an issue out of Limited Atonement is a waste of time. If Christ died a thousand deaths for the 'non-elect' they would still go to Hell."[215]

I agree with James White's statement: "It is not that the Bible's teaching on the atonement is unclear or confusing." However, his claim that any non-Reformed doctrine concerning the atonement of Jesus remains "without the first shred of meaningful biblical support" is puzzling.[216] We can look to the Bible to see the truthfulness of such a bold assertion. [The following italics are mine.]

> *John 1:29b: "Behold! The Lamb of God, who takes away the sin of the world!"*
>
> *John 3:16–17: "For God so loved the world that He gave His only begotten Son, that whoever believes in Him should not perish but have everlasting life. For God did not send His Son into the world to condemn the world, but that the world through Him might be saved."*
>
> *2 Corinthians 5:14–15: "For the love of Christ compels us, because we judge thus: that if One died for all, then all died; and He died for all, that those who live should live no longer for themselves, but for Him who died for them and rose again."*
>
> *1 Timothy 2:3–6: "For this is good and acceptable in the sight of*

---

[215] Vance, *The Other Side of Calvinism*, 409.

[216] White, in *Debating Calvinism*, 169.

God our Savior, who desires all men to be saved and to come to the knowledge of the truth. For there is one God and one Mediator between God and men, the Man Christ Jesus, who gave Himself a ransom for all, to be testified in due time."

1 Timothy 4:10: "For to this end we both labor and suffer reproach, because we trust in the living God, who is the Savior of all men, especially of those who believe."

Titus 2:11: "For the grace of God that brings salvation has appeared to all men."

1 John 2:2: "And He Himself is the propitiation for our sins, and not for ours only but also for the whole world."

The doctrine of Limited Atonement clearly stands in contradiction to the Bible's message of Jesus dying for the sins of the whole world. Few other doctrines are as important to the Christian faith as the atonement of Jesus and its active relationship to mankind. To distort in any way the salvific message of Jesus' saving work on the cross is cultishly suspect.

Tulip

Irresistible Grace Explained

The "I" in TULIP stands for *Irresistible Grace*. This term means that God's grace cannot be resisted. Calvinists give the word "grace" many different meanings. It is the particular grace that pertains to salvation that Calvinists presume to be irresistible. As the first three doctrines of TULIP theology deny that man has free will, so too does the doctrine of Irresistible Grace. In their book, *Five Points of Calvinism, Defined, Defended, Documented*, David Steele, Curtis Thomas, and Lance Quinn explain:

Although the general outward call of the gospel can be, and often is, rejected, the special inward call of the Spirit never fails to result in the conversion of those to whom it is made. This special call is not made to all sinners but is issued to the elect only. The Spirit is in no way dependent upon their help or cooperation for success in His work of bringing them to Christ. It is for this reason that Calvinists speak of the Spirit's call and of God's grace in saving sinners as being "efficacious," "invincible," or "irresistible." The grace which the Holy Spirit extends to the elect cannot be thwarted or refused; it never fails to bring them to true faith in Christ.[217]

Again, we must notice that an imaginary "general call" is mentioned. Calvinists claim that though this general call is often resisted by people, it works as a pedestal to yet another illusory concept of the "inward" or "special" call that supposedly cannot be resisted.

The Canons of Dort state that salvation is not "ascribed to the proper exercise of freewill." Rather, it:

. . . must be wholly ascribed to God, who as he has chosen his own from eternity in Christ, so he confers upon them faith and repentance, rescues them from the power of darkness, and translates them into the kingdom of his own Son . . . according to the testimony of the apostles in various places. [218]

The Westminster Confession of Faith further expresses the idea of Irresistible Grace by stating:

---

[217] Steele, Thomas, and Quinn, *The Five Points of Calvinism*, 54–54.

[218] "Canons of Dort (1619 AD)," Third and Fourth Head, Article 10 [online]; accessed 20 January 2010, available from http://www.carm.org/canons-of-dort; Internet.

All those whom God hath predestinated unto life, and those only, he is pleased, in his appointed and accepted time, effectually to call, by his word and Spirit, out of that state of sin and death in which they are by nature, to grace and salvation by Jesus Christ; enlightening their minds spiritually and savingly to understand the things of God; taking away their heart of stone, and giving unto them a heart of flesh; renewing their wills, and by his almighty power determining them to that which is good, and effectually drawing them to Jesus Christ; yet so as they come most freely, being made willing by his grace. [219]

There is a great oxymoron in the last sentence: ". . . they come most freely, being made willing by his grace." How can one come "most freely, being made . . ."? This is like saying that one is completely free while bound. Also, the Confession seems to acknowledge that man actually has a free will. It deceptively states that the elect are "being made willing by his grace." How can free will be free if it is "made"?

Yet, the doctrinal explanations for the idea of Irresistible Grace still claim biblical support. Two main verses claimed by Calvinists to support Irresistible Grace are the following:

> *John 6:37–39: "All that the Father gives Me will come to Me, and the one who comes to Me I will by no means cast out. For I have come down from heaven, not to do My own will, but the will of Him who sent Me. This is the will of the Father who sent Me, that of all He has given Me I should lose nothing, but should raise it up at the last day."*

> *John 6:44–45: "No one can come to Me unless the Father who sent Me draws him; and I will raise him up at the last day. It is written*

---

[219] "Westminster Confession of Faith," 10.1.

in the prophets, 'And they shall all be taught by God.' Therefore everyone who has heard and learned from the Father comes to Me."

Commenting on verse 44, John Calvin writes that this process of God's drawing "is not violent, so as to compel men by external force."[220]

John Gill (1697–1771), a prominent Calvinist, agrees, extrapolating that this "drawing":

> . . . is an act of power, yet not of force; God in drawing of unwilling, makes willing in the day of his power: he enlightens the understanding, bends the will, gives an heart of flesh, sweetly allures by the power of his grace, and engages the soul to come to Christ, and give up itself to him; he draws with the bands of love. Drawing, though it supposes power and influence, yet not always coercion and force: music draws the ear, love the heart, and pleasure the mind.[221]

Yes, music can draw the ear similar to the way the Holy Spirit draws sinners. But for music forcefully to pervade the ear is something quite different. John Gill and many like him downplay the obvious differences between God's drawing versus God's forcing.

John Piper also seems to mince words in his definition of Irresistible Grace by stating that it "does not mean that every influence of the Holy Spirit cannot be resisted. It means that the Holy Spirit can overcome all resistance and make his influence irresistible."[222] Yet, whether or not God has the power to overcome all resistance is not the question. The question is whether or not Scripture speaks about mankind

---

[220] Calvin, *Calvin's Commentaries: The Gospels*, 704.

[221] John Gill, *John Gill's Exposition of the Bible* [online]; accessed 15 July 2006; available from http://www.biblestudytools.com/commentaries/gills-exposition-of-the-bible/john-6-44.html; Internet.

[222] Piper, "Irresistible Grace."

having no free will and God forcing (or compelling) His salvific plan on some while withholding it from others. John Piper further explains:

> We [writing for Bethlehem Baptist Church] believe that the new birth is a miraculous creation of God that enables a formerly "dead" person to receive Christ and so be saved. We do not think that faith precedes . . . the new birth. Faith is the evidence that God has begotten us anew. . . . God begets us anew and the first glimmer of life in the newborn child is faith. This new birth is the effect of irresistible grace, because it is an act of sovereign creation.[223]

By now, it should be evident that the doctrinal statements thus far in the TULIP theology deny man of his free will. As we comprehend this, we are faced with the question of how that actually plays out in our human experiences. Although John Calvin wrote that Irresistible Grace is compatible with free will but is "not violent, so as to compel men by external force,"[224] there is a clearer definition of Irresistible Grace, believed to have been coined by Puritan scholar Perry Miller and later used by a few other Reformed theologians, notably R. C. Sproul in his novel, *Thy Brother's Keeper.* Quite simply, Irresistible Grace is equivalent to a "holy rape of the soul."[225]

While the phrase "holy rape of the soul" seems wrong on a number of theological levels, it demands our attention. We assume the Calvinist would argue that while rape goes against the victim's will, God's means of compelling changes the sinner's will to the point where it is no longer

---

[223] Ibid.

[224] Calvin, *Calvin's Commentaries: The Gospels*, 704.

[225] Perry Miller, Wikipedia, http://en. wikipedia.org/wiki/Perry_Miller, January 20, 2010. Also, accessed 21 December; available from http://www.spiritus-temporis.com/calvinism/summaries-of-calvinist-theology.html; Internet. Also, accessed 21 December; available from http://articulifidei.blogspot.com/2010/07/rc-sproul-and-holy-rape-of-soul.html; Internet.

resistant. Although the definitions and confessions given to understand the doctrine of Irresistible Grace go out of the way to portray God as not being forceful or violent against the soul of man, they do, however, depict a sort of dictatorial God who overcomes all resistance by the sinner. Ultimately, the "victim" is made willing by something other than his will. Whether God saves the soul violently or gently, the outcome of Irresistible Grace is a disregard for the free will of both the saved and the unsaved.

Attempts to make more appealing what some Calvinists themselves consider "harsh doctrines" can only go so far. Irresistible Grace means that the elect cannot help but believe. In other words, the elect are ultimately forced to believe because it is impossible to resist God's calling or salvation. Therefore, everyone who is not of the elect cannot help but *not* believe. Historical and orthodox Christianity by sound biblical exposition teaches something quite different. It shows in the Old and New Testament that believers and unbelievers can choose to resist God's will and grace in the many forms it comes in. The Bible clearly shows that human beings can resist God's saving grace.

The doctrine that God's grace cannot be resisted is completely fabricated. Like the three before it, the doctrine of Irresistible Grace disregards the free will of mankind. Nowhere is this taught or revealed in the Scriptures. It is only within the cultish side of Calvinism that "salvific rape" is held as both biblical and prosperous for humanity.

Tulip

Irresistible Grace Uprooted

Irresistible Grace means exactly what its name implies—that God's will is utterly irresistible, including His call to salvation. As Calvin himself says, "When God calls a person, His call cannot ultimately be ignored."[226]

---

[226] John Calvin, *God the Creator, God the Redeemer: Institutes of the Christian Religion*, trans. Henry Beveridge (Gainesville, FL: Bridge-Logos, 2005), 533.

To explain this doctrine in TULIP theology, we should explore the obvious question: Can God's will, calling, and grace be resisted or not? In the vast spectrum of biblical theology, a simple answer to this question is both yes and no. (Before citing examples, we must keep in mind that Calvinists believe that people, both the elect and nonelect, can resist God's will and grace in matters other than salvation.) As we have read, "The general outward call of the gospel can be, and often is, rejected."[227]

We will now consider both the possibilities and impossibilities of resisting God's will and calling. The Bible teaches in **1 Thessalonians 4:15–17** that Jesus will come back one day to receive His children:

> For this we say to you by the word of the Lord, that we who are alive *and* remain until the coming of the Lord will by no means precede those who are asleep. For the Lord Himself will descend from heaven with a shout, with the voice of an archangel, and with the trumpet of God. And the dead in Christ will rise first. Then we who are alive *and* remain shall be caught up together with them in the clouds to meet the Lord in the air. And thus we shall always be with the Lord.

In this case, God's will and desire to gather His children can in no way be resisted or ignored. His actions in gathering His holy ones cannot possibly be thwarted, regardless of what the unsaved believe, and even irrespective of His saints' beliefs about eschatology. Whether or not one believes in the claims of Jesus, the Bible's message is clear that everyone will one day find themselves in either Heaven or Hell. Someone who denies that these places exist poses no threat to Jesus assigning them to one or the other. God's will to come back and receive His church cannot be resisted, ignored, denied, or stopped by anyone.

---

[227] Steele, Thomas, and Quinn, *The Five Points of Calvinism*, 53.

However, God's will for His children to be sanctified can be, and is, resisted every day. We all know that the Christian can resist God's conviction and consequently fall into sin. But is that God's will? Is it God's will for His children to resist the Holy Spirit's conviction and choose to fulfill the lust of their flesh? The answer is clearly "No." This leads us to ask that if God's will and sanctifying Spirit can be resisted, why can His call to salvation not also be resisted? In **Colossians 1:22–23**, Paul says that Jesus "has reconciled [you] in the body of His flesh through death, to present you holy, and blameless, and above reproach in His sight—if indeed you continue in the faith . . ." Notice that Paul adds "if indeed you continue in the faith." If free will were not a factor here, why would Paul bother adding such a statement? Even more compelling is why Paul would write to Timothy about "Hymenaeus and Alexander," who had rejected "faith and a good conscience [and] . . . concerning the faith have suffered shipwreck" (**1 Timothy 1:19–20**). Although the text here does not directly read that the two men committed apostasy, or lost their salvation, it simply says that they "rejected . . . faith." How to interpret what that means is debatable. What is not debatable, however, is that their rejection of saving faith poses a problem to Calvinism's doctrine of Irresistible Grace.

Calvinists maintain that the elect cannot ever resist the will of God in regard to salvation. James White uses the account of Lazarus being raised from the dead as one example of Irresistible Grace. White writes that, "Lazarus could [not] have stopped the Messiah from commanding him to come forth."[228] He then concludes that because Lazarus could not *resist* his resurrection from the dead, God's chosen people cannot resist God's will to save the elect. He writes:

> The doctrine of "irresistible grace" is . . . simply the belief
> that when God chooses to move in the lives of His elect
> and bring them from spiritual death to spiritual life, no

---

[228] White, in *Debating Calvinism*, 206.

power in heaven or on earth can stop Him from so doing. . . . The doctrine has nothing to do with the fact that sinners "resist" the common grace of God and the Holy Spirit every day (they do) . . . Just as Christ had the power and authority to raise Lazarus to life without obtaining his "permission" to do so, He is able to raise His elect to spiritual life with just as certain a result. [229]

Once again, we can see the cultish characteristic of reinterpreting the clear teachings of Christ and His apostles. This is done by both Calvinism and Jehovah's Witnesses. From the same portion of Scripture above (**John 11:11–14**), we read that Jesus says, "Our friend Lazarus sleeps, but I go that I may wake him up." Then, Jesus says, "Lazarus is dead." Surprisingly, it is from these verses that Jehovah's Witnesses pull their unorthodox view of death. Because Jesus said that Lazarus "sleeps," concerning his death, they believe, "There is no conscious existence of the soul following death." [230] Yet this unorthodox doctrine of death or "soul sleep" opposes clear teachings within the Bible revealing that consciousness does exist after physical death, including **Philippians 1:23; Revelation 19:20; 2 Corinthians 5:8; 1 Thessalonians 4:13;** and **Mark 9:43–48**, in which Jesus says, "It is better for you to enter into life maimed, rather than having two hands, to go to hell, into the fire that shall never be quenched" (v. 43).

But while the majority of mainstream Christian apologists are quick to denounce Watchtower (Jehovah's Witnesses) doctrine, very few recognize the same kind of unorthodoxy within Calvinism. How does this Jehovah's Witnesses doctrine of "soul sleep" differ from the Calvinist's claim that God's call to salvation cannot be ignored or resisted? **Matthew 23:37; John 5:38-40; Acts 7:51; 16:30;** and

[229] Ibid., 197.

[230] Geisler and Rhodes, *Correcting the Cults*, 179.

Hebrews 4:6 clearly teach otherwise. Both unorthodox doctrines are supported by a defensive logic and misinterpreted verses, though faced with a host of passages contradicting this position.

Again, the two main passages of Scripture given as support for Irresistible Grace are the following:

> *John 6:37–39: "All that the Father gives Me will come to Me, and the one who comes to Me I will by no means cast out. For I have come down from heaven, not to do My own will, but the will of Him who sent Me. This is the will of the Father who sent Me, that of all He has given Me I should lose nothing, but should raise it up at the last day."*

> *John 6: 44–45: "No one can come to Me unless the Father who sent Me draws him; and I will raise him up at the last day. It is written in the prophets, 'And they shall all be taught by God.' Therefore everyone who has heard and learned from the Father comes to Me."*

These verses say nothing directly relating to Irresistible Grace as defined by Calvinists (that the grace "which the Holy Spirit extends to the elect cannot be thwarted or refused"[231]). At best, these verses can infer such a notion but only when interpreted with several presuppositions—namely, that "all that the Father gives me" and those whom "the Father . . . draws" cannot possibly refer to *all people* but rather to a *limited number*. Yet, because **John 6: 44–45** do not explicitly state whether the Father draws or gives all or just some, the non-Calvinist must also ask himself if the presupposition claiming that the Father's invitation was intended for all people is equivalent. The answer is simple. The non-Calvinist does not need to presuppose that God desires all to be saved because the Bible has clearly revealed this to be true. As Paul declares:

---

[231] Steele, Thomas, and Quinn, *The Five Points of Calvinism*, 53, 54.

Therefore I exhort first of all that supplications, prayers, intercessions, *and* giving of thanks be made for all men, for kings and all who are in authority, that we may lead a quiet and peaceable life in all godliness and reverence. For this *is* good and acceptable in the sight of God our Savior, who desires all men to be saved and to come to the knowledge of the truth. For *there is* one God and one Mediator between God and men, *the* Man Christ Jesus, who gave Himself a ransom for all . . . (**1 Timothy 2:1–6**).

Paul also writes:

For to this end we both labor and suffer reproach, because we trust in the living God, who is the Savior of all men, especially of those who believe (**1 Timothy 4:10**).

Jesus also states:

"And as Moses lifted up the serpent in the wilderness, even so must the Son of Man be lifted up, that whoever believes in Him should not perish but have eternal life. For God so loved the world that He gave His only begotten Son, that whoever believes in Him should not perish but have everlasting life. For God did not send His Son into the world to condemn the world, but that the world through Him might be saved. He who believes in Him is not condemned; but he who does not believe is condemned already, because he has not believed in the name of the only begotten Son of God" (**John 3:14–18**).

Jesus also issues this invitation:

"On the last day, that great day of the feast, Jesus stood and cried out, saying, 'If anyone thirsts, let him come to Me and drink. He who believes in Me, as the Scripture has said, out of his heart will flow rivers of living water'" **(John 7:37–38**).

Because there are no verses that directly support Calvinism's claim that God does not desire everyone to be saved, we are safe to conclude it is the Calvinist who presupposes that God draws a limited number of people to salvation. Calvinism's defense for Irresistible Grace is supported only by misinterpretations and inferences.

James White shows how this is done. After alluding to the raising of Lazarus passage, White further "defends" Irresistible Grace with the following verses:

Ephesians 2:8–9: "For by grace you have been saved through faith, and that not of yourselves; it is the gift of God, not of works, lest anyone should boast."

Philippians 1:29: "For to you it has been granted on behalf of Christ, not only to believe in Him, but also to suffer for His sake."

Colossians 1:3–4: "We give thanks to the God and Father of our Lord Jesus Christ, praying always for you, since we heard of your faith in Christ Jesus and of your love for all the saints."

Hebrews 12:2: ". . . looking unto Jesus, the author and finisher of our faith, who for the joy that was set before Him endured the cross, despising the shame, and has sat down at the right hand of the throne of God."

James White concludes that, "The consistent way of interpreting all of these passages is to see that divine and saving faith is a gift of God . . . Simple consistency demands it."[232] Again, however, White's whole point rests upon the presupposition discussed earlier. While some of

---

[232] White, in *Debating Calvinism*, 203.

these verses can be interpreted to reveal "divine and saving faith [as] a gift of God," they do not give proper support for the doctrine of Irresistible Grace because they fail to imply that "saving faith" is limited or given only to certain people. Orthodox Christianity has always maintained that eternal life is a free gift. All men can either receive or resist it. As **Romans 5:15–17** states:

> But the *free gift* is not like the offense. For if by the one man's offense many died, much more the grace of God and the *gift* by the grace of the one Man, Jesus Christ, abounded to many. And the *gift* is not like that which came through the one who sinned. For the judgment which came from one offense resulted in condemnation, but the *free gift* which came from many offenses resulted in justification. For if by the one man's offense death reigned through the one, much more those who receive abundance of grace and of the *gift* of righteousness will reign in life through the One, Jesus Christ. [Italics mine]

The "gift" mentioned in the passage, whether it be salvation itself or just the means to obtain it (saving faith), is offered to all men and can be resisted as much as any other gift of God. Dave Hunt states early in his dialogue with White:

> Irresistible Grace is an oxymoron. Grace is the opposite of irresistible. Moreover, if God's grace can irresistibly cause every sinner to believe in Christ, the fact that it is limited to the elect disparages His love. And why is irresistible grace no longer irresistible once a person is saved, so that Christians can so often be carnal?[233]

---

[233] Hunt, in *Debating Calvinism*, 209.

Tulip

Perseverance of the Saints Explained

The "P" in TULIP stands for *Perseverance of the Saints* and is usually associated with the Christian catch phrase, "Once saved, always saved." Yet this last point of TULIP is not quite so simple. Many Calvinists hold different meanings of "perseverance." Some, like Sproul, understand it to mean eternal security, while others like A. W. Pink do not. Though many ideas have been expressed as to the meaning of "perseverance," the generally accepted view of this doctrine is articulated in the Council of Dort:

> Just as God himself is most wise, unchangeable, all knowing, and almighty, so the election made by him can neither be suspended nor altered, revoked, or annulled; neither can his chosen ones be cast off, nor their number reduced.[234]

The Westminster Confession of Faith states:

> They, whom God hath accepted in His Beloved, effectually called, and sanctified by His Spirit, can neither totally nor finally fall away from the state of grace, but shall certainly persevere therein to the end, and be eternally saved.[235]

Note that the perseverance of the saint "shall" persevere as opposed to "should." The Westminster Confession further explains:

> This perseverance of the saints depends not upon their own free will, but upon the immutability of the decree of

---

[234] "The Canons of Dort," Article 11[online]; accessed 20 January 2010; available from http://www.creeds.net/reformed/dordt/index.htm; Internet.

[235] "The Westminster Confession of Faith," 17.2.

election, flowing from the free and unchangeable love of God the Father; upon the efficacy of the merit and intercession of Jesus Christ, the abiding of the Spirit, and of the seed of God within them, and the nature of the covenant of grace: from all which ariseth also the certainty and infallibility thereof.[236]

Boettner asserts that the doctrine of Perseverance of the Saints:

. . . does not stand alone but is a necessary part of the Calvinistic system of theology. The doctrines of Election and Efficacious Grace logically imply the certain salvation of those who receive these blessings. If God has chosen men absolutely and unconditionally to eternal life, and if His Spirit effectively applies to them the benefits of redemption, the inescapable conclusion is that these persons shall be saved.[237]

In *The Five Points of Calvinism, Defined, Defended, and Documented*, authors Steele, Thomas, and Quinn write that the doctrine:

. . . does not maintain that all who profess the Christian faith are certain of Heaven. It is saints—those who are set apart by the Spirit—who persevere to the end. It is believers—those who are given true, living faith in Christ—who are secure and safe in Him. Many who profess to believe fall away, but they do not fall from grace, for they were never in grace.[238]

---

[236] Ibid.

[237] Boettner, *The Reformed Doctrine of Predestination*, 182.

[238] Steele, Thomas, and Quinn, *The Five Points of Calvinism*, 64.

The verses typically used as a foundation for Perseverance of the Saints are as follows:

John 3:16: "For God so loved the world that He gave His only begotten Son, that whoever believes in Him should not perish but have everlasting life."

John 5:24: "Most assuredly, I say to you, he who hears My word and believes in Him who sent Me has everlasting life, and shall not come into judgment, but has passed from death into life."

John 6:37–40: "All that the Father gives Me will come to Me, and the one who comes to Me I will by no means cast out. For I have come down from heaven, not to do My own will, but the will of Him who sent Me. This is the will of the Father who sent Me, that of all He has given Me I should lose nothing, but should raise it up at the last day. And this is the will of Him who sent Me, that everyone who sees the Son and believes in Him may have everlasting life; and I will raise him up at the last day."

John 10:28–29: "And I give them eternal life, and they shall never perish; neither shall anyone snatch them out of My hand. My Father, who has given them to Me, is greater than all; and no one is able to snatch them out of My Father's hand."

Romans 5:9–10: "Much more then, having now been justified by His blood, we shall be saved from wrath through Him. For if when we were enemies we were reconciled to God through the death of His Son, much more, having been reconciled, we shall be saved by His life."

Romans 8:35–39: "Who shall separate us from the love of Christ? Shall tribulation, or distress, or persecution, or famine, or nakedness, or peril, or sword? As it is written: For Your sake we are killed all day long; We are accounted as sheep for the slaughter.' Yet in all these things we are more than conquerors through Him who loved us. For I am persuaded that neither death nor life, nor angels nor principalities nor powers, nor things present nor things to come, nor height nor depth, nor any other created thing, shall be able to separate us from the love of God which is in Christ Jesus our Lord."

Romans 11:29: "For the gifts and the calling of God are irrevocable."

1 Corinthians 1:4–9: "I thank my God always concerning you for the grace of God which was given to you by Christ Jesus, that you were enriched in everything by Him in all utterance and all knowledge, even as the testimony of Christ was confirmed in you, so that you come short in no gift, eagerly waiting for the revelation of our Lord Jesus Christ, who will also confirm you to the end, that you may be blameless in the day of our Lord Jesus Christ. God is faithful, by whom you were called into the fellowship of His Son, Jesus Christ our Lord."

Ephesians 1:13–14: "In Him you also trusted, after you heard the word of truth, the gospel of your salvation; in whom also, having believed, you were sealed with the Holy Spirit of promise, who is the guarantee of our inheritance until the redemption of the purchased possession, to the praise of His glory."

Ephesians 4:30: "And do not grieve the Holy Spirit of God, by whom you were sealed for the day of redemption."

Philippians 1:6: "being confident of this very thing, that He who has begun a good work in you will complete it until the day of Jesus Christ."

Hebrews 13:5: "Let your conduct be without covetousness; be content with such things as you have. For He Himself has said, 'I will never leave you nor forsake you.'"

Jude 1:24: "Now to Him who is able to keep you from stumbling, and to present you faultless before the presence of His glory with exceeding joy . . ."

Together, these verses support the biblical truth held by orthodox Christians that God keeps those who remain in Jesus. However, they fail miserably in proving the last point of TULIP. The question is not whether God has the ability to keep those committed to Him but whether Christians have the ability to give up their faith. Again, why would Paul command the elect to "keep the faith" if there is no possibility to do otherwise? To whom was Paul speaking? The Calvinist might reply that Paul was not even speaking to the elect. Yet, if this was the case, why would Paul encourage unbelievers to continue in something they could never have started?

Many Evangelicals seem to be in general agreement on the teaching that salvation in Christ is secure. Many Christians find it hard to disagree with this doctrine of Calvinism as opposed to the more doubtful and arguable TULIP teachings. Dave Hunt writes, "Once I had thought that I agreed with at least one Calvinist point, the Perseverance of the Saints. I learned, however, that this fifth point of TULIP offers an unbiblical basis for eternal security: that of being one of the elect."[239] Though many Christians may think that they align themselves with this teaching, the idea of "eternal security" behind Perseverance of the Saints is misleading.

Although "eternal security" and "once saved always saved" can seem as if they are one and the same, we must probe more deeply into what exactly Perseverance of the Saints looks like to the Calvinist. How to determine if a Christian is "eternally secure" is a crucial part of understanding the doctrine. Although Perseverance of the Saints and eternal security are assuredly related, they are indeed different from each other. Vance points out that "Perseverance of the Saints . . . is not the

---

[239] Hunt, in *Debating Calvinism*, 392.

same thing as eternal security."[240] We must understand the difference. Even the "lowly regarded" Wikipedia Dictionary does:

> Traditional Calvinists also believe that all who are born again and justified before God necessarily and inexorably proceed to sanctification. Indeed, failure to proceed to sanctification in their view is evidence that the person in question was not truly saved to begin with. Proponents of this doctrine distinguish between an action and the consequences of an action, and suggest that after God has regenerated someone, the person's will cannot reverse its course. It is argued that God has changed that person in ways that are outside of his or her own ability to alter fundamentally, and he or she will therefore persevere in the faith.[241]

Read again: ". . . failure to proceed to sanctification in their view is evidence that the person in question was not truly saved to begin with [and that] he or she will therefore persevere in the faith." We find then a criterion of persevering in sanctification or good works that the Christian must meet in order to know that they are indeed one of the elect. This idea started with Calvin's successor, Theodore Beza, who believed that in order to be assured of salvation, the elect would look to a life of obedience to faith. Joseph C. Dillow writes that according to Beza, "Since Christ did not die for all men, assurance must be based on works."[242]

---

[240] Vance, *The Other Side of Calvinism* , 555.

[241] www.wikipedia.com, s.v. "perseverance of the saints", accessed 20 January 2010; Internet.

[242] Joseph C. Dillow, *The Reign of the Servant Kings: A Study of Eternal Security and the Final Significance of Man* (Haysville, NC: Schoettle Publishing Company, 1992), 269.

Likewise, A. W. Pink states that, "Those who persevere not in faith and holiness, love and obedience, will assuredly perish." [243]

Murray has also stated that the elect "entertain the faith of our security in Christ only as we persevere in faith and holiness to the end." [244]

John Piper agrees, writing, "Our final salvation is made contingent upon the subsequent obedience which comes from faith."[245]

Although Christians of all denominations interpret the concept of "once saved always saved" differently, Calvinism claims that the elect *will* (without choice), instead of *should* (with choice), persevere in faith and holiness until their physical death or until the Lord's second coming. Calvinism also maintains that a life of good works and holiness is imperial evidence in determining if one is of the elect. This is contrasted to historical and orthodox Christianity, which teaches that it is by the power of God that the believer *should* persevere in faith and holiness but will not necessarily do so as a consequence of free will.

In closing, we must remember when thinking of the last doctrine of TULIP that because the elect did not choose to be saved, and could not resist His calling, it now makes it impossible for them to deny the faith: they must continue in faith and holiness. If they had a choice in the matter, it would mean they had never really been saved.

---

[243] A. W. Pink, *Eternal Security* [online]; accessed 28 January 2010; available from http://www.theologue.org/EternalSecurity-AWPink.html; Internet.

[244] John Murray, *Redemption Accomplished and Applied* (Grand Rapids: Eerdmans, 1955), 155.

[245] John Piper and Bethlehem Baptist Church Staff, "What We Believe about the Five Points of Calvinism" [online]; accessed -----; available from http://www.desiringgod.org/resource-library/resources/what-we-believe-about-the-five-points-of-calvinism; Internet.

Tulip

Perseverance of the Saints Uprooted

I have always disliked the question: Can someone lose their salvation? The question likens salvation to a set of car keys or eyeglasses. "Has anyone seen my salvation? I seem to have lost it. Can you help me find it?" As aforementioned, the issue is not whether God has the power to keep those who believe but whether the elect have the free will to renounce their faith. In the last step of uprooting Calvin's TULIP, we must first show that apostasy is possible and that the peculiar logic of Calvinism used to determine who is of the elect only leaves them in a confusing state of uncertainty.

In questioning Calvinism's exegetical foundation, Ben Witherington writes, "The idea of 'once saved always saved,' or the idea that it is impossible for a 'saved person,' a true Christian, to commit apostasy, is simply not found in the NT. More to the point, much in the NT flatly contradicts such an idea."[246] One of Witherington's conclusions about how Calvinists can still claim the doctrine is true is that they exclude certain Scriptures. He writes, "It is perfectly possible to argue consistently and logically about something, but draw the circle of argumentation too narrowly, and so wrongly exclude some of the most important data."[247]

Use of the verses that were given in defense of Perseverance of the Saints ignores the real issue. Most of the verses used to support Perseverance of the Saints are interpreted with the Calvinistic presupposition that man has no free will. For example, in **John 10:28–29**, Jesus states, "I give them eternal life, and they will never perish, and no one will snatch them out of my hand. My Father, who has given them to

---

[246] Witherington, *The Problem with Evangelical Theology*, 4.

[247] Ibid., 4–5.

me, is greater than all, and no one is able to snatch them out of the Father's hand." Yet, Calvinists completely ignore that the "snatching" would have to come from an outside source. It is generally agreed within Christianity that nothing can take God's children from His all-powerful hand, yet Calvinism claims that there is no choice whatsoever in regard to being placed there. The Bible clearly reveals that humans (fallen and redeemed) can make good or poor decisions concerning their faith.

According to Calvinism, if God is the sole author of regeneration, sanctification, and glorification, without the slightest regard to the "free will" of the human, then He will also be the sole author of preserving His elect. And because the chosen must prove their election with a life of good works, it must lie within the sole work of God to bring these good works to pass. Again, the basic Calvinist interpretation of the doctrine means that the elect *will* (without choice) persevere in faith and holiness until their physical death or until the Lord's second coming.

Here are some verses that exhort the Christian to remain in the faith.

1 Corinthians 9:25–27: "And everyone who competes for the prize is temperate in all things. Now they do it to obtain a perishable crown, but we for an imperishable crown. Therefore I run thus: not with uncertainty. Thus I fight: not as one who beats the air. But I discipline my body and bring it into subjection, lest, when I have preached to others, I myself should become disqualified."

1 Timothy 1:5–7: "Now the purpose of the commandment is love from a pure heart, from a good conscience, and from sincere faith, from which some, having strayed, have turned aside to idle talk, desiring to be teachers of the law, understanding neither what they say nor the things which they affirm."

1 Timothy 1:18–20: "This charge I commit to you, son Timothy, according to the prophecies previously made concerning you, that by them you may wage the good warfare, having faith and a good conscience, which some having rejected, concerning the faith have suffered shipwreck, of whom are Hymenaeus and Alexander, whom I delivered to Satan that they may learn not to blaspheme."

2 Timothy 2:17–18: "And their message will spread like cancer. Hymenaeus and Philetus are of this sort, who have strayed concerning the truth, saying that the resurrection is already past; and they overthrow the faith of some."

2 Peter 2:20: "For if, after they have escaped the pollutions of the world through the knowledge of the Lord and Savior Jesus Christ, they are again entangled in them and overcome, the latter end is worse for them than the beginning."

Colossians 1:21–23: "And you, who once were alienated and enemies in your mind by wicked works, yet now He has reconciled in the body of His flesh through death, to present you holy, and blameless, and above reproach in His sight—if indeed you continue in the faith,"

Revelation 3:2, 4–5: "Be watchful, and strengthen the things which remain, that are ready to die, for I have not found your works perfect before God. You have a few names even in Sardis who have not defiled their garments; and they shall walk with Me in white, for they are worthy. He who overcomes shall be clothed in white garments, and I will not blot out his name from the Book of Life; but I will confess his name before My Father and before His angels."

While these verses are not intended to lead the believer to be constantly questioning his faith or salvation, they unarguably show the responsibility of the believer to continue in the faith. But Calvinism takes this idea of Christian responsibility a step further by saying that a lifetime of good works is the indicator of whether one was actually saved or not. If a professed believer has "too few" or "not enough" good works in his lifetime, he can question if he really was saved after all, whether he believes in Jesus Christ or not. Because of this works-based perception, Calvinism's view of eternal security is, ironically, insecure.

In fact, both Laurence Vance and Dave Hunt conclude in their research that this last point of Calvinism is surprisingly incongruous with any teaching of eternal security, based on the Calvinist's premise that the outward manifestation of being one of the elect is based on good works. As Calvinists have claimed this to be true, the problem then lies in the subjective nature of what actually constitutes "good works." Dave Hunt, who has written many respected books on cults, makes a bold comparison of the last point of Calvinism to the following major cult doctrines. He writes:

> Following Calvin's teaching, however, like the Jehovah's Witnesses and Mormons, many Calvinists believe that the only way to make one's "calling and election sure" (**2 Peter 1:10**) is not through faith but through good works. Oddly, although the first four points of Calvinism insist that man can do nothing, the fifth depends, in the view of many, upon human effort.[248]

After questioning why R. C. Sproul would doubt his own salvation, Hunt answers, "Because for a Calvinist the question is not whether one has believed the gospel but whether or not one was from eternity past predestined by God to be among the elect, and that is the elusive question, as many a Calvinist has discovered to his dismay."[249]

Even though all the points of TULIP beg this "elusive question," it is the doctrine of Perseverance of the Saints that really calls the Christian to look to his good works and thereby to question the validity of his salvation. Calvinism's method for determining who is of the elect and who is not can only be legitimate if the prior four doctrines of TULIP are legitimate. Once

---

[248] Hunt, *What Love Is This?*, 381.

[249] Ibid., 382.

again, if the "golden chain" of TULIP is broken anywhere, one's faith and trust in predetermined election will be completely ruined. The Calvinist would then have no assurance of salvation.

Calvinists get around this problem by claiming that God causes the elect to persevere in faith and holiness, thus securing their salvation. While this view, once again, strips the elect of the possibility of freely worshiping, it also causes the elected believer to look back on his life of good works and holiness as proof of his election. Dave Hunt writes of this folly:

> . . . finding assurance in one's works always leaves questions unanswered in view of the undeniable fact . . . that the apparent good works of the unsaved sometimes put Christians to shame. Furthermore, one's performance could be excellent most of one's life, but if failure comes at some point, one has lost the performance-based assurance. [250]

Denying the biblical validity of the last point of Calvinism does not, in any way, force one to deny the idea of eternal security for the Christian, just as denying Calvinism as a whole does not disregard God's sovereignty. Vance comments that, "The fifth point of the TULIP, as it was originally formulated and commonly interpreted, [is] at enmity with eternal security." [251]

George Bryson writes:

> Christians are repeatedly encouraged to persevere. Just as clearly they are warned of the consequences for not persevering throughout the pages of the New Testament. To challenge Perseverance of the Saints in the Calvinistic sense is not to deny Eternal Security, but to affirm Perseverance of the Saints in the Calvinistic sense, is to

---

[250] Ibid., 381.

[251] Vance, *The Other Side of Calvinism*, 555.

deny the believer assurance. [252]

The last doctrine of the TULIP theology is founded more on progressive logic than on the plain sense of Scripture. In Sproul's defense of Perseverance of the Saints in *What Is Reformed Theology?* he quotes the Westminster Confession of Faith, Joel R. Beeke, and Sir Isaac Watts far more than he does Scripture. This is common for any Calvinist's defense of TULIP. Many seem to trust the Westminster Confession as though it were the divinely inspired and final interpretation of God's Word. We should contrast this approach to that of Laurence M. Vance, who, after forty-two pages and two hundred scriptural quotes, concludes, "We can now add Perseverance of the Saints to the list of the philosophical speculations and theological implications of the other side of Calvinism." [253]

Romans: Tulip's Taproot

[The book of] Romans more than any other source has determined Evangelical exegesis when it comes to the nature of salvation. [254]

—Ben Witherington III

The book of Romans has long been interpreted in a Calvinistic sense. Ben Witherington writes that the "English Reformation or Revival of the eighteenth century did not produce any great commentaries on Romans." Thus, "The Protestant tradition of interpretation of the nineteenth and twentieth centuries continued to be dominated by Lutheran or Calvinistic interpretation."[255] In more exhaustive explanations and thorough descriptions of the TULIP doctrines, many of

---

[252] Bryson, *The Five Points of Calvinism*, 107.

[253] Vance, *The Other Side of Calvinism*, 596.

[254] Witherington, *The Problem with Evangelical Theology*, 4.

[255] Ibid., 9.

the verses cited in its defense are often used interchangeably—meaning that the same verse is used to support different points. This is not surprising, since each of the five points essentially leads to the same conclusion: the denial of humanity's free will. Consequently, Calvinists are able to use the same verse(s) to support every point within TULIP. Most of those verses are found in **Romans 9**.

My copy of the *Reformation Study Bible*, edited by R. C. Sproul, came with a CD of Max McLean reading the book of Romans. It only seemed fitting for the "Calvinist Study Bible" to come with a reading of its primary source of doctrinal fuel. **Romans 9** is, after all, the taproot of TULIP theology. It is used to support every point in TULIP. The Scripture index in any Calvinistic writing is filled with references to **Romans 9**. This observation is very important because once a Calvinistic interpretation was drawn from **Romans 9**, this portion of Scripture began to serve as a foundation for understanding and interpreting verses that proved problematic or antithetical to TULIP theology. Thus, in exposing the errors of TULIP theology, we cannot overlook these pivotal verses in Romans that give rise to every doctrine associated with Calvinism. This section of Scripture above any other is the backbone of Calvinist theology.

We will now look at **Romans 9** and a rather simple interpretation for this complex area of theology. I will give a "simple interpretation" because my intent is not to offer a commentary on Romans 9, but to show how Calvinism pulls doctrine from this chapter and draws what I believe to be unbiblical conclusions. My interpretation will demonstrate that Calvinism's essential deductions are incomplete. Although the middle of the chapter is the section most used by Calvinism, we will look at the chapter in its entirety.

In the book of Romans, the apostle Paul is writing to the Christian Church in the city of Rome. The letter is generally thought to have been written in the fall of AD 57. Chapters 9 through 11, out of the book's thirteen chapters, deal mainly with the Jewish people and their standing with God in the New Covenant. From the advent of Jesus and the New Covenant, many questions had been raised regarding how God would now interact with the people of Jewish ancestry. Even today, there remain many valid questions and beliefs about what changes were brought about by the promises and tenets of the New Covenant in light of the Old Covenant. While Paul does mention those in Jesus as being "Israel" in the spiritual sense, he mainly focuses on those who are Jewish by blood. Paul frequently quotes Old Testament Scriptures concerning God's election prior to the New Covenant, with similarities and contrasts to the new church of Christ. Although Paul was a Jew himself and had passionately desired to bring his "brethren" to the faith, his attempts were usually met with anger, envy, and violence. In chapter 9, Paul assures the audience of his evangelistic burden for his lost brethren:

(Verse numbers have been left in for clarity).

> [1]I tell the truth in Christ, I am not lying, my conscience also bearing me witness in the Holy Spirit, [2]that I have great sorrow and continual grief in my heart. [3]For I could wish that I myself were accursed from Christ for my brethren, my countrymen according to the flesh, [4]who are Israelites, to whom pertain the adoption, the glory, the covenants, the giving of the law, the service of God, and the promises; [5]of whom are the fathers and from whom, according to the flesh, Christ came, who is over all, the eternally blessed God. Amen.

Why would Paul have "great sorrow" and "continual grief" for his Jewish brethren if he believed in a theology of unconditional election and limited atonement? Already, chapter 9 contradicts the Calvinistic doctrine of determinism. Paul continues:

> [6]But it is not that the word of God has taken no effect. For they are not all Israel who are of Israel, [7]nor are they all children because they are the seed of Abraham; but,

"In Isaac your seed shall be called."[8] That is, those who are the children of the flesh, these are not the children of God; but the children of the promise are counted as the seed.

Because of the New Covenant of faith and grace, in which Jews and Gentiles are equally received into God's kingdom, we see that verses 6–8 echo John's words: "But as many as received Him, to them He gave the right to become children of God, to those who believe in His name: who were born not of blood, nor of the will of the flesh, nor the will of man, but of God" (**John 1:12–13**). Paul writes that it is not the "children of the flesh" who are God's children, but that it is "the children of the promise" who "are counted as the seed." Thus, Gentiles (anyone not Jewish by birth) are counted as God's children by believing or "receiv[ing] Him." Again, the children of promise are not limited to just a physical bloodline (as Jews commonly thought). The promises made by Jesus for becoming a child of God are dependent upon God's calling and one's subsequent reaction. Paul continues:

> [9]For this is the word of promise: *"At this time I will come and Sarah shall have a son."* [10]And not only this, but when Rebecca also had conceived by one man, even by our father Isaac [11](for the children not yet being born, nor having done any good or evil, that the purpose of God according to election might stand, not of works but of Him who calls) . . .

According to New Testament soteriology, salvation is clearly not of human works but of God's grace through faith, as declared by Paul in **Ephesians 2**. It should be of no surprise that God's purpose by election would stand while the children (Jacob and Esau) were still in their mother's womb. Because we are not saved by works, Paul repeats the New Covenant proclamation that salvation is of "Him who calls." Accordingly, this lines up with the doctrines taught by Jesus that salvation is of "Him who calls." Calvinism assumes that the "call" must not be offered to all people. Yet, as we have already noticed, Scripture tells otherwise, in verses such as **Matthew 7:13–27, 10:32–33, 11:28–30, 16:24–26, 28:19–20; John 3:14–18, 7:37–38, 11:25–26, and 20:30–31**. The question, then, that must be asked by non-Calvinists is: If God calls all, draws all, and desires all to be saved, why did He not call, draw, or in the end, desire to elect Esau? Some might answer that it was due to the foreknowledge of God—that God, by His foreknowledge, knew the future rejection of God's grace by Esau. There are many speculative explanations, which we will not deal with here. The issue is that Calvinists assume that the association of election in the above passage deals with personal salvation. Yet, the context is far from personal and says nothing about salvation, (especially as we know it in the New Testament).[256] This will become more apparent as the chapter continues.

> . . . [12]it was said to her, *"The older shall serve the younger."* [13]As it is written, *"Jacob I have loved, but Esau I have hated."*

Many Calvinists use these verses to show that God does not desire all men to be saved, did not die for the sins of the world, and so forth. Yet we must make a distinction in verse 12. When Rebecca inquired of the Lord, the Lord said to her, "Two nations *are* in your womb, two peoples shall be separated from your body; One people shall be stronger than the other, and the older shall serve the younger" (**Genesis 25:23**). We see that God never told Rebecca whom He would love or hate. In reading **Romans 9:12–13**, people often mistake the two verses as coming from the same Old Testament source.

It is important to note that is was not God who said to Rebecca, "Jacob I have loved, but Esau I have hated." Rebecca would never hear those words. What God did tell her was that the two children in her womb were "two nations." The twins are estimated to have been born

---

[256] While salvation in the New Testament is clearly taught, salvation in the Old Testament can be viewed differently. The doctrine of salvation under the Old Covenant is much more difficult to understand than under the New.

roughly around 1800 BC. Although in the time of Jacob and Esau, the Jewish nation of Israel was still in the first stages of becoming a distinct nation, it was not until 350 years later that God would give the commandments to Moses, bringing Abram's, Isaac's, and Jacob's personal covenant with God to a fully public and national level. This act would then cause the nation to separate from the other nations in the land.

We now consider **Romans 9:13**, where Paul says, *"As it is written, Jacob I have loved, but Esau I have hated."* Paul quotes this from the book of Malachi, written nearly 1,370 years after the birth of Jacob and Esau in 430 BC concerning the "two nations." The book of Malachi begins:

> *[1]The burden of the word of the LORD to Israel by Malachi. [2]"I have loved you," says the LORD. "Yet you say, 'In what way have You loved us?' Was not Esau Jacob's brother?" says the LORD. "Yet, Jacob I have loved; [3]But Esau I have hated . . ."*

The beginning of Malachi emphasizes the blessings upon the nation of Jacob (Israel) and the lack thereof on the nation of Esau (Edom), which not only tells us that God was speaking about national superiority (not personal favoritism) but also gives us a good context in which to interpret the implications of the word "hate." We must acknowledge that the word "hated" in the Greek (**Romans 9:13**) can also mean "to love less." This definition is a grammatical option in this passage. *The Nelson Study Bible* notes that on many occasions "in the Old Testament, the verb 'hate' has the basic meaning 'not to choose.'"[257] This specific definition might apply in this case. Although in light of the context of **Romans 9**, the definition "not to choose" would seem appropriate, I do not think this meaning is a reasonable option for interpretation of the passage.

---

[257] Ronald B. Allen, Old Testament ed., *The Nelson Study Bible*: NKJV, ed. Earl D. Radmacher (Nashville: Thomas Nelson Publishers, 1997), 1557.

Understandably, some Calvinists staunchly assert that the word "hate" "simply means hate." I too essentially argue that the word "world" means world and the word "love" means love, for example. Consider, however, the words and logic of Calvinist D. A. Carson in his commentary on **Matthew 6:24**:

> The contrast between love and hate is a common Semitic idiom, neither part of which may legitimately be taken absolutely. To hate one of two alternatives and to love the other simply means the latter is strongly preferred, especially if there is any contrast between the two. This idiom sheds light on other words of Jesus: "If anyone come to me and does not hate his father and mother, his wife and children, his brothers and sisters—yes, even his own life—he cannot be my disciple" (**Luke 14:26**). This same Jesus elsewhere insists that people should honor their parents with integrity (**Mark 7:9–13**); so clearly, he is not advocating hatred. He means that any man's best love and first allegiance must be directed toward the Father and toward the Son Whom He sent, and that even family ties must be considered secondary. [258]

Even the Calvinist who is assured that the word "hate" means hate here in **Romans 9:13** must consider what the word means when used as a "Semitic idiom," as Carson suggests. That the word is used this way in Scripture (in Malachi and Romans) seems very reasonable.

Regardless of how people define the word "hate," God's blessing was undoubtedly on and extended through the nation of Israel and not Edom. Indeed, Jesus Himself came from the people of Israel.

---

[258] D. A. Carson, *Jesus' Sermon on the Mount and His Confrontation with the World: An Exposition of Matthew 5–10* (Grand Rapids: Baker Books, 2008), 86.

Furthermore, in Malachi, the majority of God's words concerning Jacob and Esau are in the context of the nations—referring to their nationality and not to individual persons. Although in their lifetimes, the older (Esau) did, in fact, serve the younger (Jacob), we see in both Genesis and Malachi that God emphasizes the two brothers as nations—not as individuals.

Calvinists apply these Old Testament acts of God in dealing with nations to uphold their New Testament doctrine of personal salvation. However, God does not save people according to nationality or ethnicity. God clearly saves on an individual basis, not on a national one. Even in the Old Testament, though God's blessings were clearly with and upon the children of Israel, His work in relation to the world was meant to be intimate and personal.

To continue in Romans:

> [14]What shall we say then? *Is there* unrighteousness with God? Certainly not! [15]For He says to Moses, *"I will have mercy on whomever I will have mercy, and I will have compassion on whomever I will have compassion."*[16] So then *it is* not of him who wills, nor of him who runs, but of God who shows mercy.

Whether or not God "hated" Esau or simply did "not choose him," our natural inclination almost automatically questions God's decision, judging it to be either good or bad. We might ask ourselves, "Is there unrighteousness with God?" Paul quickly retorts, "Certainly not!" The verse that Paul quotes is **Exodus 33:19**, in which God says to Moses, "I will be gracious to whom I will be gracious, and I will have compassion on whom I will have compassion." The words of God spoken to Moses are somewhat difficult to understand. At the time He spoke them, Moses was on Mount Sinai, asking God to reassure him by letting him see His glory (**Exodus 33:18–20**):

> And he [Moses] said, "Please show me your glory." Then He [God] said, "I will make all My goodness pass before you, and

I will proclaim the name of the LORD before you. I will be gracious to whom I will be gracious, and I will have compassion on whom I will have compassion." But He said, "You cannot see My face; for no man shall see Me, and live."

What we gather from the Exodus account is that because of God's compassion and mercy, He allowed Moses to experience a glorious blessing that no one had ever experienced before. It was not given to reward Moses' efforts or holiness. It was granted because God's goodness allowed it.

As Paul states, "It is not of him who wills, nor of him who runs, but of God who shows mercy" (**Romans 9:16**). This simple statement should clarify the question, "What shall we say then? Is there unrighteousness with God?" (**Romans 9:14**). Christians are saved by God's grace through faith, and not by works. Moses was blessed as no one had ever been before by God's goodness, just as we, God's children, are blessed because of His goodness. If we consider this part of Paul's argument without bringing in the issue of salvation, we can conclude that Moses was simply blessed above and beyond everyone else in the nation, as they awaited Moses' return at the bottom of Mount Sinai.

It is important to note that just because God chose to answer Moses' request on Mount Sinai, He was not obligated to answer the individual requests of His people below. God can give to and withhold blessings from His people without being unrighteous. Furthermore, it is not that He gives blessings only to His "chosen" people, nor that He withholds blessings from those He "hates." Calvinists wrongly believe that God withholds salvation from those unfortunate people that He "hates." While this account of God's special favor towards Moses in Exodus reveals His sovereignty in His particular works towards men, it does not reveal the essence of TULIP theology. For one to consider God unrighteous for privileging Moses in allowing Himself to be seen, while not allowing Himself to be seen by others, would be like having an "evil eye," because God is good (**Matthew 20:1–16**).

We pick up Paul's argument in **Romans 9**:

[17]For the Scripture says to the Pharaoh, *"For this very purpose I have raised you up, that I may show My power in you, and that My name may be declared in all the earth."* [18]Therefore He has mercy on whom He wills, and whom He wills He hardens.

The pharaoh of the Exodus is now brought into the picture. In contrast to Moses, the pharaoh was a man who was especially cursed by God. It would be very speculative to conclude that God's dealings with both Moses and Pharaoh were done without their free will. Yet Calvinism assumes just that. Pharaoh is mentioned as an instrument used by God to reveal His wrathful power, while Moses was used by God to reveal His glorious power. As we must note, it was God who had raised Pharaoh up. Again, however, the presupposition held by Calvinists is that God's "raising him up" was done so without Pharaoh's free will. But the Scriptures imply otherwise. Directly after God said to Pharaoh in **Exodus 9:16** (revealing His sovereignty), "But indeed, for this *purpose* I have raised you up, that I may show My power in you, and that My name may be declared in all the earth." The Lord said (revealing Pharaoh's free will), "As yet you exalt yourself against My people in that you will not let them go" (**Exodus 9:17**). It was Pharaoh's choice to reject God's will, which he did repeatedly. We know this because we see God pleading with Pharaoh multiple times in the Exodus account to obey His commands given through Moses and Aaron (**Exodus 7–11**).

Both Moses and Pharaoh were used by God to display many things. God's work and sovereignty in both men is coupled with their free will, allowing God's dealings with humans to come as both blessings and curses. This is why Paul says, "He has mercy on whom He wills, and whom He wills He hardens."

Paul uses the word "hardens" here because in the Exodus account,

God hardened Pharaoh's heart multiple times. Non-Calvinists do not deny that God "hardened" or "set" Pharaoh's heart, but as already noted, this was done so in response to Pharaoh's repeated rejection of God's commands. This is more than just an assumption. The first reference to Pharaoh's heart being hard is in **Exodus 7:14**: "So the Lord said to Moses: 'Pharaoh's heart is hard; he refuses to let the people go.'" The next reference is in **Exodus 7:22**: "Then the magicians of Egypt did so with their enchantments; and Pharaoh's heart grew hard, and he did not heed them, as the LORD had said. And Pharaoh turned and went into his house. Neither was his heart moved by this." The third time we read of Pharaoh's hard heart is **Exodus 8:15**. This time, Pharaoh hardened his own heart: "They gathered them together in heaps, and the land stank. But when Pharaoh saw that there was relief, he hardened his heart and did not heed them, as the LORD had said." Accounts of Pharaoh hardening his own heart occur four more times, in **Exodus 8:19, 32; 9:7, and 34.** From this point on in the Exodus account we read of God hardening Pharaoh's heart—first in **Exodus 9:12** and finally in 11:10. Out of the eleven times we read of Pharaoh's heart, only five times does the text refer to God actually hardening his heart. And those five references occur after the first five, in which Pharaoh hardens his own heart. God's hardening of Pharaoh's heart was always done after his initial rejection of God's commands. It would be one thing for God to harden a heart that has followed and obeyed Him. It is another thing to harden a heart that has persistently rejected His will.

As we continue through these passages, we should note the lack of direct support for Calvinism's deterministic claims. As these verses elevate our understanding of God's sovereignty in His relationship to humanity's free will and the nation of Israel, we have yet to see a direct denial of anyone's free will to maintain God's decrees. So far, we can conclude that God does not save or give blessings to someone based on works but according to His mercy and compassion. And, though there are legitimate questions concerning how God's election interplays with human choices, they should not be raised to the point of validating the unfounded conclusions of Calvinism.

In light of God hardening Pharaoh's heart, Paul raises some rhetorical questions in **Romans 9**:

> [19]You will say to me then, "Why does He still find fault?
> For who has resisted His will?"

In other words, Paul asks: If God has the ability to harden a person's heart, why would He later find fault with him? We must remember that whether God hardens a heart or not, He is right to find fault with everyone. As the Scriptures claim, "All have sinned and fall short of the glory of God" (**Romans 3:23**). Because of this scriptural and spiritual truth, the next question ("For who has resisted His will?") is answered. *Everyone* has resisted His will—from Pharaoh to Moses. Everyone to one degree or another has opposed His will. Therefore, God has the right to find fault with everyone. Could God find fault with Pharaoh before He hardened his heart? The answer is yes. Yet, some still press the questions, to whom Paul replies:

> [20]But indeed, O man, who are you to reply against God?
> Will the thing formed say to him who formed it, "Why have you made me like this?"

In order to understand this, we must figure out what "like this" means. What exactly is meant by this question, and who is asking it? If we conclude, as Calvinism suggests, that God purposes or desires some people to be sinful and reject His salvific work, it is very difficult to maintain that the Bible does not contradict itself. As we have previously covered in addressing each of the five points, God is not and cannot be the author of sin in any fashion. Could "like this" be interpreted as the general doctrine of mankind being born in a sinful state? Is this verse referring to the sinner posing the question to God, "Why have you made me like this?" This option is also doubtful. The Bible reveals all of humanity as being equally fallen, while Paul's argument seems to deal only with a certain group of people. Out of many options for what the question might mean, Paul's rhetorical question is likely asked by those who can be likened unto Pharaoh, whose actions are used by God to reveal His wrath and justice. In the end, the reader can be sure only that although Paul's question can be understood in many ways, Calvinism's interpretation positions itself too far from orthodoxy to be right.

Paul continues in Romans 9:

> [21]Does not the potter have power over the clay, from the same lump to make one vessel for honor and another for dishonor? [22] *What* if God, wanting to show *His* wrath and to make His power known, endured with much longsuffering the vessels of wrath prepared for destruction, [23]and that He might make known the riches of His glory on the vessels of mercy, which He had prepared beforehand for glory, [24] *even* us whom He called, not of the Jews only, but also of the Gentiles?

While these questions might seem to substantiate Calvinist theology, we must note that they are rhetorical. Despite the nature of these questions, Calvinists are still quick to draw from them doctrinal support. Because Christians acknowledge that God can do as He pleases (for example, making a vessel for dishonor), the Calvinist believes that God not only *can* do this; He *does* do this. The problem with this understanding is its plain contradiction of both Scripture as a whole and its declaration of the nature of an all-loving and good God. To understand these passages, one can regard the "vessel of dishonor [or] wrath" as a type of Pharaoh. Paul then writes that these vessels were "prepared for destruction." In the same vein, the "vessels of mercy" can be understood as representing the children of Israel, who "endured with much longsuffering" as slaves under Pharaoh. These "vessels of honor [or] mercy" are those "which He had prepared beforehand for glory, even us whom He called, not of the Jews only, but also of the Gentiles."

At first glance, this verse would seem to imply that if *God* "prepared" beforehand "those vessels of mercy . . . whom He called, not of the Jews only, but also of the Gentiles," then he must have likewise "prepared" those "vessels of wrath prepared for destruction." This understanding would seem logical and would indeed fit the systematic theology of Calvinism. However, we do not read that God created beforehand those "vessels of wrath prepared for destruction." That is a Calvinistic assumption. The text only says that He prepared those "vessels of mercy . . . whom He called" beforehand for glory. This is different from the "vessels of wrath prepared for destruction." In this verse, 22, Calvinists avoid the original language. The word "prepared" or "fitted" in verse 22 (Strong's 2675)[259] is completely different from "prepared" in verse 23 (Strong's 4282)[260]. As explained in commentary on these verses in *The Nelson Study Bible*, "The grammatical structure of the first 'prepared,' referring to the vessels of wrath, is different from the second 'prepared,' referring to the vessels of mercy. The first literally means 'prepared themselves,' while the second is 'which He prepared.'"[261]

---

[259] James Strong, *The New Strong's Exhaustive Concordance of the Bible*, (Nashville: Thomas Nelson Publishers, 1995, 1996) Greek Dictionary 47. Accessed 22 December 2010 from: http://www.blueletterbible.org/lang/lexicon/lexicon.cfm?Strongs=G4282&t=KJV; Internet.
  1) to render, i.e. to fit, sound, complete
  a) to mend (what has been broken or rent), to repair
  2) to complete
  b) to fit out, equip, put in order, arrange, adjust
  2) to fit or frame for one's self, prepare
  c) ethically: to strengthen, perfect, complete, make one what he ought to be

[260] Ibid., Greek Dictionary 75. Accessed 22 December 2010 from: http://www.blueletterbible.org/lang/lexicon/lexicon.cfm?Strongs=G4282&t=KJV; Internet.
  1) to prepare before, to make ready beforehand

[261] H. Wayne House, New Testament ed., *The Nelson Study Bible: NKJV*, ed. Earl D. Radmacher (Nashville: Thomas Nelson Publishers, 1997), 1896.

The difference then lies in who (or Who) is doing the preparing. While unbelievers prepare themselves for doom by rejecting Jesus, God prepares them for glory. This understanding of preparing is compatible with the whole of New Testament soteriology. While they are still on earth, God prepares His children for glory. In contrast, unbelievers prepare themselves for doom. This understanding makes sense of **Romans 9** and poses no threat to the rest of Scripture. In order to faithfully hold to Calvinistic doctrine, one must misread the text with an interpretation that it is seriously at odds with a host of other passages.

We should now consider the questions raised by Paul in Romans 9:

1. "What shall we say then? *Is there* unrighteousness with God?" (v. 14).
2. "Why does He still find fault? For who has resisted His will?" (v. 19).
3. "But indeed, O man, who are you to reply against God?" (v. 20).
4. "Will the thing formed say to him who formed it, 'Why have you made me like this?'" (v. 20).
5. "Does not the potter have power over the clay, from the same lump to make one vessel for honor and another for dishonor?" (v. 21).
6. "*What if* God, wanting to show *His* wrath and to make His power known, endured with much longsuffering the vessels of wrath prepared for destruction, and that He might make known the riches of His glory on the vessels of mercy, which He had prepared beforehand for glory, *even* us whom He called, not of the Jews only, but also of the Gentiles?" (vv. 22–24).

Again, these questions are merely rhetorical. Because of this, some people have considered these verses to hold no doctrinal weight at all, dismissing even the thoughts they provoke. While I do not think Paul's questions should be completely ignored or deemed worthless, I do think it wise to avoid pulling doctrine from rhetorical questions. Calvinism, however, places Paul's rhetoric above a multitude of clear proclamations that the New Testament offers.

If the assumptions of Calvinism were held by the apostle Paul, why would he not be straightforward about teaching them? If Paul was convinced that God died only for the elect and did not desire for all to be saved, why would he veil the Calvin-like teachings in rhetorical questions while dogmatically asserting contradictory doctrines in other places within Scripture? In the end, we must know the facts. A good portion of Paul's argument in **Romans 9** consists of rhetorical questions, which do not teach any major doctrine in and of themselves. If any doctrine is safely to be interpreted from them, it should be merely to express that God has the authority to do what He wants to do without the help or aid of humanity.

Below are the remaining verses of chapter 9:

[25]As He says also in Hosea: *"I will call them My people, who were not My people, And her beloved, who was not beloved." There they shall be called sons of the living God."* [26] *"And it shall come to pass in the place where it was said to them, 'You are not My people,' There they shall be called sons of the living God."* [27]Isaiah also cries out concerning Israel: *"Though the number of the children of Israel be as the sand of the sea, The remnant will be saved.* [28] *For He will finish the work and cut it short in righteousness, Because the* LORD *will make a short work upon the earth."* [29]And as Isaiah said before: *"Unless the* LORD *of Sabaoth had left us a seed, We would have become like Sodom, and we would have been made like Gomorroah."* [30]What shall we say then? That Gentiles, who did not pursue righteousness, have attained to righteousness, even the righteousness of faith; [31]but Israel, pursuing the law of righteousness, has not attained to the law of righteousness. [32]Why? Because *they did* not *seek* it by faith, but as it were, by the works of the law. For they stumbled at that stumbling stone. [33]As it is written: *"Behold, I lay in Zion a stumbling stone and rock of offense, And whoever believes on Him will not be put to shame."*

In ending our study on **Romans 9**, we must note the recurring theme that salvation and blessings are not brought about by the works of the law, nor by a blood lineage tied to Abraham. It is God who calls us by His grace through faith. While the last verse of the chapter tells us that there will be those who will stumble on Jesus, the "rock of offense," it also indicates that the theology of Calvinism sets itself against the whole of Scripture, contradicting the very essence of New Testament soteriology summed up in verse 33: "Whoever believes on Him will not be put to shame." Paul concludes his argument in Romans 10 in the same way he begins: "Brethren, my heart's desire and prayer to God for Israel is that they may be saved" (10:1). Again, why would Paul feel the need to pray for those who were predestined by God to Hell?

Hopefully, it is evident that the taproot of TULIP theology is not as strong as Calvinism makes it out to be. But it stands to reason that if every point of Calvin's TULIP is of itself weak and unsubstantiated, then the taproot would be as well. I do not believe that Christians will ever quite understand or mutually agree on the meaning of Paul's argument in **Romans 9** as he originally intended, but it should be apparent to Bible students that there is a wide gap between the words of **Romans 9** and the claims of Calvinism. Paul's message undoubtedly reveals the sovereign choices of God, substantiating **Proverbs 21:1**: "The king's heart is in the hand of the LORD, *Like* the rivers of the water; He turns it wherever He wishes." [262] It does not, however, give validation to the essential claim of Calvinism that humanity is denied free will.

No Such Thing as a "T U I P" and No Such Need

It is usually true (especially today) that any Calvinist, other than a "five-point Calvinist," lacks knowledge of true Calvinist theology. I had a friend a number of years ago who was unsure of what it meant to be a Calvinist. Her father claimed to be one, so she considered herself to be

---

[262] NKJV, Proverbs 21:1.

one as well. I challenged her to know what she assumed to believe. About a year later, she came to me and told me that after some searching and questioning, she still considers herself a Calvinist. Her response, when I asked her why, was roughly as follows:

- Because I believe most of the points. (not all)
- Because I believe that man is totally depraved.
- Because I believe that God has chosen an elect people.
- Because I believe in the eternal security of the believer.
- Because I believe that God is truly sovereign.

After explaining each point in TULIP, I encouraged her to further consider her beliefs. I told her that while I disagree with Calvinistic doctrine, I, too, believe in man's complete depravity (*not* inability), God's complete sovereignty, and the security of His elect. Like so many others I know, this baffled her. George Bryson also understood this when he professed to a listener on the airwaves that while he was not a Calvinist he believed in God's complete sovereignty. He recalled that in response to him, "The caller's surprise then turned to confusion."[263]

Many people struggle with the concept of denying Calvinism while remaining true to the scriptural truths of God's grace, sovereignty, and eternal protection of His elect. Although this fear stems mainly from a surface-level understanding of Calvinism, it also reflects a tendency mistakenly to associate anything not pro-Calvinist with Arminianism. Jacobus Arminius, a student of John Calvin, questioned the biblical veracity of Calvin's anti-Catholic, election-based salvation. Since that time, anyone who has disagreed with Calvinistic theology has been deemed as heretical and labeled Arminian. Vance writes that throughout history, the "terms Arminian and Arminianism . . . were broadened to impugn anyone who was opposed to

---

[263] Bryson, *The Five Points of Calvinism*, 1.

Calvinism."[264] George Bryson writes, "The idea that an Evangelical could be neither Calvinist nor Arminian, or some kind of theological hybrid called a 'Cal–minian,' is simply unthinkable to most leading Calvinists."[265] Boettner agrees:

> It must be evident that there are just two theories which can be maintained by evangelical Christians upon this important subject; that all men who have made any study of it, and who have reached any settled conclusions regarding it, must be either Calvinists or Arminians. There is no other position which a "Christian" can take. [266]

According to Reformed theologian G. T. Shedd, "Ultimately, there can be only two alternatives in evangelical understanding of the Christian Faith, the Calvinistic and the Arminian."[267] Shedd also reasons that for Christian believers, these two views are the only options that are, "logically possible [and] in the future, as the past, all evangelical believers will belong either to one dogmatic division or the other."[268]

Simply said: One cannot pick and choose what letters of TULIP to believe or neglect. Theological decision-making is not like shopping for clothes according to which items fit and which do not. TULIP is a systematic theological structure that cannot be divided without essential damage. Taking the doctrines in the order of the letters of the acronym, each doctrine is built upon the prior one(s) and is extended in the next. Geisler states that "if one [point] is rejected, then logically all should be."[269]

---

[264] Vance, *The Other Side of Calvinism*, 139.

[265] Bryson, *The Dark Side of Calvinism*, 32, 36.

[266] Boettner, *The Reformed Doctrine of Predestination*, 333.

[267] Shedd, *Calvinism, Pure and Mixed*, 35-36.

[268] Ibid., 32.

[269] Geisler, *Chosen but Free*, p. 57.

Likewise, Calvinist theologian Gise J. Van Baren says, "The five points of Calvinism are closely related. One point presupposes the other."[270]

Another Calvinist advocate and spokesman, J. I. Packer, writes:

> The very act of setting out Calvinistic soteriology (the doctrine of salvation) in the form of five distinct points (a number due merely to the fact that there were five Arminian points for the Synod of Dort to answer) tends to obscure the organic character of Calvinistic thought on this subject. For the five points, thought separately stated, are really inseparable. They hang together; you cannot reject one without rejecting them all, at least in the sense in which the Synod meant them. For to Calvinism there is really only one point to be made in the field of soteriology.[271]

The "one point" mentioned by Packer has two sides. The first is that God damns people to Hell for sins they were forced to commit. The other side is that God saves only a few people by forcing them to place faith in Him. Regardless of how it is viewed, both camps can agree that Packer's "one point" is the denial of man's free will or the proclamation of God's sovereignty—two things that Calvinists believe are mutually exclusive.

As a last resort, many people refer to themselves as four- or three-point Calvinists. Rather than rejecting Calvinism as a whole (lest they, too, be tagged as Arminian heretics), they settle on the points they like, and ignore all the rest. Not only is this an incorrect way to deal with one's knowledge of biblical truth, it misrepresents Calvinism. This

---

[270] Gise J. Van Baren, "The Perseverance of the Saints," in *The Five Points of Calvinism* (Grandville, MI: Reformed Free Publishing Association, 1976) [online]; accessed 28 January 2010; available from http://www.prca.org/fivepoints/chapter5.html; Internet.

[271] J. I. Packer, "Introductory Essay to John Owen's *Death of Death in the Death of Christ* [online]; accessed 28 January 2010; available from http://www.all-of grace.org/pub/others/deathofdeath.html; Internet.

picking and choosing of which letters of TULIP one adheres to inevitably leads to being tagged as a two-, three-, or four-point Calvinist and is common among those not conversant with Calvinistic doctrine. The first letter to be done away with is usually "L," Limited Atonement. With "L" gone, a four-point Calvinist will call himself a "TUIP." The doctrine of Limited Atonement is no more unbiblical than the rest, but the others are buried in theological and grammatical doublespeak, or as Vance writes, "the confusing labyrinth of Calvinistic terminology."[272]

There have been many "four-point Calvinists." Laurence M. Vance points out that the original four-point Calvinist was Moyse Amyraut (1596–1664), a French professor and theologian. Many have followed in his footsteps, including Lewis Sperry Chafer (1871–1952), founder of Dallas Theological Seminary. Vance also writes that there are presently "many Baptists in the general association of regular Baptists churches [who] are four-point Calvinists."[273] These are considered to be "closet Calvinists." Surprisingly, these followers of Calvin fail to see the folly of adhering to anything less than all of the five points. It is also important to know that the difference between a five-point Calvinist and a four-point Calvinist is not small. James White even says, "Upon examination, the vast majority of those who call themselves 'four-point Calvinists' are actually not Reformed at all."[274] And Calvinist James Smith agrees writing, "Indeed, I wonder how many people who describe themselves as "Calvinists" today are actually more "Lutheran.""[275]

While some Calvinists understand that the five points are intrinsically dependent upon each other, very few understand that if

---

[272] Vance, *The Other Side of Calvinism*, 556.

[273] Ibid., 147.

[274] White, in *Debating Calvinism*, 178.

[275] Smith, James, *Letters to a Young Calvinist*, 102.

any one point of the five is proven false, the other four must also be false. Likewise, if one is proven true, then the rest should also be. It has always somewhat amazed me that so-called four- or three-point Calvinists fail to see the common thread woven through all five points. Knowing that Limited Atonement means Christ only died for the elect, I wonder how it can be so unfavorably looked upon to the average four-point Calvinist in the light of the rest of the points: **T** is understood that God only regenerates the Elect, **U** means that God's choice of the Elect is unconditional, **I** makes God's offer of salvation to the Elect irresistible, and **P** means that God forces the Elect to persevere. All five are essentially the same! They rob mankind of free will and responsibility while making God's determined decrees of "love" quite confusing. Although each doctrine is based in Scripture, the conclusions contradict logic and sound biblical interpretation.

Claiming four-point Calvinism is not a viable option for anyone serious about biblical theology or Calvin's systematic theology. Ben Witherington warns of the danger of not adopting the systematic theology as a whole:

There is then a logical consistency to this cluster of linked ideas, and it is the logic and coherency that seem to make it compelling, rather than its real exegetical viability. And of course the danger of any such necessary linking of ideas is that if one link in the chain is dropped off then the chain ceases to hold. For example, if it can be demonstrated that apostasy from the true faith is not merely possible but is an idea that Christians are regularly warned against in the NT, then there is something wrong not only with the notion of perseverance but also with the ideas of irresistible grace and predetermination.[276]

James White understands this problem as well, writing, "Objections to irresistible grace are, by and large, actually objections to

---

[276] Witherington, *The Problem with Evangelical Theology*, 5.

the previously established truths of the doctrine of grace." [277]

Correctly understood, Calvinism does not allow for anything other than a full five-point Calvinist. Either to reject one point and cling to four or to reject four points and cling to one is inconsistent with the heart of Calvinism. As the authors of *The Five Points of Calvinism: Defined, Defended, and Documented* state, "The five points . . . must not be evaluated on a purely individual basis. For these five doctrines are not presented in the Bible as separate and independent units of truth. . . . *they mutually explain and support one another.*" They must be "viewed together as a system."[278] Ultimately, then, there is no such thing as a "TUIP" and no such need.

---

[277] White, in *Debating Calvinism*, 198.

[278] Steele, Thomas, and Quinn, *The Five Points of Calvinism*, 18; italics in original.

CHAPTER THREE

The Marks of a Cult within Calvinism

> Calvinism encompasses many of the features which are characteristic of a Christian cult. [279]
>
> —Kent R. Rieske

B efore we compare the theological implications of Calvinism to those of classic cults, we must understand the actual makeup a cult. With so many religions, sects, denominations, churches, creeds, and belief systems, the Christian is called to the difficult task of at least understanding those essential differences between them. Jude understood that other Christianity-like faiths can infiltrate and pollute the true faith taught by the Lord and His apostles. Jude exhorted the church to resist this threat and to "contend earnestly for the faith" (**Jude 3**). To define the makeup of a cult, we must identify where its essential doctrines differ from orthodox faith. Apologists give different opinions as to the features typically exhibited by cults, but few, if any, would disagree with the following list of characteristics. A Christian cult will usually:

---

[279] Kent R. Rieske, "Calvinism: False Doctrines of the 'Pope' of Geneva: Total Depravity, Unconditional Election, Limited Atonement, Irresistible Grace, and Perseverance" [online]; accessed 22 January 2010; available from http://www.biblelife.org/calvinism.htm; Internet.

1. take away from the deity of Jesus;
2. hold to man's merits or works rather than God's grace for salvation;
3. uphold a leader as the sole interpreter of their Scripture;
4. twist Scripture to fit their belief system;
5. claim to be the only "true church" with a sort of higher knowledge.

From the exhaustive checklist of "Characteristics Associated with Cultic Groups" by Janja Lalich and Michael D. Langone, I marked six out of fifteen characteristics for Calvinism.[280] Although the word "cult" is not found in the Bible, Wayne Jackson writes, in "How to Identify a Cult": "[The] idea is there—at least in seed form. It is represented by the Greek term *hairesis*, rendered 'sect,' which derives from a root meaning 'to choose.'" [281]

At first glance, this working list of cultish characteristics may not seem to apply strongly to Calvinism. First of all, the theology of Calvinism in no way diminishes the deity of Jesus. Even though Calvinism's portrayal of Jesus does not quite match the biblical account of Jesus—who is compelled by love to save the world and not just a select few—He is still recognized as the Son of God. Also, although Perseverance of the Saints is a works-based indicator of salvation, Calvinists strongly believe in and rely on God's grace alone for salvation.

However, though Calvinists claim to believe in the priesthood of the saint (that each of the elect is gifted by God individually to understand Scripture), their extreme admiration of John Calvin and/or faith in his interpretation of the Scriptures implies otherwise. Calvinists are Calvinists for the very reason that they align themselves with the founder of their

---

[280] Janja Lalich and Madeleine Tobias, "Appendix A. Characteristics Associated with Cultic Groups," in *Take Back Your Life: Recovering from Cults and Abusive Relationships*, 2nd ed. (Berkeley, CA: Bay Tree Publishing, 2006).

[281] Wayne Jackson, "How to Identify a Cult" [online]; accessed 28 August 2000; available from http://www.christian courier.com/articles/250-how-to-identify-a-cult.

particular theology. Also despite their claim to superior biblical exegesis and sound hermeneutics,[282] Calvinists find themselves twisting orthodox doctrine while systemizing a less than biblical theology of God.

Lastly, despite the fact that Calvinists generally do not publicly confess to be the "only true church," they do seem to believe that they alone have a higher knowledge of who God is and how He works. This is apparent in their attempts to proselytize other believers.

Although Calvinism does not necessarily exhibit every characteristic of a cult, Josh McDowell's general definition of a cult as "a perversion, a distortion of biblical Christianity" certainly applies to Calvinism.[283] In addition, Calvinism is in line with Walter Martin's definition of a cult as "a group of people polarized around someone's interpretation of the Bible."[284] Hank Hanegraaff, president of the Christian Research Institute, is "regarded as one of the world's leading Christian apologists."[285] He warns people to avoid any religious group that reveals any cultish characteristic. He writes, "If a religious group exhibits one or more of the marks mentioned above, that group may well be considered a cult."[286] Josh McDowell likewise concludes:

---

[282] Although this assertion that Calvinists "claim...superior Biblical exegesis and sound hermeneutics" is a general statement based on reading many of their writings, the thought has been pulled from Calvinism's intellectual heritage and will be expanded on the sub-chapter, "Its Elitism (us vs. them)" on page 235.

[283] McDowell, *Handbook of Today's Religions*, 17.

[284] Walter Martin, *The Kingdom of the Cults*, rev. and updated ed., ed. Hank Hanegraaff (Minneapolis: Bethany House Publishers: 2003), 17.

[285] Hank Hanegraaff bio "About Hank Hanegraaff" [online]; accessed 22 December 2010; available from http://www.equip.org/site/about_hank_hanegraaff; Internet.

[286] Hank Hanegraaff, "What Are Some Common Marks of a Cult," Christian Research Institute Statement: CP0201 [online]; accessed 26 January 2010; available from http://www.equip.org/perspectives/common-characteristics-of-cults; Internet.

While not every group that possesses these characteristics can be labeled a cult, beware of a group that embraces some of these features. The sure mark of a cult is what it does with the Person of Jesus Christ. All cults ultimately deny the fact that Jesus Christ is God the Son, second Person of the Holy Trinity, and mankind's only hope.[287]

This statement implicates Calvinistic doctrine in its staunch denial of "the fact that Jesus Christ is . . . mankind's only hope." Calvinists clearly believe that Jesus Christ is the only hope for the elect, but not for all. As Geisler and Rhodes write in their book *Doctrinal Characteristics of a Cult*, "Many cults set forth a distorted view of God and Jesus."[288] Calvinism, by altering various terms, definitions, and doctrines, distorts the orthodox understanding of the character of God. Ironically, Calvinist spokesman R. C. Sproul states, "Reformed theology . . . is driven first and foremost by its understanding of the character of God."[289] Besides the other cultish characteristics within Calvinism, arguably the misrepresentation of God poses the most severe consequences to Christianity. Based on its altering of the character and knowledge of the Bible's trinitarian God, Calvinism ultimately is too cultish for comfort.

This section will focus on additional problems with Calvinism—its evangelism, its elitism, its maligning of Scripture, and its fluctuating terminology. But before we explore these areas, we will start with observing its founder, John Calvin.

---

[287] McDowell, *Handbook of Today's Religions*, 25.

[288] Geisler and Rhodes, *Correcting the Cults*, 10.

[289] Sproul, *What Is Reformed Theology?* 20.

Its Leader John Calvin

A cult might also be defined as a group of people gathered about a specific person or person's misrepresentation of the Bible.[290]

—Walter Martin

We call ourselves Reformed because we're part of that historic branch of the Christian church that follows the teachings of 16th-century reformer John Calvin.[291]

—The Christian Reformed Church

As word spread about this man and his radical approach, his popularity increased.[292]

—Kristina Jones, former "Children of God" cult member

Norman Geisler and Ron Rhodes have written a chapter in their book, *Correcting the Cults*, on "Sociological Characteristics of a Cult." Although this chapter tries to make a distinction between "cult prophets/founders" and "legitimate reformers/revivalists, such as Martin Luther and John Wesley," their reasoning portrays John Calvin as more of a cult leader than a Reformer. Geisler and Rhodes claim:

> The differences are significant. A reformer, in contrast to a cult founder, leads people by love, not by fear. He influences by love, not by hate. He tries to motivate the

---

[290] Martin, *The Kingdom of the Cults*, 17.

[291] Official website of The Christian Reformed Church [online]; accessed 28 January 2010; available from http://www.crcna.org/pages/aboutthecrc.cfm; Internet.

[292] Kristina Jones, "Eyewitness: Why People Join Cults," BBC News 24 March 2000 [online]; accessed 28 January 2010; available from http://news.bbc.co.uk/ 2/hi/africa/688317.stm; Internet.

heart but makes no attempt to control the mind. He leads his followers like a shepherd leads sheep; He does not drive them like goats. [293]

The suggestion that John Calvin could be characterized as a cult leader would be absurd to the Calvinist. Yet it would be difficult legitimately to disagree with Geisler and Rhodes' distinctions between a genuine Reformer and a cult leader. Even the unbiased portrayal of Calvin by the Reformed historian John T. McNeill speaks volumes:

> . . . the repressive discipline, harsh laws, and paternalistic controls, the positive and constructive elements of Calvin's system were becoming more and more effective. The people of Geneva listened to preaching several times weekly. A new generation was arising, trained in Calvin's Sunday school, instructed by his sermons, able to recite his catechism, to sing the Psalter, and to read the Bible with understanding. Possibly no community had ever before existed so well indoctrinated and broken to discipline. [294]

As you read about Calvin's iron-fisted rule over Geneva, draw your own conclusion. Calvinist Charles Spurgeon stated, "A man cannot have an erroneous belief without by-and-by having an erroneous life."[295] Ironically, he wrote this in his famed book, *A Defense of Calvinism*. Perhaps he was not well informed regarding the founder of Calvinism.

---

[293] Geisler and Rhodes, *Correcting the Cults*, 11.

[294] John T. McNeill, *The History and Character of Calvinism* (New York: Oxford University Press, 1954), 190.

[295] Spurgeon, "A Defense of Calvinism."

His Control

One mark of a cult leader is the desire to control every aspect of his followers' lives. Usually the cult leader's control extends far beyond his theological views; the leader tends to have little or no tolerance of dissent in any degree. In larger cults, in which there might be many leadership positions, and in other areas of such organizations, the cult leader still remains in charge of all decisions.

As Jackson notes:

> Cult members are focused on a living leader to whom members seem to display excessively zealous, unquestioning commitment. The leader is a strong-willed, domineering character who rules the group with tight control. He lets it be known in subtle ways that he is "in charge" of the movement. He makes the plans, he orchestrates the movements of the group.[296]

Of Mormon leader Joseph Smith, author Charles L. Wood writes:

> The self-proclaimed prophet claimed that his authority over his flock was granted to him by God and he used this "God given" authority to demand obedience from his followers . . . This fear of God's and the self-proclaimed prophet's wrath caused his followers to endure great suffering and anguish.[297]

Yet, "great suffering and anguish" was not limited to those purely within the church. Many outside the church but within the city felt the impact of Smith's leadership so that the Mormon leader even exercised

---

[296] Jackson, "How to Identify a Cult."

[297] Charles L. Wood, *The Mormon Conspiracy: A Review of Present Day and Historical Conspiracies to Mormonize America and the World* (Chula Vista, CA: Black Forest Press, 2004), 167.

some control over nonreligious affairs. William Godbe, a British Latter-day Saint, started his own sect within the Mormon Church in part because of a need for political reform—"namely breaking Brigham Young's control over secular matters in the territory in October 1869— that could help spur religious reform."[298] After Joseph Smith's death, Brigham Young was one of five main successors leading the growing cult. Joseph Smith died in 1844 at the age of thirty-nine after being shot multiple times by a violent mob.

David Koresh, another cult leader had a similar fate. On February 28, 1993, the FBI raided the Branch Davidian compound in Waco, Texas, to search for illegal weapons and arrest David Koresh. The Branch Davidians were a group of small but well-known Christian cultists. David Koresh, with much help from the media, brought national attention to Waco. After finding that Koresh possessed illegal weapons, indoctrinated his followers, and confined them in a secure compound, while claiming himself to be the "Lamb of God," the FBI intervened. The raid led to a gun battle in which four agents and six Branch Davidians died. Fifty-one days later, the standoff ended. On April 19, the sect's compound was burned down, killing cult leader, David Koresh, and nearly eighty of his loyal followers. Government attorneys observed that Koresh "exercised complete control over sect members."[299] The official U.S. Department of Justice Report further stated that Koresh had "established absolute control over the sect."[300] We now know that:

---

[298] Ronald Walker, "Godbeites" Utah History Encyclopedia, [online]; accessed 23 December 2010; available from http://www.media.utah.edu/UHE/g/ GODBEITES.html; Internet.

[299] Lee Hancock, "U.S. Lawyers Detail Sect's Waco Arsenal," *Dallas Morning News* 7 July 2000 [online]; accessed 27 January 2010; available from http://www.cesnur.org/testi/waco99.htm#Anchor-35882; Internet.

[300] "Report to the Deputy Attorney General on the Events at Waco, Texas, February 28 to April 19, 1993; U.S. Department of Justice Washington, D.C. 20530 [online]; accessed 28 January 2010; available from http://www.justice. gov/05publications/waco/wacoone.html; Internet.

As the sect grew, so did Koresh's control over its members' lives. He would preach for hours, while depriving his listeners of food, sleep, and bathroom breaks. He established rules of behavior for those living at the compound, and publicly berated those who broke these rules. Whenever possible, he urged members of the sect to turn over their worldly possessions and funds to his control. He also controlled what they ate and read, what they viewed as entertainment, and where they traveled.[301]

From Charles Taze Russel, Jehovah's Witness leader, to Jim Jones, to David Koresh, cult leaders undoubtedly control and "become the absolute authority for weak individuals . . . in some cases, [this control] can extend to every aspect of life."[302] Josh McDowell notes that the cult leader will always "exercise enormous influence over the group."[303] John Calvin fit this description, exercising enormous influence not only over the church in Geneva but also over the city as a whole.

Calvin regulated the behavior of his followers by using the civil authority of the city to carry out the punishment of those who disobeyed church laws to all the civilians of Geneva, both members of the church and nonmembers. So great was his control over the city of Geneva that he was known as the "Genevese Dictator" and the "Pope of Geneva." He is known by many to have brought the controlling Catholic "spirit of Rome" into the heart of Geneva. Laurence Vance writes that Calvin "was involved in every conceivable aspect of city life."[304] After all, his income for preaching was not paid by the church but by the city treasury. While cult leaders are typically funded from the contributions of their members,

---

[301] Ibid.

[302] Geisler and Rhodes, *Correcting the Cults*, 17.

[303] McDowell, *Handbook of Today's Religions*, 24.

[304] Vance, *The Other Side of Calvinism*, 85.

Calvin's role in Geneva was as much civil as it was ecclesiastical. This might have made him feel the need to govern all facets of religious and civil affairs. Philip Yancey notes the danger of a theocracy such as what Calvin established in Geneva:

> When the church has occasion to set the rules for all society, it often veers towards the extremism Jesus warned against. Consider just one example, the Geneva of John Calvin. There, officials could summon anyone for questioning about matters of faith. Church attendance was compulsory. Laws covered such issues as how many dishes could be served at each meal and the appropriate colors of garments.[305]

The typical cult leader is compulsive in his attempt to control and manipulate the free will of his congregation—who and when people can marry, how to dress and act, how to spend their money, and so on. Calvin took this sort of control a step further by imposing his religious convictions on those outside of his church. Although Geneva had already maintained strict religious ordinances for its civilians due to the recent overthrow of Catholic offenses, these were only bolstered under Calvin's authority when he entered Geneva in 1536. Five years later on November 20, 1541, the city—not the church—of Geneva had already adopted Calvin's *Ecclesiastical Ordinances*. In light of these ordinances, historian Diarmaid MacCulloch writes:

> Ultimately it is fairly safe to add the conclusion that many people opposed Calvin because they detested him. If one would have been justified in anticipating a good night out in the company of Martin Luther, the same cannot be said for the buttoned-up French exile who wanted to stop

---

[305] Philip Yancy, *What's So Amazing about Grace?* (Nashville: Thomas Nelson, 2007), 212.

the citizens of Geneva dancing.[306]

Calvin is reported to have imprisoned a hairdresser for two days for styling the hair of a new bride in an unseemly manner. Naming a child after a Catholic saint was also a penal offense. In the newly reformed city of Geneva, over twenty people were burnt alive after being charged for practicing witchcraft in 1545 alone. Calvin was involved in the persecutions. From 1542 to 1546, fifty-eight people were executed and seventy-six were banished from the city of Geneva. It is also believed that "torture was freely used to extract confessions."[307] The "lucky" opponents of Calvin and his control over religious and secular Geneva were merely banished. Others were tortured and/or put to death.

Diarmaid MacCulloch writes that, to curb a spirit of sedition within the city, "The patrician city authorities in Geneva, in contrast to those of Münster, were determined to keep the immigrants from challenging their authority."[308] One simple way of doing this was to make a large schism between city/church officials. MacCulloch writes, "Apart from the hundreds of ordinary laypeople who arrived, all the ministers in the city were immigrants, mostly French; in fact, astonishingly between the 1540s and 1594, the Genevan ministry did not include a single native Genevan."[309]

It is no wonder, then, that a majority of the city (especially natives) was not too fond of the new church and state dictates. It should be noted that people who disagreed with the rule of Geneva were free to leave the city at any time, but choosing to stay was most likely at the high cost of sacrificing their own conscience in matters of biblical religion. While all cults

---

[306] Diarmaid MacCulloch, *The Reformation: A History* (New York: Penguin Group, 2003), 241.

[307] Vance, *The Other Side of Calvinism*, 85.

[308] MacCulloch, *The Reformation*, 239.

[309] Ibid.

look down upon members leaving, some simply do not allow it. Many present-day "rebels"—those who dare to disagree with a cult leader or attempt to flee his control—are forced to undergo some sort of psychological or physical punishment. This was true in the account of Tom Roberts, ex-member of "People's Temple" and friend of Jim Jones.

"Jim" or James Warren Jones was born on May 13, 1931. He was the founder of the cult called "People's Temple." After deviating from the Disciples of Christ, Jim led a growing congregation with radically unorthodox beliefs. At forty-seven years old on November 18, 1978, Jim led his congregation in "a mass murder/suicide by poison in their isolated agricultural community called Jonestown, located in Guyana. Over nine hundred people died from cyanide poisoning or gunshot wounds in the aftermath of Jones' ordering his men to kill Congressman Leo Ryan and others with him.

After years of service and commitment to the cult and Jonestown, Tom Roberts and his wife made an attempt to leave the compound. But in the morning of their intended departure, their children had been taken to another location, resulting in their prolonged three-year stay. Roberts attested that during this time, at "cathartic" commission meetings, members were stripped naked, beaten, and forced to engage in sexual acts. Jones had "threatened dissidents and defectors with murder."[310] Two years before the mass murder/suicide at Jonestown, Roberts and nearly all of his family finally escaped the compound.

As sad and as evil as the events in Jonestown were, they could pale in comparison to the troubles that faced the entire city of Geneva. At least the People's Temple was limited to those who willingly followed Jim Jones, compared to the entire population of Geneva being held to John Calvin's civil and private regulations. Like many challengers of Calvinism today, a doctor by the name of Jerome Bolsec

---

[310] Lowell D. Streiker, *Cults: The Continuing Threat* (Nashville: Abingdon Press, 1983), 127–28.

(1520–1584) did not agree with Calvin's view of biblical predestination. He was arrested and threatened when he attested that "those who posit an eternal decree in God by which He has ordained some to life and some to death make him a tyrant, and in fact an idol, as the pagans made of Jupiter."[311] MacCulloch also writes of Jerome Bolsec, an ex-Carmelite friar and French refugee who "tackled the question of predestination in a lecture audaciously delivered to the Company of Pastors in 1551, declaring that the formulation which Calvin had made of double predestination to salvation and reprobation (damnation) effectively made out God to be . . . [not only] "a tyrant . . . [but] the author of sin."[312] Because of his challenge to Calvin, Bolsec was banished from the city. MacCulloch writes:

> Bolsec did not forgive and forget, and he devoted the rest of his career to attacking both predestination and Calvin. In old age once more a member of the Roman Catholic Church, he got his revenge by producing a viciously vituperative anti-biography of Calvin and his successor Theodore Beza; there, among other choice morsels, he accused them both of sodomy.[313]

Soon after Bolsec's banishment, a city notary of Geneva named Jean Trolliet opposed Calvin's stance on God's complete sovereignty by claiming that would make God out to be the author of sin. Because of the challenge to Calvin's *Institutes*, the city council ruled that "no one should dare to speak against this book and its doctrine."[314]

Similarly, many cult leaders will censor reading material that is

---

[311] Vance, *The Other Side of Calvinism*, 86.

[312] MacCulloch, *The Reformation*, 242.

[313] Ibid., 243.

[314] Vance, *The Other Side of Calvinism*, 86.

contrary to the leader's writings or teachings. The cult leader's doctrine and writings are not to be challenged. Jackson explains that the leader of a cult usually "discourages reading any material, examining any ideas that he does not generate. He seeks to control the inflow of knowledge relative to 'his group.'"[315]

This is clearly seen in the case of Mormonism. When the Scriptures of the Bible and of *The Book of Mormon* (written by Joseph Smith) contradict each other, one must take a back seat to the other. Mormons, of course, uphold their book as more authoritative than the Bible. This is apparent when Joseph Smith states in the introduction to *The Book of Mormon*, "The Book of Mormon was the most correct of any book on earth, and the keystone of our religion and a man would get nearer to God by abiding by its precepts, than by any other book."[316] This was also true in the case of the Branch Davidians. David Koresh controlled what his followers "ate and read" as well as what they "viewed as entertainment."[317]

Calvin not only controlled what some people ate and read, he literally controlled the city of Geneva. Even Calvinist historian, John T. McNeill confesses that, "The sway Calvin exercised in Geneva was very real, and at some points unduly harsh."[318] Because of Calvin's control of Geneva, the city was nicknamed "Protestant Rome." It was "Protestant" because its inhabitants *protested* against the Catholic Church. In Calvin's grasp, however, Geneva ironically mirrored Catholicism's authoritative capital, Rome. As the Pope ruled in Rome, so Calvin governed Geneva.

Geisler and Rhodes write about cult leaders constructing a

---

[315] Jackson, "How to Identify a Cult."

[316] Joseph Smith, *The Book of Mormon* (Salt Lake City: The Church of Latter-day Saints, 1948), Introduction.

[317] Report to the Deputy Attorney General on the Events at Waco, Texas, February 28 to April 19, 1993.

[318] McNeill, *The History and Character of Calvinism*, 186.

situation called *isolationism*, explaining that:

> . . . the more extreme cults sometimes create fortified boundaries, often precipitating tragic endings, such as the disaster in Waco, Texas, with the Branch Davidian cult. The erection of such barriers, whether physical or psychological, creates an environment of isolation, which in turn often leads to antagonism.[319]

In this manner, Joseph Smith "owned" Utah and Jim Jones owned Jonestown, just as John Calvin owned Geneva. Calvin's iron-fisted rule of Geneva cannot be overlooked by those who boast of adhering to his doctrine. McNeill readily admits that under Calvin, Geneva's laws "became more detailed and more stringent."[320] On February 2, 1554, at Calvin's prompting, "the Council of two hundred, with uplifted hands, together swore henceforth 'to live according to the Reformation, forget all hatreds and cultivate concord.'"[321] As the facts of ecclesiastical and civil punishment read, we can only interpret that their "concord" was meant for those who agreed to and obeyed their systematic theological tenets. Religious freedom was obviously not promoted by Calvin or his successors. As we will see later, this pattern was carried into colonial America years later.

Another contemporary Calvinist and historian, Robert Godfrey, describes Calvin as "a rather medieval man on several important political issues. He did not believe that democracy was the best form of government, and he did not believe in religious freedom."[322] Godfrey also justifies Calvin's approach, arguing that Calvin indeed "believed

[319] Geisler and Rhodes, *Correcting the Cults*, 12.

[320] McNeill, *The History and Character of Calvinism*, 189.

[321] Ibid., 187.

[322] Godfrey, *An Unexpected Journey*, 102.

that if a government had become tyrannical, responsible citizens had a right and duty to rebel against that tyranny in the name of justice."[323] Considering the extent of Calvin's rule of Geneva, the truth of Godfrey's statement is questionable.

The extent of Calvin's control in both ecclesiastical and secular matters can make other well-known cult leaders seem almost mild. Christians have regarded David Koresh, Jim Jones, and Joseph Smith as obvious examples of cult leaders—dangerous in their warped ideas of Scripture and the extent of their control over followers. However, the overwhelming amount of evidence for John Calvin's control and even cruelty in a whole city is usually completely overlooked or dismissed by Calvinists. To look beyond his control is one thing, but his means of enforcing religious rule must be taken into account.

His Violence

Jim Jones had such control over his followers that outwardly he did not need to inflict any sort of violence or punishment to maintain the obedience of his loyal devotees. Although there were violent acts before the mass suicide, they were done mostly behind closed doors. At the peak of the Jim Jones cult, so intense was his control that most of the devotees willingly committed suicide. Over 900 people of the Jim Jones cult killed themselves by drinking poisoned Kool-Aid or Flavor Aid. (Other reports state that not all of the 900 deaths were suicides. A number of victims were forcefully injected or shot.) On April 19, 1993, David Koresh led himself with close to eighty of his loyal followers into eternity. Both David Koresh and Jim Jones defended their faith with violent acts. From micro-cults like the Branch Davidians to massive religious institutions like Roman Catholicism and Islam, violence has

---

[323] Ibid.

been used to enforce a particular theological view.

It is interesting that Evangelical Christians (including Calvinists) so easily condemn Jim Jones, David Koresh, and other violent religious fanatics, while praising John Calvin, who was responsible for the banishment, torture, and death of both the "guilty" and the innocent. What born-again believer in Jesus chooses to overlook that his theological and positional title is named not after Christ, who forgave those while He was dying, but after a man who lived fifteen hundred years after Christ and burned men and women at the stake for the mere suspicion of sin?

We read in the previous section that when a cult leader loses his controlling grip on a pawn, he can quickly turn to violence for appeasement, as was the case with John Calvin. In the heart of a cult is often found violent and sadistic behavior. This behavior can be on a private or public level. For instance, we can see that before the Jonestown mass suicide, Jones reportedly had grown violent in both private and public acts. Likewise, Mormon president Sidney Rigdon stated in his Fourth of July speech of 1838, which was reproduced in the *Comprehensive History of the Church*:

> . . . [the] mob that comes on us to disturb us, it shall be between us and them a war of extermination; for we will follow them until the last drop of their blood is spilled; or else they will have to exterminate us, for we will carry the seat of war to their own houses and their own families, and one party or the other shall be utterly destroyed.[324]

Joseph Smith approved of the speech. Soon after, it only bolstered the church, which is known to have "led battles against non-aggressive former Mormons and mistakenly led a battle against the states

---

[324] Sidney Rigdon, "Oration, Delivered by Mr. S. Rigdon, On the 4th of July, 1838" [online]; accessed 28 January 2010; available from http://sidneyrigdon.com /rigd1838.htm; Internet.

own militia."[325]

The fact that Mormons were violently punished for some crimes should be no surprise when Rigdon's publicized "Salt Sermon" mentions hanging all dissenters. And with Joseph Smith's overt approval of such disciplinary actions, Garn LeBaron Jr. was recently compelled to write "Mormon Fundamentalism and Violence: A Historical Analysis." He concludes:

> As an exploration of the relationship between Mormon fundamentalism and violence, this paper has analyzed the origins of Mormon fundamentalist doctrines and illustrated how these doctrines can become operationalized in a violent way . . . Most fundamentalists are religious, law abiding people, but sometimes this potent blend of religion, isolation, revelation and action combines to create a culture of violence.[326]

Thus, the article "Mormon Blood Atonement: Fact or Fantasy?" written by Jerald and Sandra Tanner, should not be too much of a mystery. The Mormon doctrine of "blood atonement" was the practice of "shedding the blood" of any Mormon who was guilty of committing the more offensive sins, particularly sins against the church. Although today this doctrine is never taught, rarely mentioned or even known, Brigham Young explained that the doctrine as fact. In a sermon given on September 21, 1856, Young stated:

There are sins that men commit for which they cannot

[325] "A Response to Gordon B. Hinckley's *The Mormons' Trail of Hope*" [online]; accessed 28 January 2010; available from http://www.lds-mormon.com/tmpc.shtml; Internet.

[326] Garn LeBaron, Garn Jr., "Mormon Fundamentalism and Violence: A Historical Analysis," 1995 [online]; accessed 28 January 2010; available from http://www.exmormon.org/violence.htm; Internet.

receive forgiveness in this world, or in that which is to come, and if they had their eyes open to see their true condition, they would be perfectly willing to have their blood spilt upon the ground, that the smoke thereof might ascend to heaven as an offering for their sins; and the smoking incense would atone for their sins, whereas, if such is not the case, they will stick to them and remain upon them in the spirit world. . . . I know, when you hear my brethren telling about cutting people off from the earth, that you consider it is strong doctrine; but it is to save them, not to destroy them . . . And furthermore, I know that there are transgressors, who, if they knew themselves, and the only condition upon which they can obtain forgiveness, would beg of their brethren to shed their blood, that the smoke thereof might ascend to God as an offering to appease the wrath that is kindled against them, and that the law might have its course. I will say further; I have had men come to me and offer their lives to atone for their sins.[327]

Although "blood atonement" was initially taught as a solely self-inflicted act, John D. Lee, a member of Young's underground "Council of Fifty" stated otherwise. He said, "I knew of many men being killed in Nauvoo [and] many a man who was quietly put out of the way by the orders of Joseph and his Apostles while the Church was there."[328] Later, Lee reported the punishment of dissenters by the priesthood, saying that:

[327] Jerald and Sandra Tanner, "Mormon Blood Atonement: Fact or Fiction?" *The Salt Lake City Messenger*, Issue 92, April 1997 [online]; accessed 28 January 2010; available from http://1857massacre.com/MMM/bloodatonement.htm; Internet.

[328] Ibid.

In Utah it has been the custom with the Priesthood to make eunuchs of such men as were obnoxious to the leaders. This was done for a double purpose: first, it gave a perfect revenge, and next, it left the poor victim a living example to others of the dangers of disobeying counsel and not living as ordered by the Priesthood. [329]

Lastly, he confessed that, "The most deadly sin among the people was adultery, and many men were killed in Utah for the crime."[330]

The retribution for committing adultery under Brigham Young is reminiscent of acts performed by John Calvin, "who favored the death penalty" for "incorrigible adulterers."[331] Of course, the death penalty was not limited to "incorrigible adulterers," as in the case of Jacques Gruet, a known opponent of Calvin. Gruet was thought to have left on Calvin's pulpit letters attacking him and his control over Geneva. While his house was searched, a letter was found confirming his thoughts on how the civil laws under Calvin were too intrusive in personal affairs. Vance wrote that:

> After a month of torture, Gruet confessed and was sentenced to death . . . He was beheaded on July 26th, 1547, with Calvin consenting to his death. Several years later a heretical book of Gruet's was discovered and publicly burnt on Calvin's advice in front of Gruet's house.[332]

In 1553, the rise of Calvin's theology within the civil areas of Geneva provoked many who opposed him or his doctrines to open

---

[329] Ibid.

[330] Ibid.

[331] Vance, *The Other Side of Calvinism*, 85.

[332] Ibid., 86.

altercations. "Four of his chief opponents who did not flee the city were beheaded, and their defeat, Calvin's triumph, was represented as God's triumph. Over the severed head of one of the victims was coldly inscribed:

> For having fallen into the misfortune
> Of a loving man more than God
> Claude de Geneve has his head
> Nailed up in this place."[333]

Some argue in vain that Calvin was simply a product of his times and was carrying out punishments that the Catholic Church had already been doing for years. But this logic fails to defend Calvin's use of capital punishment. Although Christians are undoubtedly affected by the culture they live in, the Holy Spirit of God is able to change how a man looks at punishing the sins of the unconverted. By the same logic that Calvinists defend their leader's violence as simply being part of those more barbaric times of history, we, too, should tolerate a number of historical and even present-day atrocities under the guise of "culture." The question must be asked: Where and in what time period in the body of Christ's church should death and torture be enforced to bring about piety of others? Where in the body of Christ is that ever acceptable?

In fact, Calvin's tendency toward inflicting religious punishment on nonreligious people, as in the case above, looks much like present-day Islamic fascism. Just like Calvin believed he serving God by beheading dissenters, Islamofascists believe they are serving "Allah" when they too sever the heads of "infidels." While Calvin publicized these acts with paper and pen, radical Muslims do so with video cameras, hoping to spread their rule of terror to the world. If Calvin terminology is correct, disciplining or putting to death the disobedient and unconverted is really just showing a form of God's "love." Calvin saw Geneva's committee of

---

[333] MacCulloch, *The Reformation*, 246.

pastors and elders (who were mainly responsible for enforcing discipline) as "demonstrating love in action" through their violent deeds.[334]

As if the biblical command to forgive others and live not by the sword is not a strong enough argument to speak for itself, Vance further refutes those who defend John Calvin's violent punishments with Calvin's own words. Vance states that all the excuses given in defense of Calvin's violence:

> . . . are immaterial if we take at face value what the Calvinists say about his knowledge of and reliance on the Scriptures. Another former Calvin College professor, Charles Miller (1919–1997), insists that "first and certainly basic in all of Calvin's thought is a dependence on Scripture." We are also told that Calvin "was willing to break sharply with tradition where it was contrary to the 'Word of God.'" So whatever the customs, traditions, and prejudices of his age, Calvin, because of his profound reverence for the authority of the Scriptures, should have been an iconoclast when it came to the Rome-like regulation of Genevan religion and society. But such is not the case, for Calvin, recognizing the errors of papal rulers, admonished Protestant rulers to emulate them: "Seeing that the defenders of the Papacy are so bitter and bold in behalf of their superstitions, that in their atrocious fury they shed the blood of the innocent, it should shame Christian magistrates that in the protection of certain truth, they are entirely destitute of spirit." It is statements from Calvin like this that prompted the Baptist historian A. H. Newman (1852–1933) to remark: . . . "Calvin's view of the subordination of the

---

[334] Ibid., 238.

civil power to the ecclesiastical does not appear to be radically different from the papal." And although Calvin's actions are repeatedly dismissed because of the spirit of his age, it is not true that all Christians maintained a persecuting spirit. The Anabaptists, against whom Calvin wrote in 1544, certainly did not believe in persecuting their opponents.[335]

But John Calvin did. Michael Servetus was born in the early 1500s in Aragon, Spain. Of his many published works, two attacked the Trinity and seven pertained to the "errors" of the Trinity. He also held that infant baptism insulted true Christianity. It was through a bookseller in Lyons that Servetus and Calvin would later engage. Servetus gave Calvin a manuscript full of questions to be answered. But rather than spend time answering Servetus's questions, Calvin simply gave him a copy of his *Institutes*. Servetus returned Calvin's document full of critical remarks in the margins. Calvin later said that there was not a page that was not "defiled by his vomit."[336] Seven years before Servetus's death, Calvin wrote in a letter to fellow Reformer, Guillaume Farel, that he would "never permit him to depart alive, provided [his] authority be of any avail."[337]

Historian Diarmaid MacCulloch writes:

Calvin was as clear as the Roman Catholic inquisitors in Lyon or the papal Antichrist in Rome that Servetus must die. The Genevan city authorities determined that the heretic's fate should be the traditional one of burning at the stake, and although Calvin would have preferred a

---

[335] Vance, *The Other Side of Calvinism*, 88.

[336] Ibid., 90.

[337] Ibid., 92.

more mercifully summary method of execution, he did not oppose the burning on 27 October 1553.[338]

As Servetus was burned at the stake, his last words were noted: "O, Jesus, Son of the eternal God, have pity on me!"[339] Eight years after the death of Servetus, Calvin encouraged Marquis the Poet to follow his lead and rid the country of "zealous scoundrels." He wrote that, "Such monsters should be exterminated, as I have exterminated Michael Servetus the Spaniard."[340] Despite this evidence, there remain supporters of Calvinism who claim Calvin had little or nothing to do with Servetus's execution. They pass the blame wholly on the Catholic Church, which set the precedent of enforcing religious rule. Even those who admit Calvin's overt involvement in the death of Servetus (though claiming it as an exception) would do well to read John Calvin's *Defense of the Orthodox Trinity Against the Errors of Michael Servetus*, in which he defended his actions against the so-called heretic, stating, "Whoever shall now contend that it is unjust to put heretics and blasphemers to death will knowingly and willingly incur their very guilt."[341]

Apparently, Calvin felt no guilt for using the sword to defend his theology. While this might not seem too strange for many in religious movements throughout history (and even some today), it cannot help but stand out for Christians claiming to be obedient to the sole authority of the Bible. Although the Bible has recorded periods of violence and war, its New Testament teachings far from condone it. The Bible teaches that a mark of a mature Christian is submission to the Spirit of God rather than conformity to the "spirit of the age." If the Holy Spirit of God is powerless to bring about

---

[338] MacCulloch, *The Reformation*, 245.

[339] Vance, *The Other Side of Calvinism*, 91.

[340] Ibid., 95.

[341] Ibid., 94.

change in a person, then He will be powerless to bring about change in a culture. Oppositely, marks of a "carnal Christian," as mentioned in 1 Corinthians 3, include caring for the things of the world, disregarding the Holy Spirit's work, and conforming to the spirit of the age. On a number of occasions, Jesus showed His submission to the Holy Spirit and disregard for the spirit of the age. He touched lepers, talked to women, healed Samaritans, called out the sins of the religious elite, and most importantly, forgave those who sinned against Him. John Calvin, on the other hand, embodied papal punishment under the guise of the newly reformed faith of Martin Luther.

Calvinism in Colonial America

C. S. Lewis observed that almost all crimes of Christian history have come about when religion is confused with politics.[342]

—Philip Yancey

Calvin and his ideas have had a shaping role in American history, one that goes far beyond matters of church polity and religious doctrine. From Jonathan Edwards to William Faulkner, American writers have worked within an intellectual framework marked by beliefs and attitudes shaped by Calvin's Institutes and the Geneva Bible, both of which came to America with the Pilgrims on the Mayflower.[343]

—Timothy George

Unfortunately, the use of the sword to maintain Christian "orthodoxy" did not end when Calvin died. His interpretation of Scripture was adopted by nearly every Puritan who would later come to America. It was a spiritual Manifest Destiny that led to the predominant Presbyterian and Baptist churches in New England. Not only had these

---

[342] Yancey, *What's So Amazing about Grace?* 211.

[343] George, "John Calvin: Comeback Kid."

Puritans aligned themselves with Calvin's theology, but they followed the precedent he had set in governing Geneva as well. Philip Yancey notes, "Early on, America teetered on the brink of becoming a theocracy along the lines of Calvin's Geneva." [344]

We can see this clearly illustrated by an incident in Massachusetts Bay when one man was ostracized not for his lack of piety but for his condemnation of religious officials who enforced civil law by inaccurately interpreting Scripture. Although Roger Williams (1603–1683) was considered by some to be somewhat of a Calvinist by default, this colonial theologian and advocate of religious freedom fought vehemently against the use of the sword to enforce religious policy. While historians have different opinions about Williams' theology and philosophy, all certainly recognize his pursuit of religious freedom. It is also universally accepted that the heart of the theological practices of persecution that Williams so defied was Calvinism.

"Progressive historians" like Vernon Louis Parrington and James Ernst considered Roger Williams "an Enlightened thinker before his time—a liberal who rejected the harsh Calvinistic theology of his Puritan contemporaries."[345] Author and historian James P. Byrd, Jr. refers to Calvin's theology as a "persecuting theology" (reflecting Williams' sentiments).[346] Byrd also concludes that while "Williams revered Calvin's theological genius and considered him a great man . . . he attacked Calvin's biblical interpretation, calling it a dangerous perversion that turned the Holy Word into a bloody instrument of persecution."[347]

---

[344] Yancey, *What's So Amazing about Grace?* 213.

[345] James P. Byrd, Jr., *The Challenges of Roger Williams: Religious Liberty, Violent Persecution, and the Bible* (Macon, GA: Mercer University Press, 2002), 27.

[346] Ibid., 140.

[347] Ibid., 190.

Although Williams held no grudges against Calvin himself, the biblical interpretation and philosophy mimicked by the Christian leaders of the day was the main source of the tension between Williams and his adversaries. Williams believed that true religious reform could never come from the civil sword or ostracism. He believed that spiritual change came from the heart and not from mandatory obedience. Williams also condemned how his fellow colonists viewed the neighboring Native Americans. While Williams believed that they were in need of the saving gospel of Christ, he was outspoken about his disapproval of his fellow Christians' arrogant posture towards the people they referred to as "savages."

Many people, then and now, consider Williams as having been before his time. Historian Vernon Parrington views Williams as a "philosopher caught in an age dominated by gloomy Calvinists."[348] According to Byrd, Parrington also holds that "Puritans committed many errors, the greatest being their appalling relish for John Calvin's theological government."[349] Byrd explains that:

> In sixteenth-century Geneva, Calvin had established a theocratic rule that ministers guided and magistrates enforced. Because Calvin combined religious and secular authority, Parrington considered him a "tyrant" who used the power of the state to enforce God's commands— with violence when necessary.[350]

As Parrington says in his own words, "A few splotches of blood on the white garments of the Church did not greatly trouble" Calvin.[351] Because Puritans brought Calvin's theology regarding the relationship of church and

---

[348] Ibid., 28; Vernon L. Parrington, *Main Currents in American Thought*, vol. 1 (New York: Harcourt Brace, 1927), 64.

[349] Byrd, *The Challenges of Roger Williams*, 28.

[350] Ibid.

[351] Parrington, *Main Currents in American Thought*, 20–21.

state to the new land of America, LeRoy Moore believes that Parrington deems the Puritans to be "an anomaly on the American scene, foreign to everything true, good, and beautiful in the maturing national culture."[352]

Roger Williams believed that John Calvin and other respected leaders of Christianity who followed in his footsteps of governmental/church rule "were actually *'bloody Persecutors'* who drew arrows from *'the Quiver of Scripture'* and used them 'to pierce the tender heart of Christ Jesus' in their errant exegesis."[353] Supposedly, however, the Puritans boasted of their "nearness to Christ." Again, according to Byrd, "Williams believed, because despite their arrogant profession, *'to draw nearer to Christ Jesus than other states and churches,'* New England Puritans were avid believers in the *'Bloody Doctrine'* of persecution." [354]

The point is clear. Because of John Calvin's great influence in civil religion, the majority of seventeenth-century Christians, Protestants, Lutherans, Baptists, and Puritans had a Calvinistic framework in understanding Scripture that remained largely unchallenged until Roger Williams did so. In his exegesis, Williams not only revealed that religious freedom is a biblical concept but also that Calvin's tyrannical roles, along with his scripturally supportive interpretations, were misguided.

His Writing

Calvin goes on from the original Protestant experience of conversion to build a system, to extrapolate, to raise all the dark questions and give without flinching the dark answers.[355]

—C. S. Lewis, on Calvin's *Institutes*

---

[352] Byrd, *The Challenges of Roger Williams*, 28.

[353] Ibid., 6.

[354] Byrd, *The Challenges of Roger Williams*, 19.

[355] C. S. Lewis, Quote 139, "Calvin, John," taken from the Introduction to *English Literature in the Sixteenth Century*, para. 61, p. 42, in *The Quotable Lewis*, ed. Wayne Martindale and Jerry Root (Wheaton, IL: Tyndale House Publishers, 1898), 83.

Cult leaders rarely lead without their own writings. Mary Baker Eddie penned her *Science and Health with Key to the Scriptures*; Joseph Smith wrote *The Book of Mormon*; Ron Hubbard, *Dianetics: The Modern Science of Mental Health*; and John Calvin has his famed *Institutes*. Out of all his writings and commentaries, which by his own words were subordinate to his *Institutes*, no other writing has so "determined the course of history and changed the face of Europe" as have Calvin's *Institutes*.[356] So influential are the *Institutes* that comparing them to other cultish writings might at first seem absurd.

To refresh our memory, John Calvin was eight years old when Martin Luther penned his *Ninety-Five Theses* in 1517. Born in one of the most tumultuous times in church history, John Calvin grew up in the midst of heavy Roman Catholic influence. Although Calvin officially broke allegiance to the Catholic Church at the age of twenty-five, a majority of his education had been completed under its authority. He studied at the University of Paris and later studied law at the University of Orleans. He wrote the first edition of his *Institutes of the Christian Religion* in 1536 at the age of twenty-seven. Because Calvin was so young, some scholars question his credibility. Dave Hunt states that the *Institutes:*

> . . . could not possibly have come from a deep and fully developed evangelical understanding of Scripture. Instead, they came from an energetic enthusiasm of a recent law graduate and a fervent study of philosophy and religion, a young genius devoted to Augustine and a newly adopted cause.[357]

It is also important to note that five years after writing the *Institutes*, the Genevan authorities asked Calvin to draft the *Ecclesiastical Ordinances*, an outline of church structure and doctrine. "Calvin borrowed

---

[356] Alister McGrath, *A Life of John Calvin* (Oxford: Basil Blackwell, 1990), xiii, 209.

[357] Hunt, *What Love Is This?* 39.

Bucer's assertion that the New Testament indicated four functions of ministry: pastors, doctors, elders, and deacons [but] was himself never ordained as priest or minister in any Church." Nevertheless, he classified himself as a doctor. "Together the pastors and the senior doctors, who were obviously close to them in ministry, notably Calvin himself, formed a company of Pastors." [358]

Although people have said that Calvin gave Protestantism its first systemized theology, it can hardly be said that he was the sole mind in formulating it. Calvin was well-read in the works of Reformers before him, and he relied heavily upon Bucer and Luther. However, he referred to no other theologian more than Augustine of Hippo, who is quoted in Calvin's *Institutes* over 400 times. Spurgeon, acknowledging Calvin's use of Augustine's works, observes, "Perhaps Calvin himself derived it [sotereological system] mainly from the writings of Augustine," and affirms that "Augustine obtained his views, without doubt, through the Spirit of God, from the diligent studies of the writings of Paul, and Paul received them from the Holy Ghost, from Jesus Christ." [359]

If Augustine "without doubt" received his views from the Holy Spirit and Calvin heavily received his views from Augustine, then one could nearly conclude that the *Institutes* of John Calvin are divinely inspired. Many Calvinists seem to have concluded just that. From the *Institutes*, Calvinism draws its doctrine, interpretation of Scripture, systemized theology, and distorted view of God. Claiming to be a Calvinist is nothing less than trusting that the *Institutes* are unparalleled in defining "true" Christianity. After the *Institute*'s twenty-three years of revisions, it was finally finished in 1559, just five years before Calvin's death on May 27, 1564.

---

[358] MacCulloch, *The Reformation*, 238.

[359] Charles H. Spurgeon, message delivered at the opening ceremony of the inaugural ceremonies for the new Metropolitan Tabernacle, in "Expositions of the Doctrines of Grace," sermons 385-388 of *The Spurgeon Archive* [online]; accessed 28 January 2010; available from http://www.spurgeon.org/sermons/ 0385.htm; Internet.

In most cults, the leader's writings and doctrines determine the followers' involvement with and interpretation of the Bible. Instead of plain Scripture leading to doctrine, doctrine leads the interpretation of Scripture. Although we will look at this in more depth in the next chapter, here are two examples: Those who follow *The Book of Mormon* consider it to be the *fullness of the gospel*. Thus, they deem it as more authoritative than the Bible itself. Those who follow the doctrines of Charles Taze Russell consider any translation of the Bible other than the *New World* to be incorrect. Cult members also interpret the Bible to fit the theology of their leader. For example, the audience of Mary Baker Eddie's *Key to the Scriptures* interprets the Scripture from a very mystical, nonliteral perspective. The same can be said of Jehovah's Witnesses and Mormons. Likewise, when Calvinists read the Scriptures, they usually do so in the light of John Calvin's *Institutes*, confirming the words of Kent R. Rieske:

> Calvinists hold John Calvin in such a high esteem that his writings and teachings are studied and quoted in preference to Scripture. His teachings are used by Calvinists to interpret Scripture rather than the sound doctrine of using Scripture to interpret Scripture.[360]

In Calvin hotbeds, the *Institutes* is referred to as often as the Bible, and is even studied in the same manner. Latter-day Saints are educated in the book of Mormon just as students at Calvin Theological Seminary in Grand Rapids, Michigan, can take classes on Calvin's *Institutes* and commentaries. Brigham Young founded the Mormon Brigham Young College (BYC) in Logan, Utah, on July 24, 1877, just two years after he founded Brigham Young Academy (Brigham Young University from 1903) in Provo, Utah. In the Mormon schools, students learn theology and read the Scriptures as interpreted by Joseph Smith, just as students in both Calvin Seminary and Calvin College learn the Bible as interpreted by

---

[360] Rieske, "Calvinism."

John Calvin. At one school, Joseph Smith is highly esteemed; in the other, John Calvin is greatly revered.

Other than his *Institutes*, John Calvin offered much commentary in the marginal notes of the *Geneva Bible*. When England was ruled under Queen Mary I, many Protestant scholars escaped her persecution to Geneva. The city of Geneva was ruled by John Calvin who we know lead both church and civil matters. The *Geneva Bible* was partially printed in England in 1575 and fully printed a year later. There were over 150 editions made. With John Knox collaborating with Calvin in the new Bible, a law was passed in Scotland in 1579 requiring all houses to purchase a copy if financially possible. The commentary in the Bible's margins was prized by Calvinists but was not liked by the Church of England nor King James, who later commissioned the "Authorized Version" or King James Version to replace it in 1611. Until the English Civil War, the *Geneva Bible* was widespread among all Puritans and Calvinists.

Kent Rieske astutely notes the apparent "need" for the *Geneva Bible* to be full of Calvin's commentary. He writes, "Calvin's theology could not be ascertained by the typical student of the Bible without the external study of Calvin's *Institutes* . . . Calvin wrote commentary notes in the margin of the Bible to be used as the interpretation of the Scripture."[361] Although soundly translated from Greek and Hebrew, the marginal notes of the *Geneva Bible* made it what is was. To its credit, the *Geneva Bible* was in fact the first "'Study Bible,' with extensive commentary notes in the margins."[362] With Calvin's commentaries included in its 1599 edition, the *Geneva Bible* was "the most complete study aide for Biblical scholars and students" at that time; the "extensive collection" of commentary was not a trivial part of the new Bible,

---

[361] Rieske, "Calvinism."

[362] Greatsite Marketing website, [online]; accessed 23 December 2010; available from http://www.greatsite.com/facsimile-reproductions/geneva-1560.html; Internet.

for it is still considered the "greatest distinction of the *Geneva Bible.*"[363] Calvin's notes comprise nearly 300,000 words, or nearly one-third the length of the Bible itself, and they are justifiably considered "the most complete source of Protestant religious thought available."[364] As a result, the *Geneva Bible* became:

> . . . the most widely read and influential English Bible of the 16th and 17th centuries. It was continually printed from 1560 to 1644 in over 200 different editions. It was the Bible of choice for many of the greatest writers, thinkers, and historical figures of the Reformation era. [365]

With men such as William Shakespeare, John Milton, John Bunyan, and Oliver Cromwell using the *Geneva Bible*, we can again see why Calvinism has had a strong foothold on theology.

Despite the wide acceptance of *the Geneva Bible*, its place in history was relatively short. Although the Geneva translation was accurate, the "not so marginal" notes of John Calvin so angered the Catholic Church, namely King James of England, that it was promptly replaced by the widely known 1611 King James translation, which was published without commentary. From then on, the *Geneva Bible* has gone mostly unnoticed in Christianity. And now that Calvinism is making a comeback, the new *Reformation Study Bible*[366] has recently appeared on the scene. Although it

---

[363] "1599 Geneva Bible," Introduction from L. L. Brown Publishing [online]; accessed 25 June 2010; available from website, http://www.reformedreader. org/gbn/en.htm; Internet.

[364] Ibid.

[365] Ibid.

[366] "Widely considered one of the best tools available for Bible study and previously only available in the New King James translation, The Reformation Study Bible has been updated to the readable and accurate English Standard Version (ESV). This foundational resource was created by more than fifty scholars and features thousands of in-depth study notes, 96 theological articles, 19 in-text maps, colored maps, and 12 charts to help you understand the Bible better." [online];

uses both the New King James Version and English Standard Version translations, it is full of marginal notes written by leading Calvinists.

One could rightly argue that this fact is unimportant, since most of today's Calvinists are not even familiar with the *Geneva Bible*. However, although many Calvinists might not use either the new *Reformation Study Bible* or old *Geneva Bible* or hold them in the same light that past Calvinists have, the readers are indeed affected by their adherence to Calvin's biblical interpretation. This point is made clear by a conversation I had recently with a Jehovah's Witness as my truck was being fixed. We briefly discussed the *New World Translation*. (This purposely mistranslated Bible was proved in a court of law to have mangled the original language of the Bible for the intent of substantiating unorthodox views of Jesus and other biblical doctrines that accompany salvation). He was quick to mention that he reads all translations of the Bible. Regardless of this fact, the damage has already been done for him. Whenever this man had read other translations, his views of God, which are based on ideas by Charles Taze Russell, twisted his interpretation of even correctly translated verses that reveal the deity of Jesus.

Ultimately, no matter what translation of the Bible the man may read, his unorthodox views of Jesus will remain unchanged, because he holds to Russell's teachings. The same can be said of the Mormon. Mormons read orthodox translations of the Bible. Yet, the unorthodoxy from Joseph Smith's writings has horribly corrupted the sound interpretation found in other Bibles. Likewise, the *Key to the Scriptures* and *Watchtower* magazines can pervert the minds of readers and obscure their vision of plain scriptural truth.

This is true for many Calvinists today. They might not have a clue that the footnotes in the *Geneva Bible*s are unorthodox, but they still understand John 3:16 to mean something other than that Christ died for all of humanity. When one professes to be a Calvinist or a Reformed

---

accessed 23 December 2010; available from website http://www.ligonier.org/store /reformation-study-bible-esv-genuine-leather-black/?gclid=CNf_vLXvgq YCFQwCbAodWlolng; Internet.

Christian, the damage has already been done. Calvinists align themselves with John Calvin's beliefs and his interpretation of selective salvation. They align themselves with all his writings and footnotes—both the orthodox and the unorthodox.

Collin Hansen has recently noted that John Calvin, "appear[s] not to be a major figure among the latest generation to claim the theology he made famous."[367] How can one not acknowledge John Calvin in Calvinism? Despite the claims from most cultists that they hold their leader's writings as merely being *equal* to the Bible, in practice, the Bible usually takes a back seat. *The Book of Mormon* is blatantly tagged as "the fullness of the gospel." Ellen G. White, the Seventh-day Adventists' prophetess, claims that she writes not her own ideas but "what God has opened before me in vision."[368] Although most Calvinists would never be so bold as to say that the *Institutes* are as authoritative as Scripture, the outcome of their biblical theology suggests otherwise. As with Joseph Smith, Charles Russell, Ellen White, Mary Eddie, and many other cult leaders, John Calvin's writings have radically changed the way his followers interpret the Bible.

Its Twisting of Scripture

The fact is, the cults are notorious Scripture-twisters. When dealing with cults, one must keep in mind that they are always built not upon what the Bible teaches but upon what the founders or leaders of the respective cults say the Bible teaches.[369]

—Norman L. Geisler and Ron Rhodes

---

[367] Hansen, "Young, Restless, Reformed."

[368] Ellen G. White, *Testimonies for the Church Volume 5*, 67 [online]; accessed 2 February 2010; available from http://www.truthfortheendtime.com/SOPText/Testimonies_for_the_Church.pdf; Internet.

[369] Geisler and Rhodes, *Correcting the Cults*, 18.

I am deeply troubled over the Reformed version of grace because through it, the precious and scriptural truths concerning grace are so maligned.[370]

—George Bryson

Manipulation of Scripture in order to construe a certain meaning that was not or could not be intended for the reader is the hallmark of a cult. The "Bible Answer Man," Hank Hanegraaff, writes, "The first mark of a cult is its manipulation of Scripture. The Bible is twisted to fit the leader or group's interpretation."[371] Nothing has done more damage in Christianity than the use of unorthodox hermeneutics. As an example, there has been no more flagrant forgery of Scripture than the *New World Translation* of the Bible. Jehovah's Witnesses claim that this so-called Bible was translated by Greek, Aramaic, and Hebrew scholars and theologians. However, not only did the purported translators lie about having an education in Greek and Hebrew, the entire translation committee was sponsored solely by Jehovah's Witnesses and composed by members of the Watchtower Bible and Tract Society.

Because Jehovah's Witnesses do not believe that Jesus Christ was God, verses from the Bible that reveal His being more than a man or an angel, were altered to support their heretical belief. Correct words were purposely omitted and false words were intentionally added in order to change an essential doctrine of the Bible— namely, that Jesus is God. Here are some examples of their twisting of Scripture.

The *New World Translation* (NWT) has exchanged the truth for a lie. In the NWT, Zechariah 12:10 reads, "They will look upon the one whom they have pierced." Here the Hebrew ". . . look upon me whom they have pierced"—in which God is the speaker—has been altered in order to avoid the implication that the one who is to be pierced (on the cross) is God Himself.

---

[370] Bryson, *The Dark Side of Calvinism*, 30.

[371] Hanegraaff, "What Are Some Common Marks of a Cult?"

Again, because the cult teaches that Jesus was a created being rather than the Creator God, Colossians 1:15–17 in the NWT reads:

> He is the image of the invisible God, the firstborn of all creation; because by means of him all [other] things were created in the heavens and upon the earth, the things visible and the things invisible, no matter whether they are thrones or lordships or governments or authorities. All [other] things have been created through him and for him. Also, he is before all [other] things and by means of him all [other] things were made to exist.[372]

The word "other" has been inserted several times to avoid the deity of Jesus. The first edition of the NWT was printed without brackets.

The NWT version of **Hebrews 1:8** reads: "God is your throne forever."[373] Despite that the translation makes no grammatical or logical sense, it continues to be used in place of the correct translation, which is, "Your throne, O God, is forever."[374] Again, the text was altered because the original statement is referring to the Christ.

The most famous of the Watchtower mistranslations is found in **John 1:1**, where one letter, the article "a," is slipped into the passage with huge theological consequences. The NWT translates **John 1:1** as, "In the beginning was the Word, and the Word was with God, and the Word was a god."[375] The correct translation is, ". . . and the Word was God." The distorted translation of the NWT implies that Jesus was merely an angelic or supernatural being rather than God Himself.

---

[372] *New World Translation of the Holy Scriptures* (NWT) (New York: Watch Tower Bible and Tract Society of Pennsylvania, 1961).

[373] NWT, Hebrews 1:8.

[374] NKJV, Hebrews 1:8.

[375] NWT, John 1:1.

Although the Watchtower Bible and Tract Society has been proven guilty of lies and perjury in an American court of law (March 17, 1913, *Russell v. Ross*) the incorrect renditions have not been retracted. Because the Jehovah's Witnesses use the NWT as their scriptures they are continually misled and intellectually compromised, believing unbiblical doctrine. The NWT is a "translation" of the Bible written to fit a particular group's beliefs by means of deception through the manipulation of God's revealed words.

Since Mormons adhere to *The Book of Mormon* more than the Bible, a need to distort the Bible's message is less essential. When essential contradictions are found between *The Book of Mormon* and the Bible, Mormons look to *The Book of Mormon* as their ultimate authority. Therefore, the need for Mormons to alter biblical doctrines is not as great as for Jehovah's Witnesses, whose doctrine is supposedly derived directly from the Bible itself. Because Jehovah's Witnesses do not have the option to claim another source of authority, they must make their peculiar doctrine seem as sound as possible. Mormons, nevertheless, do their fair share of mangling Scripture in hopes of passing their theology off as orthodox.

Because the founders of Mormonism were polygamists, Mormon doctrine concludes that a man should practice polygamy in order to enter the highest heaven.[376] This doctrine supposedly came from Joseph Smith's "revelation." Today, polygamy is still practiced among various sects of Mormonism even in light of the Bible's denouncing of it. Mormon theology has purposefully misconstrued many biblical verses showing God's *tolerance* of the practice in the Old Testament, for He clearly commanded His people not to "multiply wives" in **Exodus 20:14–17**. Other like verses include **Deuteronomy 17:17; 1 Kings 11:1;** and **Matthew 19:9**. There are also a number of other verses referring to the folly of practicing polygamy that are either ignored or twisted to confuse their intended purpose.

---

[376] Smith, Introduction to *The Book of Mormon*.

The *Catholic Answers* Web site also notes the Mormons' misinterpretation of God's Word. Concerning **Ezekiel 37** they write:

> Mormons neglect the plain sense of the words and ignore their true interpretation, given by God—in the very same chapter. The text makes clear, this is a prophecy of national reunification, not about the appearance of hidden scriptures. The Hebrew term translated as "stick" (aits) is never used anywhere in the Old Testament to mean "book," "scroll," "writing" or anything similar. It is variously translated as "wood" or "branch," "timber," or "tree." Needless to say, the Book of Mormon was allegedly written on metal plates, not scrolls or sticks. Only Mormonism can manage to mistake "timber" for "scrolls" and "nations" for "metal plates."[377]

Mormons also teach that God the Father has a physical body. They pull the doctrine from **Genesis 1:26–27**, in which God says, "Let Us make man in Our image" (NKJV). From this statement, Mormons conclude that God has a body.[378] This idea contradicts what Jesus says, "God is Spirit, and those who worship Him must worship in spirit and truth"[379] (**John 4:24, NKJV**). Jesus also points out that "a spirit has not flesh and bones" (**Luke 24:39,** NKJV).[380] Mormons choose to disregard any verse that clearly counters their doctrine. More verses distorted or ignored by Mormons about the nature of God include **Numbers 23:19; Isaiah 45:12; Hosea 11:9;** and **Romans 1:22–23**.

---

[377] Isaiah Bennett, *Catholic Answers* (San Diego, CA, 1979-2008) [online]; accessed 5 July 2006; available from http://www.catholic.com/thisrock/quickquestions/keyword/Mormons; Internet.

[378] Smith, *The Book of Mormon*, Doctrine and Covenants 130:3.

[379] NKJV, John 4:24.

[380] NKJV, Luke 24:39.

Likewise, unorthodox "Word Faith" leaders like Kenneth Hagin, Kenneth Copeland, Paul Crouch, and Benny Hinn also misconstrue **Genesis 1:26–27**. They teach that according to these verses, God's followers are themselves "little gods."[381] Although this belief is held at different levels of intensity by Word Faith followers, it is an unbiblical doctrine needing correction. The complete and "purest" meaning of **Genesis 1:26–27** can indeed be argued and debated (as with many other verses), but its interpretation cannot fly in the face of other parts of Scripture if it is to be true. The two errant doctrines teaching that Christians are little gods and that God the Father has a physical body arise from poorly interpreted verses and discount others verses relevant to the subject. Despite claiming a biblical foundation for these doctrines, both Mormon and Word Faith teachers set themselves clearly against biblical orthodoxy.

John Calvin's practice of manipulating Scripture is obvious to those who have taken a careful look at his theology. Although the majority of his commentaries are accurate, he was not afraid to change the words and meanings of certain verses in order to make his particular interpretation work. Historian Diarmaid MacCulloch writes:

> Like the mainstream tradition of Judaism, he [Calvin] felt that imagery in relation to the divine was best restricted to words, where it could be extravagant or as startling as he pleased: in one sermon on Deuteronomy preached in 1555–6, for instance, he radically adapted some words of Jesus in order to compare God's coming in flesh in the birth of Jesus Christ to a hen stooping down to the ground.[382]

As we remember the words of historian James P. Byrd, Jr. when he states what Roger Williams thought of Calvin's poor interpretive skills

---

[381] Geisler and Rhodes, *Correcting the Cults*, 21.

[382] MacCulloch, *The Reformation*, 249.

concerning ecclesiastical government over civil affairs, we see the validity of Williams' claim. Byrd writes, "Williams revered Calvin's theological genius and considered him a great man, but he attacked Calvin's biblical interpretation, calling it a dangerous perversion that turned the Holy Word into a bloody instrument of persecution."[383]

We will see many examples of how Calvin and his followers have misinterpreted portions of Scripture for the sake of TULIP. Calvinists have not invented their own religious books, as have the Mormons, nor have they created a new translation of the Bible, as have the Jehovah's Witnesses, but they have taken a step in that direction. Although the *Geneva Bible* was once banned by King James of the Catholic Church, Thomas Nelson Publishing began printing the *New Geneva Study Bible*, or the *Reformation Study Bible* (RSB) in 1995 with the English Standard Version (ESV). Leading Calvinist R. C. Sproul gives the introduction, titled "Reformation Truth," to the RSB with its explanations of Scripture. The Christian must ask: can absolute biblical truth be reformed? Sure, it can . . . but only into something less than absolute biblical truth. Look how clearly we can see this in the following attempts of the *Reformation Study Bible* to do away with the biblical doctrine of man's free will and God's offer of salvation to the whole world.

The ESV correctly translates **John 3:16** as, "For God so loved the world, that he gave his only Son, that whoever believes in him should not perish but have eternal life." However, under the guise of "Reformation Truth," the RSB footnote interprets the verse to mean something quite different:

> Some have insisted that God sent Jesus to die for the purpose of bringing salvation to everyone without exception, but only as a possibility . . . The point made by the "world" is that Christ's saving work is not limited to

---

[383] Byrd, *The Challenges of Roger Williams*, 190.

one time or place but applies to the elect from all over the world.[384]

Again, knowing that the message of **John 3:16** does away with Calvin's third point of TULIP, Calvinists twist the Scripture at all cost. Leading Calvinist James White says that "whosoever believeth on him should not perish" actually means "in order that everyone believing on him should not perish."[385] With the addition of a few words, White defends Calvinism by saying that the elect alone believe and thus Christ died for them only. How does this differ from the Jehovah's Witnesses' practice of adding words to the text and thereby changing its meaning?

The twisting of Scripture in the *Reformation Study Bible* is no less devious than that of the *New World Translation*. Orthodox Christian leaders often speak against Jehovah's Witnesses for their new interpretation of the Bible while remaining silent regarding Calvinists, who also add words to scriptural texts in order to support their false claims.

First **Timothy 2** speaks of God's concern for all men and women of all classes. We are commanded to pray, intercede for, and give thanks for all people. In the RSB, **1 Timothy 2:1** reads, "First of all, then, I urge that supplications, prayers, and thanksgivings be made for all people . . ." (ESV). Here, however, a footnote appears, explaining that "all people" really does not "mean 'every human being' but rather 'all types of people,' whatever their station of life" (RSB).[386]

In verse **1 Timothy 2:3–4**, Paul continues his thought: ". . . God our Savior, who desires all people to be saved and to come to the

---

[384] R. C. Sproul, ed., *The Reformation Study Bible* (RSB), (Orlando, FL: Ligonier Ministries, 2005) p. 1,514.

[385] James White, "Blinded By Tradition: An Open Letter to Dave Hunt Regarding His Newly Published Attack Upon the Reformation, *What Love Is This? Calvin's Misrepresentation of God*" [online]; accessed 13 July 2007; available from http://vintage.aomin.org/DHOpenLetter.html; Internet.

[386] RSB Footnote, p. 1,752.

knowledge of the truth" (ESV). Once again, the RSB attempts to "reform" this truth in its footnote:

> . . . who desires all people to be saved. This does not mean that God sovereignly wills every human being to be saved . . . It may refer to God's general benevolence in taking no delight in the death of the wicked, or to God's desire that all types be saved (i.e., God does not choose His elect from any single group).[387]

With many verses contradicting TULIP theology within the English Standard Version, the RSB must rely on its footnotes to provide some connection between the actual text and its Calvinistic ideas and undertones.

Another example of the *Reformation Study Bible*'s mutilation of the intended meaning of the Word is in **2 Corinthians 5:14**. The ESV reads, "For the love of Christ controls us, because we have concluded this: that one has died for all, therefore all have died." Without reading into the verse's meaning, we understand that Christ is the "one" who "died" literally "for all." If Christ died for all, then all—*not some*—have died. Because this Scripture affirms what the five points of Calvinism deny, the footnote in the RSB reads, "The ones He died for are the same as the 'all' who 'died' with Him as a result of His death . . ."[388] No. The verse does not say nor give any indication that the ones for whom He died are the "ones who died with Him." The verse clearly reads that the "one," who is Christ, "has died for all." Christ has died for all, regardless of whether or not we who have placed faith in Him undergo the salvific process of dying "with Him as a result of His death."

This kind of biblical interpretation illuminates Kent R. Rieske's radical statement that, "Calvinists have typically taught from the margin

---

[387] RSB Footnote, p. 1,752.

[388] RSB Footnote, p. 1,679.

notes in the Calvinist's *Geneva Bible* in preference to the Scriptural text."[389] Although Calvinists would vehemently disagree, the few examples above show that when a verse clearly contradicts a doctrine of TULIP, it is usually supplemented by a footnote misinterpreting the verse to fit the doctrine. Like most cults, when confronted with scriptural truth that affirms what they deny, the followers are led by the founder's interpretation.

Biblical footnotes can be very useful, but they can only be trusted when Scripture is interpreting Scripture. Did the above footnotes from the *Reformation Study Bible* sound like Scripture was being used to interpret Scripture or like Calvin's TULIP was being used to interpret Scripture? We will answer this question in more detail later.

Many Calvinists praise John Calvin in an unhealthy and unbalanced way, heralding him as the apostle Paul's "faithful interpreter."[390] By this selective mentality, a Reformed conscience can be held captive by Calvin's radical and unorthodox interpretations. Josh McDowell claims that one of the key characteristics of a cult is its offering "new interpretations of the Scripture." He states, "Some cults make no claim to know truth or extra-biblical revelation, but believe they alone have the key to interpreting the mysteries in the Bible."[391] Let's stop here and note that a great mystery found within the Bible is how man's free will and God's sovereignty work together. But Calvinism claims to have the answer! This theological system does away with the mystery by doing away with man's free will. Calvinists believe that, "they alone have the key to interpreting the mysteries in the Bible."[392] Reformed Theology, as Calvinist W. Robert Godfrey asserts, even has a

---

[389] Rieske, "Calvinism."

[390] Godfrey, *An Unexpected Journey*, p. 60

[391] McDowell, *Handbook of Today's Religions*, 20.

[392] Ibid.

"Reformed interpretation of Romans."[393] Godfrey assumes that non-Reformed churches likely "miss the real meaning of the Word of God," as well as "the real need of the un-churched—namely, the gospel of the grace of Jesus Christ." He then concludes that, "To find that real meaning, we must turn from stories to a system."[394]

Also note that Calvinism has cleverly interpreted the mysteries of the Bible without claiming (as most cults do) to have "new truth" or "extra-biblical revelation." Instead, as McDowell states:

> The scriptures are their only acknowledged source of authority, but . . . are interpreted unreasonably and in a way different from that of orthodox Christianity. They testify that the historic beliefs and interpretations of Scripture are based upon a misunderstanding of the Bible or were pagan in origin.[395]

Is it a coincidence that leading Calvinists claim that the traditional doctrines of orthodox Christianity are at odds with TULIP theology? Since Calvinists believe that their interpretation is the "true gospel" message (coming on the scene 1500 years after the birth of Christianity), every Christian doctrine before their time must have been somewhat unorthodox. Could this be true?

Were the doctrines of the free will of man, God's desire for all men to be saved, and Christ's universal offer of atonement merely man-made teachings, having their roots in humanistic *tradition* rather than Scripture?

Leading Calvinist James Whites believes that:

> If we derive our beliefs from the Bible (rather than assuming them as a *tradition* . . .), we will conclude that the phrase,

---

[393] Godfrey, *An Unexpected Journey*, 26.

[394] Ibid., 36.

[395] McDowell, *Handbook of Today's Religions*, 21.

"God is love" does not mean that God has the same kind and level of love for all things, including for each and every single individual human being.[396] [Italics mine.]

He continues:

Surely it is part of the modern evangelical tradition to say, "God loves you and has a wonderful plan for your life," but providing a meaningful biblical basis for this assertion is significantly more difficult. Unfortunately, most are never challenged to think through their *traditions*.[397] [Italics mine.]

Though the Bible-believing Christian should be challenged to think through traditions, to say that God's love for humanity stems from tradition rather than "biblical truth" is simply ludicrous—but then again, so are most twisted interpretations of the Bible. Mormons defend their trust in *The Book of Mormon* by asserting that the Bible has been corrupted, whereas Calvinists defend their trust in TULIP theology by asserting that the mainstream understanding of God's universal offer of salvation is a man-made tradition and a "denial of biblical truth."

McDowell concludes that cults reinterpret the Bible:

. . . usually out of context, to justify the peculiar doctrines of a cult. Without an objective and reasonable way to understand what the Bible teaches, the cult member is at the whims of the cult leader.[398]

Again, we see a perfect example of this through John Calvin's attempt to justify one of his peculiar doctrines concerning his strict ecclesiastical rule over Geneva. Concerning Jesus' parable of the weeds in **Matthew 13**, American historian James P. Byrd, Jr. states:

---

[396] White, in *Debating Calvinism*, p. 268.
[397] Ibid., 265.
[398] McDowell, *Handbook of Today's Religions*, 21.

Above all, Calvin believed that the parable of the weeds contained valuable instruction on church discipline. . . . Calvin's argument that the parable had to do with church discipline rested on his belief that the field signified the church. This presented an embarrassing dilemma because, as Jesus himself explained, "the field is the world (**Matt 13:38**)." Calvin's exegesis of the parable therefore seemed to contradict the explanation that Christ gave to his disciples. In treating this delicate problem, Calvin argued that although Christ called the field the world, he intended "to apply" the field "to the Church, about which, after all, he was speaking,". . . Calvin solved the apparent conflict by not taking literally Jesus' interpretation of the field as the world. Calvin claimed that Jesus "transfers by synecdoche to the world what is more apt a part of it." Jesus did not mean that the field was the world itself, but rather the church that existed within the world.[399]

James Byrd concludes that "Calvin rejected a simple reading of the Christ's interpretation of the field as the world, preferring instead a figural interpretation at this crucial juncture in the parable."[400] Therefore, Calvin arrogantly altered the actual meaning of Jesus' words in this parable because they posed a threat to his conscience and his systematic approach to understanding the Bible.

Apart from changing the definitions of biblical words, the main aspect of twisting Scripture is taking a verse out of its immediate context, placing it in a different area of Scripture, and then using it to uphold a false doctrine. Sometimes this is done innocently and sometimes not. As we have seen before, the account of Jesus raising Lazarus from the dead

---

[399] Byrd, *The Challenges of Roger Williams*, 94–95; Byrd quotes Matthew 13:38 and Calvin, *Harmony of the Gospels*, Vol. 2 of *Calvin's Commentaries*, 75.

[400] Ibid., 261.

has been used a number of times by Calvinists to support their false doctrine of Total Depravity, as well as other doctrines in TULIP. We also see an example of this in James White's book, *Debating Calvinism*. White uses **Ezekiel 37:1–14** to support "man's inability" to come to Christ. However, Ezekiel 37 narrates a one-time event, experienced by one man, that took place in the Old Covenant, and it is meant to point to the future restoration of the nation and people of Israel. But White moves this passage from its context and places it as central to the salvation of all New Covenant believers, in order to support the belief that regeneration somehow precedes faith.

In responding to James White's book, *The Potter's Freedom* (a refutation of Geisler's book, *Chosen but Free*), Norman Geisler states:

"Another technique employed by PF [*Potter's Freedom*] to further its position is to *redefine terms* that cover the harsh reality of a biblically, morally, and rationally indefensible view."[401] [italics mine] Geisler also says:

> A similar problem emerges when PF [*Potter's Freedom*] employs a kind of theological doublespeak to forward its view. For example, it affirms that fallen humans can will, but yet they have no will (192); that grace is irresistible, but yet it is not coercive (161); that depraved humans are dead but are alive enough to hear and reject the gospel (101); that God does not force anyone, but He regenerates them contrary to their will (200). [402]

Calvinists have not produced a whole new book to support their theology as did the Mormons. They need only to explain away those verses that contradict TULIP. As Geisler states above, this is done by redefining terms and theological doublespeak. Kent Rieske also explains how this is accomplished:

---

[401] Geisler, *Chosen but Free*, p. 261.

[402] Ibid.

Calvinism consists of theological doctrines which use words found in the Bible. However, Calvinism consistently redefines those words, takes them out of context, applies the doctrines inappropriately, exaggerates the meaning of the words to the extreme, or in some other way distorts the Word of God to match the theology written by John Calvin in his book, *Institutes of the Christian Religion*.[403]

While an orthodox Christian can easily point out the flaws found within the *New World Translation*, the theology of Calvinism is not so blatantly twisted since there is not a Calvinistic translation of the Bible. In dissecting Calvinism's TULIP, one must point to the ill *interpreted* as opposed to ill *translated* verses. In either case, both pose serious problems with similar consequences. Using twisted footnotes, words, and contexts are all ways to pull unintended meanings from the Bible. And yet it is under an intellectual guise of spiritual fervency that Calvinism shows just how it's done.

Its Ignoring of Scripture

When certain Scripture is ignored, the most ridiculous teachings can easily fool the novice and usher in a tidal wave of theological confusion. Although this practice varies among cults, it is indeed found to some degree in every cult. Radical cults with more glaringly unorthodox doctrines disregard hosts of passages, whereas more conservative cults may choose to overlook only the few passages that obstruct their beliefs. Either way, ignoring parts of Scripture to any degree has huge theological consequences for the cult's followers.

---

[403] Rieske, "Calvinism."

A tragic example of a cult that excluded a vast majority of Scripture, despite claiming to have a biblical foundation, was the "Children of God" or "The Family" cult. The biblical "foundation" this cult claimed was from **Matthew 4:19**, in which Jesus says, "Follow me, and I will make you fishers of men." Yet in the hands of Children of God leader David Berg, **Matthew 4:19** was bizarrely twisted into a justification of religious prostitution. This cult formed in 1974 and ended in 1987 (partially due to the AIDS scare). In David's theology, being a fisher of men was the call for women to win converts by sexual attraction. These women were called "hookers for Jesus" and their offspring were sadly referred to as "Jesus Babies." Prostitution was widely used as a means for "converts" or solicitors to donate or raise money for the cult. David's foul "teaching" of the Scriptures were so perverted they insult and degrade common sense. Yet, internal records of the *Children of God* indicate that over 223,000 people or "fish" took the bait. These naïve people believed the lie and were sexually loved between 1978 and 1988.[404] The point is made: any doctrine, no matter how absurd, can amass a large cult following by claiming biblical roots and godly motives when Scripture is picked apart and discarded.

A fundamental difference between orthodox Christianity and Calvinism is that one holds two truths equally whereas the other holds one truth to the detriment of the other. The non-Calvinist does not rail against the truth that God is completely sovereign. The Calvinist, however, would have you believe that if you accept that God is sovereign, you cannot also believe that man has a free will. Orthodox Christians hold both to be true.

Think of it this way: If I were to debate a Calvinist, I would never deny the scriptural fact that God is completely sovereign. My opponent

---

[404] www.xfamily.org/index.php/Main_Page; Under "Flirty Fishing" (*CAUTION: The article under 'Flirty Fishing' contains explicit text and/or images that some may find disturbing or offensive.*), [online]; accessed 25 June, 2007; Internet.

could go through a plethora of verses revealing that God is sovereign over creation and has an elect people. I would not argue or debate with these. We are not discussing whether or not God is sovereign. That is a biblical fact. But because the Calvinist ignores the biblical truth that man has a free will and that God offers salvation to all men, he must do one of two things when handling the Bible. Like a typical cultist, he must either falsely interpret any verses that testify to whatever he does not believe in, or more simply, to ignore those portions of Scripture altogether. Again, while the orthodox Christian should hold both truths in equality, Calvinists hold one truth—*God's sovereignty*—over the other—*man's free will.*

If I were trying to persuade you to believe that God is not sovereign and that there is no such thing as the elect, I would have to ignore that part of Scripture that teaches otherwise. I would only teach and focus on those passages that support my theology—and that would be absurd. Could I make a case that man has free will and that God desires to save all men, without regard to God's sovereign elect? Of course . . . as long as I ignore the part of Scripture about God's sovereign elect. Could the Calvinist make a case that God is sovereign and that He has an elect, without regard to man's free will and God's desire to save all men? Of course . . . as long as he ignores the part of Scripture about man's free will.

To ignore means to refuse to notice or pay attention to somebody or something. The word stems from the Latin word *ignorant*, which means "to not know" or "to be without knowledge."[405] But to ignore is different than simply not knowing. To ignore is purposefully to disregard. I might understand the reasoning behind Calvinistic theology if its followers withheld those scriptural texts that teach man's free will and God's universal offer of salvation to mankind. But no Scripture is withheld from the Calvinist, and they are accountable for purposefully ignoring parts of Scripture.

---

[405] *Webster's New World Dictionary*, s.v. "Ignorant".

Dave Hunt argues, in his response to James White's defense of "man's inability":

> To support Calvinism's denial of human ability and responsibility, White gives a few favorite proof texts while ignoring a plethora of passages that present the other side. He offers inferences but not one Scripture that clearly states that unregenerate man is unable to believe the gospel.[406]

In his book, *Problems with Evangelical Theology*, Ben Witherington notes this particular problem within Calvinism (especially among those who like to debate). He states, "It is perfectly possible to argue consistently and logically about something, but draw the circle of argumentation too narrowly, and so wrongly exclude some of the most important data."[407] Excluding Scripture, or "important data," is precisely the error of all cults. In order to practice prostitution and fulfill his own lusts, David Berg paid no attention to the parts of Scripture that deals with sexual purity, monogamy, and marital faithfulness. To uphold his book and writings, Joseph Smith disregarded the part of the Bible that condemned adding to it or subtracting from it. He upheld his book as the "fullness of the gospel" anyway, caring nothing for the words of Paul written to the Galatian believers: "But even if we, or an angel from heaven, preach any other gospel to you than what we have preached to you, let him be accursed" (**Galatians 1:8**, NKJV).[408] Likewise, in holding their belief that the apostle Peter was never married (being the supposed first pope), Catholics close their eyes to **Matthew 8:14**, "Now when Jesus had come into Peter's house, He saw his wife's mother lying sick with a fever." In believing Jesus to be less than God, Jehovah's Witnesses choose not to take into account that Jesus "is the image of the invisible God

---

[406] Hunt, in *Debating Calvinism*, 75.

[407] Witherington, *The Problem with Evangelical Theology*, 5.

[408] NKJV, Galatians 2:8.

. . . For by Him all things were created . . . All things were created through Him and for Him. And He is before all things, and in Him all things consist" (**Colossians 1:15–17**, NKJV).[409] Lastly, to believe that man has no free will and that God does not desire all to be saved, Calvinism simply glosses over verses like **John 3:16**, "For God so loved the world that He gave His only begotten Son, that whoever believes in Him should not perish but have everlasting life," and **1 Timothy 2:3–4**, "For this is good and acceptable in the sight of God our Savior, who desires all men to be saved and to come to the knowledge of the truth" (NKJV). While very few cults would ever admit to purposefully ignoring certain verses, some attempt to get around any verse that appears to threaten the validity of their doctrines by simply redefining the meanings of words. This maneuver is not easy to detect and usually misleads those not familiar with the details of the passage at hand. We see this clearly in Calvinism.

Its Twisted Terminology

[Cults] manipulate the Scriptures to fit their own beliefs. Although they may claim to serve Jesus Christ, and may even use the same terminology orthodox Christians use, their definitions are vastly different.[410]

—Hank Hanegraaff

Monergism can, however, be defined unscripturally—as it is in Reformed Theology. The same can be said for just about any theological term. In the wrong hands, an otherwise good term can be used to convey a bad concept. So it is with monergism in the hands of a Calvinist.[411]

—George Bryson

---

[409] NKJV, Colossians 1:15 - 17.

[410] Hanegraaff, "What Are Some Common Marks of a Cult?"

[411] Bryson, *The Dark Side of Calvinism*, 352.

Having a proper understanding of a cult's terminology is paramount in differentiating the orthodox from the unorthodox. The novice might ask:

How does the Latter-day Saint differ from me? They believe that we all need God's grace, and that we are all sinners. They believe in the Holy Spirit and in the work of Jesus on the cross and redemption.

The key words in the statements above are *God, grace, sinners, Holy Spirit, Jesus,* and *redemption.* Jonathan Rowe, a critic of Mormonism writes, "There is a lot of Christian terminology on the official [Mormon] website, but upon examination, you come to understand that though the terms are familiar, the meanings of those terms are foreign and heretical."[412]

Although cults use Christian words, their definitions of them are far from orthodox. Some examples include the following:

The orthodox Christian believes in one God. The Mormon believes in many gods. The orthodox Christian believes that Jesus is the Son of God and Creator of all. Jehovah's Witnesses believe Jesus was created and that He is not God. The orthodox Christian believes that sin is disobedience to God. Christian Science believes that sin is an illusion and merely an err in humanity. The orthodox Christian believes that salvation is reconciliation to God by Jesus' death and resurrection. The New Age follower believes that salvation is being one with the universe. The orthodox Christian believes that God desires all of mankind to be saved. The Calvinist must logically believe that God desires a majority of mankind not to be saved but eternally punished in Hell.

In a frustrating argument with a Calvinist, in which no progress was made, Josh McDowell's warning rang very true to me. He writes:

---

[412] Jonathan Rowe, "Pastore Won't Let Up," post on Positive Liberty blog, 29 April 2007 [online]; accessed 29 April 2007; available from positiveliberty.com/2007/04/pastore-wont-let-up.html; Internet.

A feature of some cultic groups is that they say one thing publicly but internally believe something totally different. Many organizations call themselves Christians when in fact they deny the fundamentals of the faith. . . . One therefore must be on the alert for the organizations that advertise themselves as "Christians" but whose internal teachings disagree with Scripture.[413]

Cult leaders form new meanings of passages by redefining the words of the text. When faced with Scripture that seemed contradictory to his own teachings, John Calvin did just that. In his commentary on **1 Timothy 2:1–4**, Calvin wrote that the modifier "all" men "doesn't mean all men but all kinds and races of men."[414] Dave Hunt writes, "Calvin's audacity in changing the meaning of Scripture is breathtaking."[415] He also writes, "For turning all men into all kinds and races of men and 'princes and foreign nations' in order to accommodate their system of theology, Calvinists will answer to God."[416]

In his classic *Kingdom of the Cults*, Walter Martin challenges the Christian to tolerate absolutely no confusion of Christian terminology. He writes:

And just as the American Bar Association will not tolerate confusion of terminology in the trial of cases, and as the American Medical Association will not tolerate redefinition of terminology of diagnostic and surgical

---

[413] McDowell, *Handbook of Today's Religions*, 22-23.

[414] Calvin, Commentary, 1 Timothy 2:3–4, also noted in, [online] accessed 2 February 2010; available from http://www.the-highway.com/Salvation_ of_ All .html; Internet.

[415] Hunt, in *Debating Calvinism*, 316.

[416] Ibid., 317.

medicine, so also the church of Jesus Christ has every right to not tolerate the gross perversions and redefinitions of historical and Biblical terminology simply to accommodate a culture and a society that cannot tolerate an absolute standard or criterion of truth, even if it is revealed by God in his Word and through the true Witness of His Holy Spirit.[417]

In order to argue effectively and dialogue with a Calvinist, one must know his language. Calvinists often refer to the term *regenerational grace* (a term nowhere found in the Bible). As we have seen earlier, the terms *total depravity of man,* and the *fall* also take on new meanings with the Calvinist, as do the words, *grace, atonement, mankind,* and *race.* Concerning the word "grace," George Bryson notes that, "It cannot be reasonably denied that Calvinists hold to a distinctive definition of grace."[418] It is when we correctly understand how the Calvinist uses these terms that the playing field of argumentation will be even.

Not only do biblical words referring to salvation have different meanings as Calvinist terminology but the invention of new words and ideas seems to have no end. For example, Sproul's *What Is Reformed Theology?* contains numerous terms in both categories, including *monergism, synergism, operative grace, cooperative grace, prescient view, external call, internal call, effectual calling, ordo salutis,* (order of salvation), *pelagianism, semi-pelagianism, moral inability, moral ability, double predestination, reprobation, active decree, antinomianism, civil virtue, common grace, condign merit, congruous merit, consubstantiation, dynamic monarchianism, determinism, decretive will, general revelation, infralapsarianism, modalism, neo-platonism, passive decree, permissive will, pluralism, perceptive will, radical corruption,* and *utter depravity.*[419] Thankfully, he

---

[417] Martin, *The Kingdom of the Cults*, 31.

[418] Bryson, *The Dark Side of Calvinism*, 28.

[419] Sproul, *What Is Reformed Theology?*

includes a "Glossary of Foreign Terms."[420] Although some of these words have the potential to clarify biblical theology, some do just the opposite. Again, in order to defend TULIP rather than the message of the Bible, Calvinists have been forced to invent new terms and redefine others. The Bible clearly reveals that God desires all to be saved and thus, *calls* all to repentance. But because Calvinists hold that God only calls those who will believe, they make a distinction regarding the word "call." As Sproul says, "In Theology, we distinguish between two kinds of divine calling: the external call and the internal call."[421] Only the theology of Calvinism and other Christian cults make such distinctions about vital biblical words pertaining to salvation. The Bible does not identify an "internal" and "external" calling, but simply a "calling." Because the Scriptures were not written only for biblical scholars, the obvious and intended meaning of this "calling" and other words like it, are intended to be straightforward, with no double or hidden meanings.

John Calvin himself redefined the word "election." Diarmaid MacCulloch explains Calvin's interpretation of the "elect" within both the Old and New Testament:

> Israel was the Old Testament equivalent of the true Church; it had been a covenanted, chosen nation. Everyone in Israel was elect: they enjoyed a "general election." But not all Israelites followed God's commandments . . .[422]

Calvin wrote, "We must now add a second, more limited degree of election . . . when from the same race of Abraham God rejected some but showed that he kept others among his sons by cherishing them in the

---

[420] Ibid., 225.

[421] Ibid., 143.

[422] MacCulloch, *The Reformation*, 244.

Church."[423] Yet the Bible does not speak of a "general election" or a "more limited degree of election." While these terms are not even mentioned in Scripture, John Calvin and his followers have taken the liberty not to only invent them but to establish doctrine on their foundation, as well.

Because many non-Calvinists believe that the doctrine of election is based upon God's foreknowledge of who will choose to receive Jesus, leading Calvinists have boldly changed the meaning of "foreknew" in **Romans 8:28** ("For those whom He foreknew He also predestined . . ."). Steele, Thomas, and Quinn write in their book *The Five Points of Calvinism* that, "The word 'foreknew' as used here is thus understood to be equivalent to 'foreloved'—those who were the objects of God's love He marked out for salvation."[424] This is what Calvinists believe.

This concept of adjusting definitions is also found with the salvific word "grace." To accurately define the word "grace" in all of its multifaceted relations to mankind and the world is impossible. Nevertheless, Calvinists have meddled with the word to make distinctions like *operative grace, cooperative grace, regenerational grace,* and *common grace,* in order to promote Calvin's TULIP. Titus 2:11 says, "For the grace of God that brings salvation has appeared to all men . . ." But because this verse and many like it give the idea that God desires all to be saved and has extended His grace to everyone, the word "grace" undergoes a butchering, or in the words of a Calvinist, a "distinction." George Bryson understands how Calvinists define grace differently than does the Bible, writing, "It cannot be reasonably denied that Calvinists hold to a distinctive definition of grace . . . I am deeply troubled over the Reformed version of grace because through it, the precious and scriptural

---

[423] John Calvin, Institutes, vol. 2, ed. John Thomas McNeill (Westminster Press, Louisville Kentucky, 1960, Reprinted in 2006), p. 929.

[424] Steele, Thomas, and Quinn, *The Five Points of Calvinism* 158.

truths concerning grace are so maligned."[425] Once again, since Titus 2:11 reads that the "grace of God has appeared to all men," the Calvinist is compelled to interpret "grace" as meaning *common grace*, as opposed to *regenerational grace*. "Common grace" does not lead to salvation and can be resisted, whereas "the grace of regeneration is irresistible."[426] Again, these words do not appear in Scripture and are not even used consistently by major defenders of Calvinism. **Ephesians 2:8** reads that grace is essential to one's salvation: "For by grace you have been saved through faith." Calvinism totally distorts this idea by redefining the word "grace."

Several more words in Calvinism's dictionary have been born from mere speculative philosophy, such as *double predestination* and *reprobation*. Sproul uses twisted and invented terminology both to defend and "sugar coat" the true doctrines of Calvinism. He even goes so far as to label himself not as a *Calvinist* but as a *Reformed* theologian. Richard Mouw, however, remains faithful to his Calvinist label, saying that such labels "serve us well when they are informative, when they tell us something important about the person who chooses to use a specific label."[427] R. C. Sproul, however, seems to shy away from traditional Calvinistic names. Thus, he titled his book: *What Is Reformed Theology?* not *What Is Calvinism?* Inside, he goes further in renaming the Five Points of Calvinism "The Five Points of Reformed Theology." He continues in this vein by revising the name of each point. Total Depravity is changed to "Humanity's Radical Corruption"; Unconditional Election is "God's Sovereign Choice"; and Irresistible Grace is the "Spirit's Effective Call." No longer is Christ's atonement "limited" (lest the word "limited" suggest that Jesus died only for a few)—Sproul calls it *Purposeful*. One specific doctrine in Calvinism that has undergone many different name changes is Limited Atonement. Whether referred to as "limited," "specific,"

---

[425] Bryson, *The Dark Side of Calvinism*, 28-30.

[426] Sproul, *What Is Reformed Theology?* 189.

[427] Mouw, *Calvinism in the Las Vegas Airport*, 18–19.

"particular," "effective," or "definite and personal," calling Limited Atonement by other names "can never change the fact of what it really is."[428]

Kent R. Rieske has also noted Calvinism's modification of words and ideas:

> John Calvin defined important doctrinal Bible words differently than the orthodox and historic Christian interpretation. These erroneous definitions are needed to give logical support to Calvin's blasphemous doctrines. This technique is typical of cults such as Mormons who hold Joseph Smith in high esteem and base their doctrines on his writings. Calvinists are so indoctrinated with these false definitions that they cannot understand the opposition to their doctrines. Naturally Calvinists believe the false doctrines of John Calvin because they believe the false definitions of major doctrinal words.[429]

No other word in the history of Calvinism has been so maligned as the word "world." How this word is interpreted determines whether Jesus' atonement was limited or not, and ultimately whether TULIP blooms or dies. Calvinist author Duane Spencer says, "Much of what we think about the atoning death of Christ will be tempered by what we understand the simple word *world* to mean."[430] At least he acknowledges that the word is indeed "simple," but ironically, in the hands of a Calvinist, it is anything but simple. The word, instead, takes on several mysteriously incorrect and inconsistent meanings. In examining the theological weight of this word, Vance rightly states that "everything hinges on the meaning of

---

[428] Vance, *The Other Side of Calvinism*, 407.

[429] Rieske, "Calvinism."

[430] Duane E. Spencer, Duane E., TULIP, *The Five Points of Calvinism in the Light of Scripture* (Grand Rapids: Baker Books, 1979), 46.

the word *world.*[431] The following verses give light to the fact that the standard meaning of the word "world" poses a great threat to the doctrine of Limited Atonement and TULIP as a whole.

John 1:29: "The next day John saw Jesus coming toward him, and said, 'Behold! The Lamb of God who takes away the sin of the world.'"

John 3:16: "For God so loved the world that He gave His only begotten Son, that whoever believes in Him should not perish but have everlasting life."

John 4:42: "Then they said to the woman, 'Now we believe, not because of what you said, for we ourselves have heard Him and we know that this is indeed the Christ, the Savior of the world.'"

John 6:33: "For the bread of God is He Who comes down from Heaven and gives life to the world."

John 6:51: "I am the living bread which came down from Heaven. If anyone eats of this bread, he will live forever; and the bread that I shall give is My flesh, which I shall give for the life of the world."

John 12:47: ". . . for I did not come to judge the world but to save the world."

1 John 2:2: "And He Himself is the propitiation for our sins, and not for ours only but also for the whole world."

2 Corinthians 5:19: ". . . God was in Christ, reconciling the world to Himself . . ."

1 John 4:14: "And we have seen and testify that the Father has sent the Son as Savior of the world."

---

[431] Vance, *The Other Side of Calvinism*, 435.

In order to remain faithful to TULIP theology, the Calvinist must reinterpret what the word "world" really means.

A. W. Pink, a popular expositor for Calvinism, goes to great lengths to avoid the plain truth of **John 1:29** (see above). He changes the meanings of two words in the text: "'Sin,' here signifies *guilt* (condemnation) as in **Hebrews 9:26**; and 'the world,' refers to the world of *believers.*"[432] The word "sin" in this verse actually has no abnormal implication of guilt or condemnation in the original language and has no connection at all to Hebrews 9:26. Furthermore, saying that "the world" refers to the "world of the elect" is completely speculative and fundamentally changes the meaning of the word, verse, and message of the Bible.

In the example below, the word "world" is again interpreted by the Calvinist as the world of the godly.

In response to **John 4:42** (see above), Pink proclaims, "This does not mean that Christ is the Saviour of the human race, but is a general term used in contradistinction from Israel, including all believing Gentiles scattered throughout the earth."[433]

Another example of how "world" equates to the world of believers is found in the Calvinist's most feared verse in all the Bible: **1 John 2:2** (see above). Regarding this verse, Pink explains:

> . . .when John says, "He is the propitiation for *our* sins" he can only mean for the sins of *Jewish believers*. . . . when John added, "And not for ours only, but also for the *whole world*," he signified that Christ was the propitiation for the sins of the Gentile believers too, for, as previously shown, "the world" is a term *contrasted* from Israel.[434]

---

[432] A. W. Pink, *Exposition of the Gospel of John, Volume One, John 1–7,* (Grand Rapids: Zondervan, 1945), 59.

[433] Ibid., 225.

[434] Arthur W. Pink, *The Sovereignty of God* (I. C. Herenedeen, 1930; Grand Rapids: Baker Books, 1984), 259.

Similarly, regarding **John 6:33** (see above), Pink again writes, "The 'world' here does not include the whole human race . . . It is the 'world' of believers who are here in view." [435]

According to Pink's interpretations, Christ came for the elect only. Christ Himself said, however, that He had come for the sick and sinful, as opposed to the healthy and righteous: "When Jesus heard it, He said to them, 'Those who are well have no need of a physician, but those who are sick. I did not come to call *the* righteous, but sinners, to repentance'" (**Mark 2:17**, NKJV).

After studying the eighty appearances of the word "world" in the Gospel of John, Vance emphatically concluded: "Not only does the word 'world' never denote the elect, it is unequivocally demeaned and condemned by God." [436] In fact, the word "world" was written over two hundred times in the New Testament and never does it denote or even vaguely imply God's elect.

The other most misused and incriminating word in Calvinist theology is the word "love." Recognizing this, Dave Hunt based the title of his book on the question Calvinists have yet to adequately answer: *What Love Is This?* Calvinism defenders, Doug VanderMeulin and Steve Watkins, have tried to answer the question by confronting Dave Hunt on the grounds that his book inaccurately portrays Calvinism. Though after a two-hour discussion, Doug and Steve might have clarified some nonessentials of their faith, they only solidified the vital claims of Mr. Hunt's book. When Dave Hunt asked, "Does God love those that he has predestined from eternity past to eternal doom?" [437] They replied, "Yes, He loves them . . . with an 'agape'

---

[435] Ibid., 325.

[436] Vance, *The Other Side of Calvinism*, 435.

[437] Dave Hunt, *Conversation on Calvinism* (Bend, OR: The Berean Call, 2002) [CD-ROM].

love."[438] To this, Hunt replied, "And that is why I titled my book, *What Love Is This?*"[439]

George Bryson also acknowledges the Calvinistic redefinition of the word "love," stating, "Even those Calvinists who believe God loves all people have redefined that love, in their thinking and theology, to exclude any kind of saving grace for some of the people they say God loves." [440] We find this to be true in how Calvinists such as Doug VanderMeulin and Steve Watkins justify the assertion that God does indeed love the people He has predestined to eternal doom by giving the definition of "love" a new meaning. Although the Greek language has four words for different kinds of love, not one of them hints of a love that is "salvific" in nature.[441] Not even *eros*, the most fleshly sort of love, would justify the act of forcing someone to suffer eternal punishment. The kind of love prescribed in Calvinism is well summarized by Hunt: "I'm going to shoot you guys, I'm going to torture you, I'm going to shoot you, but I want to show some love towards you and some mercy towards you, so I'm going to give you a good meal."[442]

Norman Geisler has also identified how Calvinist leader James White redefines certain verses in his book *The Potter's Freedom*:

> Yet PF [*Potter's Freedom*] repeatedly reads "some men" into passages that clearly and emphatically say "all men" (140, 142). It insists against the context that **2 Peter 3:9** (where God desires that all men be saved) is not speaking about salvation (146–147) . . . It distorts the word "saves"

---

[438] Ibid.

[439] Ibid.

[440] Bryson, *The Dark Side of Calvinism*, 26.

[441] Hunt, *Conversation on Calvinism*.

[442] Ibid.

to "saves himself" (64), and so on. . . . PF [*Potter's Freedom*] is permeated with logical fallacies and reveals an inadequate comprehension of the unjustified theological and philosophical underpinnings of extreme Calvinism. . . . *PF futilely attempts to make the implausible sound plausible and the unbiblical seem biblical.*[443]

Geisler provides another example of problematic Calvinist terminology:

From the time of the later Augustine this text [**1 Timothy 2:3–4**] has been manhandled by extreme Calvinists. Spurgeon summarizes their attempts to avoid the obvious. He said here is how "our older Calvinistic friends deal with this text. 'All men,' say they—'that is, some men': as if the Holy Ghost could not have said 'some men' if he had meant some men. 'All men,' say they; that is, 'some of all sorts of men'; as if the Lord could not have said 'All sorts of men' if he had meant that. The Holy Ghost by the apostle has written 'all men,' and unquestionably he means all men.'[444]

Similarly,

Of this and like passages John Owen [also] offers the dubious view that "all" does not mean "all" here.[445]

In his book, *The Apocalypse Code*, Hank Hanegraaff writes about how unorthodox views of the Bible can stem from changing the meanings of simple words. He prefaces his argument by stating that we

[443] Geisler, *Chosen but Free*, p. 262–63.

[444] Ibid., 210; Footnote 19: Cited by Murray, Spurgeon v. Hyper-Calvinism, 150–151.

[445] Ibid., 211.

should "interpret the Bible in accordance with the basic rules of language."[446] He then writes:

> Suppose I told my children, "I don't want *you* to touch this *gingerbread cake*, because we are going to have dinner *soon!*" They wouldn't need an advanced degree in English from Yale to understand that by "this" I meant *this* gingerbread cake—not *that* gingerbread cake, as in a gingerbread cake that would be baked for their twenty-first birthday. Nor are they the least bit confused about the meaning of the "you," which in context refers to them, not to children of a future generation. "Soon" is equally unambiguous. To say we were going to have dinner "soon" could possibly mean dinner in the distant future. When it comes to interpreting scripture, we should not suppose that the rules of grammar mysteriously change.[447]

Calvinists would do well to reconsider the core tenets of their theology in light of Hanegraaff's advice. Let's again ponder closely the words of Walter Martin on the danger of twisting the Bible's words:

> And just as the American Bar Association will not tolerate confusion of terminology in the trial of cases, and as the American Medical Association will not tolerate redefinition of terminology of diagnostic and surgical medicine, so also the church of Jesus Christ has every right to not tolerate the gross perversions and redefinitions of historical and Biblical terminology . . .[448]

---

[446] Hanegraaff, Hank, *The Apocalypse Code* (Nashville: Thomas Nelson, Nashville, 2007), 72.

[447] Ibid., 72.

[448] Martin, *The Kingdom of the Cults*, 31.

Despite Calvinism's historical and biblical appearance of intellectual orthodoxy, its insistence on maintaining the doctrines of TULIP has led it perilously close to "the kingdom of the cults."

Most Christians would say that Calvinism is simply a Christian theology based upon John Calvin's teachings. In my explanation of the five points, I argued that Calvinism is a Christian but cultlike theology that strips humanity of free will. Although descriptions may vary, the essential philosophy of Calvinistic religion has a name—fatalism. As George Bryson writes:

> For all practical purposes, Calvinism amounts to *Theistic Fatalism*. A theist believes in a personal God. A fatalist believes the future (especially regarding the destiny of individuals) is fixed. A Theistic Fatalist believes that a personal God unconditionally determines where individuals go when they die, that is, whether they go to heaven or hell. . . When I say that Calvinism amounts to Theistic Fatalism or that it has a dark side, it is not for the purpose of offending Calvinists, though some will no doubt take offense at my use of these words. I use the label Theistic Fatalism because it perfectly describes Reformed Theology. I use the words *dark side*, because Calvinism has, as a central tenet, a very dark and disturbing distinctive.[449]

Lawrence Vance, as well, deduces the following:

> Although Calvinists go out of their way to distance themselves from fatalism, they are in essence teaching the same thing. When a philosopher believes "what is to be will be" it is called determinism. When a stoic believes "what is to be will be" it is called fate. When a

---

[449] Bryson, *The Dark Side of Calvinism*, 21–22.

Muslim believes "what is to be will be" it is called fatalism. But when a Calvinist believes "what is to be will be" it is called predestination.[450]

Geisler likewise states that "there is no real difference . . . between the extreme Calvinists and fatalistic Islam,"[451] concluding that:

> . . . some Calvinists reject this "double-predestination" in favor of God simply "passing over" the non-elect, but even they must admit that the result is the same: since God did not give them the desire to be saved "they are condemned to eternal misery."[452]

Its Elitism (Us vs. Them)

I have never been embarrassed about being a Calvinist. In fact, I used to be a pretty big jerk about it.[453]

—Joe Thorn

While the temperament of individual Calvinists may cause some to keep their theological convictions a relatively private matter, Calvinism tends to make its adherents more theologically aggressive and spiritually hostile to non-Calvinists than they might otherwise be.[454]

—George Bryson

---

[450] Vance, *The Other Side of Calvinism*, 278.

[451] Geisler, *Chosen but Free*, p. 138.

[452] Ibid., 139; Footnote 4, Hodge, Outlines of Theology, 222.

[453] Joe Thorn, "Reformed Motivation," blog entry 22 February 2006 at JoeThorn.net [online]; accessed 28 November 2010; available from http://www.joethorn.net/2006/02/22/reformed-motivation/; Internet.

[454] Bryson, *The Dark Side of Calvinism*, 24.

In his research on cults, Hank Hanegraaff has found that cult members generally possess deeply polarizing attitudes, or "an exclusive 'us'/'them' mentality . . ."[455] This could not be more clear than in the case of Calvinists. In Calvinism, this disposition is not only manifest as intolerance towards the secularist (since "toleration is not one of the virtues of the cultic mentality"[456]) but towards those within the church, as well.

Geisler and Rhodes note that cults characteristically show "intolerance towards others," admitting that levels of intolerance within different cults and religions vary.[457] They state, "Intolerance is often manifest in antagonism. . . Both Mormon and Branch Davidian history have examples of this kind of . . . intolerance."[458] The elitism mentality inevitably leads to an unhealthy form of theological separation, fostering the idea that "those who are not for us" are somehow "against us." Wayne Jackson observes that cult members "imbibe the critical disposition. No one is really as 'sound' as 'we' are. We are an 'elitist' group." He then concludes by saying, "And so, seeds of isolationism are sown."[459]

John Rice contends that Calvinism "is not a Bible doctrine but is a perversion by proud intellectuals."[460] He also argues that Calvinism "is unscriptural, false doctrine. It tends to flourish in

---

[455] Hanegraaff, Hank, "What Are Some Common Marks of a Cult?"

[456] Matt, "Introduction to Understanding the Cults," blog entry January 26 2010 at arminiantheology.com [online]; accessed 28 December 2010; available from http://arminiantheology.com/understanding-the-cults.html under 'Moral Characteristics of a Cult', Intolerance toward Others; Internet.

[457] Geisler and Rhodes, *Correcting the Cults*, 13.

[458] Ibid.

[459] Jackson, "How to Identify a Cult."

[460] Rice, *Some Serious, Popular False Doctrines*, 274.

intellectual pride and in neglect of soul winning."[461] Even Reformed theologian John M. Frame writes:

> [T]he Reformed denominations have claimed to have a sounder formulation of the gospel than non-Reformed bodies, as well as sounder methods of evangelism and nurture. They claim, therefore, to be better equipped than others to carry out the Great Commission. If they are not reaching some ethnic and social groups, that is cause for concern."[462]

The elitist ideology cultivated by Reformed leaders continues to promote itself at the harm of other Christians. Because Calvin's theology has infiltrated most mainline denominations to some degree, those who maintain Calvinistic inclinations find themselves dividing the already divided body of the universal church. If those wanting to pursue Calvin's theology would simply join the Christian Reformed Church or the Dutch Reformed Church, many theological conflicts would be solved.

How absurd would it be if Mormons were pressing their doctrines in a Baptist Church, or if Jehovah's Witnesses were pressing their teaching of Jesus in a Lutheran Church? Many leading Calvinists, however, aggressively promote their doctrines in Christian churches of any denomination.

The theology of Calvinism has advanced itself in all forms of church governments as well. Distinguishing between the theology of Calvinism and other denominations, Vance writes, "Unlike baptism, which was the main bone of contention between the Baptists and other groups, the bitter controversy over Calvinism has infected all the various denominations at one time or another."[463] While Vance then states the

---

[461] Ibid., 289.

[462] John M. Frame, *The Doctrine of the Christian Life: A Theology of Lordship*, (Phillipsburg, NJ: P&R Publishing, 2008), 678.

[463] Vance, *The Other Side of Calvinism*, Preface, ix.

cause of this as being from "the other side of Calvinism,"[464] I attribute it to the *cultish* side.

Though Calvinists might say that pride is one of the "most heinous and palpable sins,"[465] their typical sense of doctrinal superiority cannot help but foster conceited actions. Geisler notices this in James White's book *The Potter's Freedom*: "Throughout PF [*Potter's Freedom*], the author takes great pride in his exegetical skills."[466]
Calvinist Richard Baxter admits that pride is:

> so prevalent in some of us [Reformed pastors], that it influences our discourses, it chooses our company, it forms our countenances, it puts the accent and emphasis upon our words. It fills some men's minds with aspiring desires, and designs: it possesses them with envious and bitter thoughts against those who stand in their light, or who by any means eclipse their glory, or hinder the progress of their reputation.[467]

I appreciate Baxter's honesty. Likewise, Reformed theologian John Frame concedes that:

> Historically, the Reformation has been a movement of scholars. In the churches, preaching has followed something of an academic model in style and content.

---

[464] Ibid.

[465] Richard Baxter, *The Reformed Pastor*, William, Brown (Editor) Christian Classics Ethreal Library, Grand Rapids, 2002; [online] accessed 28 December 2010; available from http://www.ccel.org/ccel/baxter/pastor.html; CHAPTER 3/APPLICATION/SECTION 1—THE USE OF HUMILIATION, 62; Internet.

[466] Geisler, *Chosen but Free*, 255.

[467] Baxter, *The Reformed Pastor*, 62.

This approach appeals to the well-educated, who are also often the relatively wealthy members of society. It tends to turn away others, in the present case the relatively poor minorities . . . Being an intellectual movement, the Reformation in some circles disparaged feelings, in my judgment to an unscriptural extent. This attracted rather stoic kinds of personalities and discouraged those who have greater need of emotional support."[468]

Because of these tendencies, to encounter a humble Calvinist seems to be rare. Although a prideful disposition might be more predominant among younger Calvinists, I have met a number of the pompous though older sort. Some years ago, for example, I worked as a chaplain in a local hospital for over a year. The chaplain staff was composed of twenty men between forty and sixty years old. It was a great time of serving God, meeting new people, and laboring with older men of God. One chaplain had just finished writing a book on the Holy Spirit and was excited that R. C. Sproul would possibly endorse it. As we conversed, he overtly mentioned that he was a Calvinist. He then asked if I was a Calvinist. When I replied that I was not, he quickly retorted: "Well, surely you're not an Arminianist?" Unfortunately, I was not surprised by his reaction because I was familiar with his Calvinistic assumption that no passionate and Bible-believing Christian would dare be an Arminianist. A general Calvinist assumption is that people who are not "Reformed" must somehow be "missing out." Because of this assumption, we find a remarkable tendency toward elitism among Calvinists. All the Calvinists I have met share a peculiar elitism on a higher level than people representing other cults. Although this is somewhat surprising, since Christians are not called to be prideful, it makes sense that God's "exclusive" elite—those who have an enlightened understanding, and align themselves with present-day

---

[468] Frame, *The Doctrine of the Christian Life*, 679.

intellectuals—have a "better than you" or "us vs. them" mentality. Calvinists themselves often readily admit this.

Laura Watkins shares how she became a Calvinist in an article in *Christianity Today*'s article titled "Young, Restless, and Reformed." She says, "When you first become a believer, almost everyone is an Arminian, because you feel like you made a decision."[469] From the very beginning, she had assumed that all Christians who are not Calvinists are Arminianists and thus inferior. It is to this audience that Calvinist James Smith wrote his newly (2010) published, *Letters to a Young Calvinist—An Invitation to the Reformed Tradition*. The first chapter or Letter is entitled "Welcome to the Family."[470] While Smith is quick to denounce spiritual pride, he admitted that he used to "spend an inordinate amount of time pointing out the error of . . .("Arminian") ways."[471]

Calvinist Curt Daniel knows this attitude is prevalent among his own. In his book, *Practical Applications of Calvinism*, he admits that one of the "Pitfalls Peculiar to Calvinists" is pride:

> I am not speaking of pride in general, for non-Calvinists have that affliction as well. Rather I am talking about Calvinist pride, or pride in being a Calvinist. This rank disease has several symptoms. One of them is personal pride. After all . . . am I not one of the elect? . . . This TULIP-flavored pride takes other forms as well. One is that Calvinists too frequently look down their noses at their non-Reformed brothers in Christ. We place

---

[469] Laura Watkins, quoted by Collin Hansen in "Young, Restless, and Reformed: Calvinism is Making a Comeback—And Shaking Up the Church," *Christianity Today* 50, no. 9 (September 2006): 1 [online]; accessed 27 September 2010; available from http://www.christianitytoday.com/ct/2006/september/42.32.html; Internet.

[470] Smith, James, *Letters to a Young Calvinist*, 1.

[471] Ibid., xi.

ourselves above them. We are the elite; we know more about the deep mysteries than they do. What good men we are. All such attitudes are proud. Then this shows in the way we too often disparage those brethren with whom we have the most serious disagreements.[472]

Along with an "us vs. them" approach, Calvinism can also instill a false sense of intellectualism as an outlet for spiritual fervency. This no doubt plays a big part in the prideful mindset of ardent Calvinists. Curt Daniels confesses this to be true:

> . . . there is the pitfall of Calvinist intellectualism. Too often we Calvinists spend more time discussing the doctrines of grace than living the grace of the doctrines. We have already shown how this is done in the area of evangelism. To be more precise, Calvinists sometimes mistake knowledge for spirituality, as if one could somehow gauge spiritual growth by how much one knows about the finer points of Calvinism, such as the order of decrees.[473]

In *Christianity Today*'s October 2010 cover story, "The Reformer—How Al Mohler transformed a seminary, helped change a denomination, and challenges a secular culture" Molly Worthen claims that the president "of the SBC's flagship school—the Southern Baptist Theological Seminary in Louisville," Al Mohler, is "the most prominent public intellectual in the convention."[474] She writes that he is "a cerebral,.

---

[472] Curt Daniel, "Appendix E: Practical Applications of Calvinism," in *The Five Points of Calvinism: Defined, Defended, and Documented*, 2nd ed., by David N. Steele, Curtis C. Thomas, and S. Lance Quinn (Phillipsburg, NJ: P&R Publishing, 2004), 192-93.

[473] Daniel, *Practical Applications of Calvinism*, 194.

[474] Molly Worthen, "The Reformer—How Al Mohler transformed a seminary, helped change a denomination, and challenges a secular culture."

. . five-point Calvinist . . . who has branded himself as one who speaks to and for evangelicals.[475] In noting his intellectualism, Worthen states:

> Mohler believes that the only intellectually robust defense of biblical inerrancy lies in the Reformed scholasticism that emerged from the Synod of Dort (1618) and enjoyed its apogee at late-19th-century Princeton Theological Seminary, where James Boyce trained. Non-Calvinist conservatives, Mohler says, "are not aware of the basic structures of thought, rightly described as Reformed, that are necessary to protect the very gospel they insist is to be eagerly shared." He thinks that Reformed theology's appeal to young people proves its unique imperviousness to the corrosive forces of 21st-century life.[476]

Time magazine has also noted Mohler, calling him the "reigning intellectual of the evangelical movement in the U.S."[477]

Calvinist pastor and author Robert Godfrey writes, "From the sixteenth century on, millions of Christians have found spiritual and intellectual fulfillment . . . in the Reformed movement."[478] Godfrey notes that it was partly his "intellectual curiosity" that would make him later herald the Calvinist theology.[479] Although he also admits that Calvinism has become an

---

Christianity Today, 1 October 2010 [online] accessed 15 December 2010; available from http://www.christianitytoday.com/ct/2010/october/3.18.html.

[475] Ibid.

[476] Ibid.

[477] Broward Laston, "Interview: Missionary Work in Iraq.". *Time*, 15 April 2003 [online] accessed 15 December 2010; available from http://www.time.com/time/world/article/0,8599,443800,00.html.

[478] Godfrey, *An Unexpected Journey*, 9.

[479] Ibid., 11, 25.

"intellectual exercise in theology" and that "Reformed Christianity is an expression of intellectual theology," he fears that "sometimes Reformed Christians are tempted to turn their churches into theological debating societies."[480] He continues to describe this drawback of Reformed Theology:

> I fear today in some Reformed circles, the head may have triumphed over the heart. Sometimes the legitimate satisfaction that we Reformed take in the profound scholarship of our heritage becomes an ugly arrogance. At other times we seem to focus excessively on a particular doctrine or set of ideas that produces a very unbalanced form of Calvinism.[481]

Because James Smith acknowledges that he came from an "anti-intellectual Christian background,"[482] he warns against the pride that too often accompanies intellectual Calvinism. He writes, "It took me a long time to be free of the pride and self-righteousness that had infected me"[483] and that "religious pride almost seems like a kind of genetic defect of the Reformed tradition, one that threatens to perpetuate itself."[484] He states further:

> Calvinism became a sophisticated theological justification for patriarchal attitudes and practices. The collective shape of the "Calvinism" they had found was not pretty—and certainly not a winsome witness to God's

---

[480] Ibid., 143.

[481] Ibid., 142.

[482] Smith, James, *Letters to a Young Calvinist,* 6.

[483] Ibid., 10.

[484] Ibid., 8.

coming kingdom. I sometimes encounter the same in the "new Calvinists" I bump into.[485]

This sense of pride is indeed more apparent in Calvinism than in any other theological group. When David Cloud wrote his article concerning the growth of Calvinism,[486] someone took the liberty to post the report as a blog on another Web site. Cloud commented, "There were 16 pages of responses and most of the replies were either in favor of or sympathetic toward Calvinism or were neutral." In addition, Cloud says, "Many of them ridiculed me in a fashion that I have found to be typical among 'young' Calvinists. A haughty smirkness characterized many of the responses."[487] It is this "haughty smirkness" of Calvinism that, as Baxter stated, "influences discourses," "chooses company," and "forms countenances." Dr. Ron Comfort accurately observes that the result of all this is "bitterness and division."[488]

William MacDonald similarly writes:

It is the practice of many Calvinists to press their views relentlessly upon others, even if it leads to church division. This theological system becomes the main

---

[485] Ibid., xii.

[486] David Cloud, "Calvinism on the March," blog entry posted on Way of Life Literature 26 March 2009 (updated; first published 18 October 2006) [online]; accessed 28 November 2010; available from http://www.wayoflife.org/files/category-calvinism.html; Internet.

[487] David Cloud, quoted by Greg Linscott on *Sharper Iron* blog entry, "A haughty smirkiness characterized many of the responses," 20 October 2006[online]; accessed 28 November 2010; available from http://sharperiron.org/2006/10/20/a-haughty-smirkness-characterized-many-of-the-responses; Internet.

[488] Comfort, "The Fruits of Calvinism."

emphasis of their conversation, their preaching, their prayers, and their ministries.[489]

As with any theology, Calvinism grips its followers and consumes their very being—their attitude, their evangelism, their service, and their leadership methods. As Calvinist Curt Daniel explains:

Christians need to have a biblical worldview. This is especially true with Calvinist Christians. No practical philosophy is complete unless it has a general blueprint. Is there, then, a distinctly Reformed worldview? Yes, there is.[490]

Unfortunately, the Calvinists who press their views upon others are not only laypeople but also pastors . . . who may not even preach in a Reformed Church. I have heard numerous stories of how a non-Reformed pastor has gone to a Reformed convention or gathering, adopted its theological view, and brought his newfound theology back to his church. Instead of resigning from pastoral leadership in the church, the pastor often remains to try and convert his parish of non-Calvinists to Calvinism. Pastor Ron Comfort has seen this pattern occur in churches frequently enough to offer the following advice:

Let me encourage you; don't be naive enough to think that you can put a Calvinist in leadership in your church and say, "Don't talk about Calvinism." That is like telling Michael Jordan not to talk about basketball. That is like telling Bill Gates not to talk about money. It just consumes their very being.[491]

---

[489] William MacDonald, to Dave Hunt (marginal note in review copy), Hunt, *What Love Is This?*, 384.

[490] Daniel, *The Practical Applications of Calvinism*, 188.

[491] Comfort, "The Fruits of Calvinism."

On October 18, 2006, David Cloud posted the following on the Fundamental Baptist Information Service Web site:

> Writing in *SBC Life*, Malcolm Yarnell, associate professor of systematic theology at Southwestern Baptist Theological Seminary, observed that TULIP theology is causing division in churches. Steve Lemke, provost of New Orleans Baptist Theological Seminary, warns: "I believe that [Calvinism] is potentially the most explosive and divisive issue facing us in the near future. It has already been an issue that has split literally dozens of churches, and it holds the potential to split the entire convention."[492]

> Speaking of Mark Driscoll's "New Calvinism," Molly Worthen in the *New York Times* writes that it "underscores a curious fact: the doctrine of total human depravity has always had a funny way of emboldening, rather than humbling, its adherents."[493]

For a number of reasons, the doctrines of TULIP are divisive for the Christian body. To believe in a God who loves the entire world is vastly different than believing in a God who loves only a small portion of it. To believe that faith in Jesus precedes God's work of regeneration is quite different than believing that regeneration precedes faith. To believe that God is sovereign in light of man's complete free will is contrary to the belief that the two are incompatible. Yet many Calvinist leaders go undetected in non-Calvinist churches, pressing their unique theology on those believers who are outside the Calvinist camp. Calvinist leaders are dividing churches that do not need or want this theology. Church splits that occur over the

---

[492] Cloud, "Calvinism on the March."

[493] Worthen, "Who Would Jesus Smack Down?"

doctrines of Calvinism paint a cultish picture of the arrogant evangelism and supposed superiority of Calvinism.

Its Evangelism: The Dichotomy of Calvinistic Evangelism

[Calvinists] actually view and treat many of the most dearly held convictions of non-Calvinist Evangelicals as symptomatic of a spiritual and theological disease, of which Reformed Theology is supposedly the CURE.[494]

—George Bryson

If God can save anyone to whom He gives the desire to be saved, then why does He not give the desire to all people?[495]

—Norman Geisler

Calvinism is unscriptural, false doctrine. It tends to flourish in intellectual pride and in neglect of soul winning, and is a symptom of moral guilt. It is Satan's effort to kill concern and compassion for souls . . . a perversion by proud intellectuals who thus may try and excuse themselves from any spiritual accountability for winning souls.[496]

—John Rice

Within Calvinistic evangelism, we find a dichotomy. Though the doctrines of TULIP do not logically present the need to carry out Jesus' "Great Command" to make disciples, we can still find the followers of TULIP evangelizing, sometimes aggressively. In this dichotomy being simultaneously faithful to Calvinism's TULIP and the biblical command to

---

[494] Bryson, *The Dark Side of Calvinism*, 27.

[495] Geisler, *Chosen but Free*, 139.

[496] Rice, *Some Serious, Popular False Doctrines*, 289, 274.

evangelize leads to an intellectual compromise of Calvinist theology. In trying to have it both ways, Calvinists present a rather confusing theology. While Calvinistic doctrines dogmatically teach that man has no free will to choose salvation, Calvinists are usually uncompromising in their call to evangelize. The most troubling aspect of their evangelism is whom they target. While it might be assumed that any religious group will set their sights on the "world," or the unsaved, Calvinists particularly seek to convert those already within Christianity. In this chapter, we will consider five issues:

1. why Calvinists are campaigning if the TULIP doctrines do not logically promote evangelism;
2. how a supposedly monergistic God uses Christian efforts to fulfill His will to evangelize;
3. how Calvinism's efforts to convert the church rather than those outside of it is a cultish tendency;
4. why Calvinism's gospel and other cult theologies are dishonestly presented; and
5. the practical fruit of maintaining Calvinism's theological view of evangelism.

(1) Why Calvinists are campaigning if the TULIP doctrines do not logically promote evangelism

Why would Calvinists evangelize if God offers most people no choice to respond? This problem has yet to be answered by anyone claiming to be Calvinist. Despite their belief that God predestines a majority of the human race to eternal Hell without the slightest regard for their will or desire, many Calvinists continue to follow the biblical command to evangelize. Yet faithfully maintaining Calvinistic doctrine must have consequences. Calvinist Curt Daniel confesses that a "pitfall" of his likeminded brothers is "that of Reformed apathy and lethargy. This is seen, for example, in the reluctance to evangelize because, 'After all, God has His elect out there and He will call them to Himself in due time.'" He argues that "the doctrines of grace . . . excuse their laziness."[497] Norman Geisler also writes that extreme Calvinism "leads logically (if not practically) to personal irresponsibility." [498]

A large number of evangelistic works have recently surfaced as a way to combat this lethargy. One example is Richard Mouw's *Calvinism in the Las Vegas Airport.* While the purpose of the book is to inform the Calvinist about how to evangelize in today's American culture, Mouw admits that the TULIP doctrines "have a harsh feel about them."[499] Although Mouw understates this problem, his honesty is refreshing. Similarly, Reformed theologian John Frame asks, "Why are there so few African-Americans, Native Americans, and Latinos in Reformed churches? That is, I think, an important question."[500] He further states, "I have no statistics on the success of Reformed churches in reaching out to American minorities, but my observation (and I trust the reader's as well) is that we have been very weak in this respect."[501]

But the honesty of other leading Calvinists should be called into question as they make statements that blatantly contradict the paradox of evangelism found within Calvinism. For instance, John Piper states, "Evangelism and missions are not imperiled by the biblical truth of election, but empowered by it, and their triumph is secured by it."[502] In his book *Don't Waste Your Life*, Piper encourages the work and calling of missions for the Christian. Likewise, Boettner, who sets the pattern for many Calvinists, says that Christians should

[497] Daniel, *The Practical Applications of Calvinism*, 194.

[498] Geisler, *Chosen but Free*, 137.

[499] Mouw, *Calvinism in the Las Vegas Airport*, 14.

[500] Frame, *The Doctrine of the Christian Life*, 678.

[501] Ibid., 679.

[502] John Piper, *The Pleasures of God* (Sisters, OR: Multnomah Publishers, 2000), 153.

pray for the unconverted, "that they may each be among the elect."[503] And Spurgeon, the so-called Calvinist, said, "Soul winning is the chief business of the Christian."[504]

While these statements of faith and Christian interaction with the world sound competent, they fail to explain why a Monergistic god of regeneration calls his followers to work with and through them to evangelize. And if soul winning was of truly utmost importance to the Calvinist, why would the Calvary Chapel founder Chuck Smith express the true concern of many that, "evangelism is so neglected in much of the Reformed community"?[505] Besides this, as Walls and Dongell point out, Calvinistic evangelism also fails to "make coherent sense of how God can have compassion for persons he has not elected to save."[506]

A common reason given from the evangelistic Calvinist as to the purpose of evangelism is that it is simply commanded in God's Word. But if the Calvinist obeys the Great Command out of sheer obedience, he must surely wonder why his God would call him to reach the unsavable, or try to reveal God to the spiritually blind and deaf. Despite what Calvinists believe and teach, they circumvent the question of evangelism because it logically contradicts the five points. In doing away with the need to fulfill Jesus' words of the Great Commission, Calvinists find themselves between a rock and a hard place. Yet their call to evangelize seems justified despite their belief in Irresistible Grace and Limited Atonement. Calvinists seemed to have "solved" this doctrinal Catch-22 by claiming that although God has an unconditional elect and even though Jesus died for a limited number of people, we must evangelize because we never know who the

---

[503] Boettner, *The Reformed Doctrine of Predestination*, 285.

[504] Charles H. Spurgeon, *The Soul Winner* (Grand Rapids: Eerdmans, 1963), 15.

[505] Chuck Smith, Foreword, in *The Dark Side of Calvinism*, 8.

[506] Walls and Dongell, *Why I Am Not a Calvinist*, 188.

elect are and are not. Geisler thankfully admits that "not all extreme Calvinists consistently live out their beliefs. Thankfully, sometimes people are better in their conduct than in their creed."[507]

James White says, "Since we do not know who the elect are, we are to preach the gospel to every creature, trusting that God will honor His truth as He sees fit in the salvation of His people."[508] John Calvin said long before:

> Since we do not know who belongs to the number of the predestined and who does not, it befits us so to feel as to wish that all be saved. So it will come about that, whoever we come across, we shall study to make him a sharer of peace . . . even severe rebuke will be administered like medicine, lest they should perish or cause others to perish. But it will be for God to make it effective in those whom He foreknew and predestined.[509]

Though these answers may sound legitimate, they are really nothing more than double-talk. If the doctrines of Calvinism were true, then a life lived in spreading the gospel message (while it might be pleasing to God) would have no influence upon the number of people who are saved. According to Calvinism, trying to save the unsavable would be directly against the will of God, and for all intents and purposes would be a wasted life. Ironically, Piper's *Don't Waste Your Life* is wildly popular among Calvinists, mainly because they claim that they can "still remain passionately evangelistic!"[510] *Don't*

---

[507] Geisler, *Chosen but Free*, 143.

[508] White, in *Debating Calvinism*, 321.

[509] John Calvin, *Concerning the Eternal Predestination of God*, trans. J. K. S. Reid (London: James Clarke and Co., Limited, 1961), 138.

[510] Greg Elmquist, Foreword to "What Should We Think of Evangelism and Calvinism?" by Ernest C. Reisinger [online]; accessed 1 February 2010; available from http://www.reformedreader.org/e&c.htm; Internet.

Waste Your Life has grown in popularity along with Piper's book, *Desiring God*, which has sold more than 275,000 copies. John Piper is a popular Calvinist who is passionate about soul winning and being effective—quite the opposite of what the doctrines of Calvinism concede. Many Calvinists look up to Piper's claims in order to justify that their doctrine is not opposed to evangelism. In fact, some Calvinists evangelize as much as or more than non-Calvinist Christians. David Cloud writes that although there are exceptions, "Calvinism tends to cool evangelistic fervor. Among Calvinists, evangelism is done IN SPITE OF Calvinism, not because of it."[511]

Another reason why many Calvinists believe they should evangelize is because the city of Geneva practiced evangelism. Ray Van Neste writes:

> Perhaps the best evidence of Calvin's concern for missions is the mission activity of the Genevan church under his leadership. Under Calvin's leadership, Geneva became "the hub of a vast missionary enterprise" and "a dynamic center or nucleus from which the vital missionary energy it generated radiated out into the world beyond." Protestant refugees from all over Europe fled to Geneva; they came not merely for safety but also to learn from Calvin the doctrines of the Reformation so they could return home to spread the true gospel. Philip Hughes notes that Geneva became a "school of missions" which had as one of its purposes to send out witnesses who would spread the teaching of the Reformation far and wide. . . . It [Geneva] was a dynamic centre of missionary concern and activity, an axis from which the light of the Good News radiated forth through the testimony of those

---

[511] Cloud, "Calvinism on the March."

who, after thorough preparation in this school, were
sent forth in the service of Jesus Christ.[512]

Yet, pointing to John Calvin as an example in support of
missionary work is misleading. Here is an example: two plus two will
always equal four no matter who says or believes otherwise. By the same
logic, the theology of Calvin has and will always contradict the need for
missions, regardless of who says and believes otherwise . . . even if it is
John Calvin. What exactly were Calvin's motives in evangelizing? Was
Calvin's Geneva really spreading the good news of the gospel to the lost,
as Jesus intended, or was he simply dispersing his new doctrines to those
Christians who wished to be officially separated from the Catholic
Church? We should be able to draw a conclusion as we continue.

The reasons behind John Calvin's push for evangelism, as
compared to the motives of evangelizing Calvinists today, are likely
different. At the time, Calvin was writing a whole new understanding of
the Bible. Therefore, his doctrines were very attractive to anyone hoping
to break away from Catholicism. Although the purpose of evangelism is
to "make disciples of all nations," it is reasonable to conclude that this
was not Calvin's true intention. As Salt Lake City was a missionary center
for the Mormons, and as was Brooklyn, New York, for Jehovah's
Witnesses, so Geneva was "a dynamic centre of missionary concern and
activity."[513] But from our knowledge of John Calvin, we can question if
Geneva was truly spreading the "light of the Good News,"[514] or, rather,
the theological thoughts of a man thrust into a position of a prominent
spiritual leadership.

---

[512] Ray Van Neste, "John Calvin on Evangelism and Missions," *Founders Journal* 33 (Summer 1998) [online]; accessed 1 February 2010; available from http://www. founders.org/journal/fj33/article2.html; Internet.

[513] Ibid.

[514] Ibid.

Although we cannot know the true intentions of John Calvin's pursuit in evangelism, for several reasons it seems unlikely that he aimed only to proclaim salvation in Christ. First, his theological view clearly makes evangelism ultimately useless. Second, cult leaders usually seek their own desires, as opposed to the desires of God as revealed in Scripture. Third, John Calvin knew that his missionaries were not spreading good news to anyone whom God would not save. In fact, as Reformation historian Diarmaid MacCulloch writes, "Calvin was perfectly aware that the determinism of predestination was 'dreadful indeed' to humanity."[515] In fact, his missionaries were spreading nothing but bad news to almost all of those who were supposedly not of the elect. According to MacCulloch, "The most discordant noises came from Basel, where one anonymous pamphlet with bitter sarcasm described the Genevan Church as proclaiming 'its good news with flames.'"[516]

In light of the evidence, the doctrines, and the backdrop of time, we are better able to understand just what Calvin was spreading, and the reasons behind his evangelism. There is also the fourth possibility that Calvin was simply deluded into thinking that *his* particular doctrine of divine determinism and earthly evangelism worked hand in hand.

(2) How a supposedly monergistic God uses Christian efforts to fulfill His will to evangelize

As we have noted before, the Calvinist believes that God uses human efforts in bringing the message of salvation to the world, while simultaneously holding to the belief "that He [God] is fully able to save without the aid of His creatures."[517] Calvinists hold that they

---

[515] MacCulloch, *The Reformation*, 244.

[516] Ibid., 245.

[517] White, in *Debating Calvinism*, 64.

should evangelize because they do not know who is predestined to believe. But knowing, or not knowing, who will choose to believe the gospel should be of no concern to the followers of Calvinism. According to Calvinistic doctrine, if every last Calvinist completely forsook the spreading of the gospel message, the predestined election of God would in no way be affected.

Many Calvinists often argue that if God alone is not the sole Regenerator of man, then He is somehow dependent upon man to help save and, therefore, is not completely sovereign. The Calvinistic idea that man somehow contributes to salvation by merely "receiving" Christ is appropriate for the TULIP believer, for only in the theology of Calvinism is "receiving" the grace of God equated with "giving aid" to Him. Thus, to explain man's lack of free will in regards to salvation, R. C. Sproul proclaims that God is *monergistic* in nature, pointing out that, "Monergism is something that operates by itself or works alone as the sole active party."[518] This is contrasted to *synergism*, which is defined as "a cooperative venture, a working together of two or more parties." [519] White believes that if God uses the aid of man to bring about regeneration, it actually gives man "the ability to control God's free and sovereign work of salvation."[520]

Despite their deterministic theology, when it comes to evangelism, Calvinists seem to do away with their idea that God is monergistic. In spreading the gospel message to unbelievers, Calvinists seem to believe that God does require some human effort. This begs the question: is Calvinism's god monergistic or synergistic? For the Calvinist, the practical answer is . . . whatever makes TULIP stay alive. Concerning the regeneration of the sinner, God is monergistic, and concerning evangelism, He is synergistic. If God can

---

[518] Sproul, *What Is Reformed Theology?* 183.

[519] Ibid., 184.

[520] White, in *Debating Calvinism*, 72.

be synergistic in regards to evangelism, why can He not be that way in regards to salvation? And if receiving God's grace is seen as "giving aid" to God (taking away from His sovereignty), how then must a life of evangelism be viewed? By asserting that God is monergistic while simultaneously maintaining a call to evangelize, Calvinism proves itself to be inconsistent and unorthodox.

(3) How Calvinism's efforts to convert the church rather than those outside of it is a cultish tendency

In a previous chapter, we considered the elitism of Calvinists among other Christians. This arrogance is evident as we see whom Calvinists target for conversion. One way that cults are distinguished from other religions is the high value placed on spreading their "superior" doctrines not only to "the lost" but to anyone who does not share the same theological distinctive. For example, Jehovah's Witnesses and Mormons regularly go door-to-door, just as the self-realizationists faithfully chant *Hare Krishna* in the streets. These forms of evangelism are unique not because of how they are conducted but because of who is targeted. I have had many conversations with both Mormons and Jehovah's Witnesses. My question to them both is their purpose in evangelizing to Christians. Their answer is simple: although someone may technically be saved, he is missing out on the "fullness of the gospel" if he does not adhere to their specific doctrine. This is seen in the case of Calvinism, in which Calvinists attempt to convert other Christians to their theological view.

George Bryson writes:

> Many Calvinists are extremely zealous in their commitment to win non-Calvinists (especially non-Calvinist Evangelicals) over to the Reformed version of the Christian faith . . . Believing they are doing all non-Calvinists a favor by winning them over to Calvinism, many Calvinists have become proselytizers for the

Reformed faith. . . . Calvinists are very good at winning non-Calvinist Christians into the Reformed faith.[521]

In his book, *Chosen by God*, R. C. Sproul writes about the excitement of converting a non-Calvinist Christian: "They say there is nothing more obnoxious than a converted drunk. Try a converted Arminian. Converted Arminians tend to become flaming Calvinists, zealous for the cause of predestination." Sproul goes on to admit: "You are reading the work of such a convert."[522] Although Calvinist James Smith acknowledges that "battling other Christians . . . should not be a very high priority" it nevertheless remains "a common malady in the Reformed tradition"[523]

The reputable founder of Calvary Chapel Church, Chuck Smith, has also noted the efforts of Calvinists to proselytize fellow Christians:

> Many Calvinist are spending time and energy trying to win the already saved to Calvinism. What this means is that Calvinists want other Christians to believe in their convoluted theology, which if fully understood, destroys the gospel to every creature.[524]

Such strong words can better be appreciated knowing the hesitancy of Chuck Smith to take sides on such a controversial issue. George Bryson clarifies:

> What if Calvinists were content to simply win the lost to Christ and then build them up in the Reformed faith? If

---

[521] Bryson, *The Dark Side of Calvinism*, 20.

[522] R. C. Sproul, *Chosen by God* (Wheaton, IL: Tyndale Publishing House, 1986), 13.

[523] Smith, James, *Letters to a Young Calvinist*, 8.

[524] Smith, Foreword to *The Dark Side of Calvinism*.

that were all that Calvinists were doing, they would hear little or nothing from me. Contemporary champions of Calvinism—men like R. C. Sproul, John Piper, James R. White, John MacArthur, and a host of others—are not simply *promoting* Reformed Theology among those new believers that *they have led to Christ* or that *have come to them* for spiritual guidance. Instead, as noted earlier, Calvinists are zealously proselytizing for the Reformed faith. If you are a part of a non-Reformed Evangelical Christian church or affiliation of churches, it is very likely that Calvinists have their sights set on winning you. Ready or not. They are coming for you and your church or church group (if they have not already arrived).[525]

The fact that Calvinism sets its sights more on the Christian world than the world itself speaks volumes and, again, seems too cultish to ignore.

(4) Why Calvinism's gospel and other cult theologies are dishonestly presented

When I share the gospel message, either from the pulpit or one-on-one, I have nothing to hide or water down about my beliefs and theology. This may sound very basic, but it must be noted. If I were a people pleaser, I would be tempted to overlook those parts of my theology that might offend a potential believer. Certain aspects of the gospel's good news, like "personal sin" and "divine judgment," are not merely a part of understanding one's need for God's grace but are imperative to receiving it. Thus, although the prospective convert might not welcome the true notion of his rebellion before God (i.e., his sin) and a time of God's future judgment, I withhold nothing and keep no secrets in laying out the full gospel.

---

[525] Bryson, *The Dark Side of Calvinism*, 26–27.

This is not the case with Mormonism and Jehovah's Witnesses. This is also not the case with the gospel according to Calvinism. George Bryson writes:

> Some Calvinists are not only less than totally up-front, but they are not even being altogether honest with the non-Calvinists whom they are targeting. In the promotion of doctrine, what is held back or not expressed (relative to those doctrines) can be very misleading.[526]

Bryson contends that "some Calvinists do not want non-Calvinists to know the full implications of Calvinism until after they have become committed Calvinists."[527] It should not be hard to figure out the reasons why a "potential" convert might not want to know intimately the core doctrines of Calvinism from the beginning.

If the forbearer of the Calvinist gospel message cannot or will not be upfront and direct about the doctrines pertaining to salvation (in public or private life), the skeptic must seriously consider why. Furthermore, we should wonder whether Jesus Himself was hiding some important aspects of His messages. Was He withholding the doctrine of double predestination when He called everyone to come and receive the Bread of Life? Did He expect the crowds to understand that when He said "all" or "world" what He really meant was "some" and "elect"? Did He assume that His followers would understand that "grace" could have multiple definitions? Did Jesus expect His apostles to understand that their efforts to evangelize would be ultimately futile? Indeed, Chuck Smith asks, "Why would the God of all truth, who speaks so sternly against lying, send His servants out to promote such a lie?"[528]

---

[526] Ibid., 23.

[527] Ibid., 22.

[528] Smith, Foreword to *The Dark Side of Calvinism*.

Yet, some Calvinists today seem guilty of being dishonest in presenting their particular gospel. One Reformed Southern Baptist pastor, in an article entitled "Instructions for Local Church Reformation," advises other Calvinist pastors:

> Choose a few men who are sincere, teachable and spiritually minded and spend time with them in study and prayer. They will help you to reform. . . . In the pulpit, don't use theological language that is not found in the Bible. Avoid terms such as Calvinism, reformed, doctrines of grace, particular redemption, etc. Most people will not know what you are talking about. Many that do will become inflamed against you.[529]

We read about dishonesty concerning the gospel early in church history. Certain men came down from Jerusalem teaching the brethren that unless they were "circumcised according to the custom of Moses," they could "not be saved" (**Acts 15:1**, NKJV).[530] Because of this threat to the gospel message, the apostles gathered and directly faced the problem. The main reason the apostles opposed this teaching was because of its false message of salvation, which added "works" to the free grace of God and limited those who could be saved to those who were circumcised. Similarly, Calvinism limits salvation to "the elect." "Certain men" (Calvinists) are teaching the brethren that some people can "not be saved" at all.

Like Paul, the Christian is called to confront those who are "not straightforward about the truth of the gospel."[531] In **Galatians chapter**

---

[529] Ernest C. Reisinger and D. Matthew Allen, *A Quiet Revolution: A Chronicle of Beginnings of Reformation in the Southern Baptist Convention* [online]; accessed 1 February 2010; available from http://www.founders.org/library/ quiet4/; Internet.

[530] NKJV, Acts 15:1.

[531] NKJV, Galatians 2:14.

2, Paul confronted Peter about his hypocrisy. Although the gospel was commanded to be taken to all of humanity, Peter would fellowship only with the Gentiles in the absence of the Jewish elite. Thus, while Peter believed the gospel was for the Gentiles as well as the Jews, his actions differed from his beliefs. He witnessed mainly to the Jewish people who came from Jerusalem. When Paul noticed Peter compromising the truth of the gospel, he said, "Now when Peter had come to Antioch, I withstood him to his face, because he was to be blamed; . . . But when I saw that they were not straightforward about the gospel, I said to Peter before *them* all . . ."[532] (**Galatians 2:11–14**, NKJV). Paul then brings Peter's hypocrisy into the light.

Likewise, those who herald Calvinism today do not practice what they preach. While on the outside, Calvinists claim that their gospel is for all people, their doctrines clearly declare otherwise. To win the minds of those around them, their doctrine of limited atonement is not openly addressed. Calvinists, as with all cultists, are not straightforward about their message. If they were straightforward, there would be no need for Calvin expositors like Pink, White, and Sproul to malign the intended meanings of simple words like "world"; there would be no need for Calvinist teachers to make unfounded distinctions in words like "love," "grace," and "calling"; and there would be no need to change the TULIP labels. The following example illustrates how far from straightforward a Calvinist can be.

I recently watched an episode of a sitcom, in which the manager of a paper resale office was offered a promotion in the company, but only if he laid off several of his employees. The manager, though close friends with many of his employees, agreed to take the new position. Not knowing their fate, his staff anxiously sought his decision. When he came out of his office, he said, "I have good news and bad news. I'll tell you the bad news first. A lot of you will lose your job here or be forced to

---

[532] NKJV, Galatians 2:11–14.

relocate to Sweden." At this, the employees were distraught and saddened. But their regional manager was quick to try and raise their spirits by finishing, "And now the good news—I was offered to be head manager over all of the U.K." As he looked for approval among his employees, they offered him none. After a minute of silence, one of the employees pointed out the stupidity of his ex-manager: "That's not good news. All you have is bad news and irrelevant news. We've just lost our jobs so you could be promoted, and you think we should be happy for you?"[533]

Likewise, the gospel of Calvinism looks into the faces of people whom their god has doomed to eternal fire and expects a joyful response to their fate. In Luke 2:10, the angel of the Lord announces the true gospel of Christ as "good tidings of great joy which will be to all people." Is one to believe that this angel from God held the same unreasonable logic of the new U.K. branch manager? Did the angel really think that the unfortunate souls would find the news of their damnation as "good tidings of great joy?"

These types of contradictions that plague Calvin's TULIP make for a confusing and inconsistent theology. Why does it maintain such contradictions? Is it because Christians would not swallow Calvinism if it were not watered down? Is it because Calvinism's "unveiled" gospel would turn potential new converts away instead of winning them over? Why unbelievers, let alone Christians, would be repulsed by Calvinism's deterministic form of Christianity should be no surprise, for it must bear a certain fruit in the lives of its followers.

(5) The practical fruit of maintaining Calvinism's theological view of evangelism

Calvinist James McGuire admits, "Deeds of real love accompanying vital evangelism are often woefully missing from

---

[533] Ricky Gervais, *The Office*, Season 1, Disc 2, Episode 6 (BBC Television); available online at http://www.amazon.com/Episode-Six-Judgement/dp/B001444N0O/ref=pd_vodsm_B001444N0O; Internet.

Reformed students of the Bible."[534] This is the practical effect from the absence of love as a motivating force of Calvinistic evangelism.

In **2 Corinthians 5:14**, Paul says, "The love of Christ compels us." The fruit of this compelling love from God led Paul and the other apostles to evangelize the entire known world and plant churches in almost every city they entered. It is clear by the evangelistic fruit of the twelve apostles what the love of God meant to them. Their lives were marked by both its joyful and painful costs.

But what does God's "love" for the lost mean to Calvinists, and how will it affect their evangelism? If I believed that man had no free will to exercise regarding salvation, I could tell you what the love of God would mean to me. As a pastor, I can testify that ministry has been a "labor of love" to certain people that God has placed in my life. I, with many other saints, have endured years of struggle, patience, and service, hoping that one day our collective efforts of love and sacrifice will be used by God to bring a certain soul to salvation and spiritual maturity. Once in a while, I will ask myself if it is all worth it. But I quickly renounce such a thought. What amount of service can ever be equal to a soul in Heaven!? There is no amount of service or tribulation too great to endure. The apostle Paul wrote that the afflictions he endured on earth were nothing compared to the glory of one day being in Heaven (**2 Corinthians 4:17**). Therefore, he endured shipwrecks, hunger, nakedness, and other severe consequences for taking the message to all men and to the whole world.

If God, in the scope of eternity, gathered all the hours of prayers, service, and sacrifice from 10,000 saints that resulted in one soul saved from the penalty of sin, indeed those 10,000 standing in the glory of God could never find a hint of remorse for their service and sacrifice, even if

---

[534] James N. McGuire, "Appendix A: The Five Points of Calvinism," in *The Five Points of Calvinism: Defined, Defended, and Documented*, 2nd ed., by David N. Steele, Curtis C. Thomas, and S. Lance Quinn (Phillipsburg, NJ: P&R Publishing, 2004), 141.

they sought it. Instead, I assume they would rejoice that God counted them worthy to be used at all in such a manner.

On those nights when I lie in bed disquieted about the future of those whom I serve as pastor, I often question my calling to continue ministering to certain people who can sometimes seem to be a burden. But my knowledge that God desires their salvation and has good plans for their future drives me. In Paul's words, "the love of Christ compels" me. I can almost say that His love constrains me. On the dark/flip side: If for a mere minute I were to entertain the doctrinal claims of Calvinism, I would not only give up ministering to the souls in need but would also regret the past service and ministry that have consumed my time and comfort. I would very easily give up self-sacrificing evangelism, knowing that my efforts, tears, frustration, and joy have amounted to nothing. What always brings reassuring comfort when I wonder if my service is worth anything it is that there really "is no trouble too great, no humiliation too deep, no suffering too severe, no love too strong, no labor too hard, no expense too large, but that it is worth it, if it is spent in the effort to win a soul."[535] Calvinist theology must deny this.

Calvin enthusiasts Doug VanderMeulin and Steve Watkins state their thoughts on "soul winning" by saying, "We are, for example very against a lot of the big event evangelism."[536] By declaring their disapproval of a certain style of evangelism, they portray the heart of true Calvinism. Usually any sort of "big event" evangelism aims specifically at the unchurched, whereas most evangelistic efforts by Calvinists are focused on those already within the church. When these words are compared to Piper's—"Evangelism and missions are not imperiled by the biblical truth of election, but empowered by it"[537]—one must only wonder how Calvinists define evangelism.

---

[535] "A Guide to Christian Workers," *The Holy Bible: The Open Bible Edition, KJV*, (Thomas Nelson Inc., 1975), p. 1,253.

[536] Hunt, "Conversation on Calvinism."

[537] Piper, *The Pleasures of God*, 153.

Even if Calvinists seem to come up with "answers" to the paradox of Calvinistic evangelism, the questions themselves pose serious threats to the theology. The first and most important flaw within Calvin's evangelism is that the TULIP doctrines do not logically promote it. Thus, what is the need for it? Secondly, one can only wonder how a supposedly monergistic God uses Christian efforts to fulfill His will to save only the elect. Thirdly, how does one make sense of Calvinists' claim truly to evangelize the world while they concentrate their efforts to convert people on those already within the church?

The gospel of Calvinism is markedly dishonest; such a message is a feature commonly shared by cults. Maintaining Calvinism's theological view of evangelism can only bear bad fruit. To think otherwise would be to mock God. What a man sows, that he will reap.

Its God

The heart and soul of Calvinistic doctrine, when carefully examined, is nothing less than the creation of a god that is foreign to the God of the Bible. We must remember that the "end of the Reformed tradition is God himself as revealed to us in Jesus Christ and present with us in the person of the Holy Spirit."[538] James Smith writes further that "the Reformed tradition is itself an invitation into the life of God" and at "its heart, Calvinism is simply a lens that magnifies a persistent theme in the narrative of God's self- revelation."[539] Thus, while the quest to "understand the character of God"[540] is what drives Reformed Theology, the picture it paints of God is grossly misconstrued. If Reformed Theology is different from traditional orthodoxy, one must ask how its god differs as well. These

---

[538] Smith, *Letters to a Young Calvinist*, xv.

[539] Smith, *Letters to a Young Calvinist*, 14.

[540] Sproul, *What Is Reformed Theology?*, 20.

differences are not small, by any means. Many prominent Bible scholars and pastors have come to the same conclusion:

> The God introduced to us by Calvin seems to be far removed and very different from the God who said, "The Spirit and the bride say, 'Come.' And let the one who hears say, 'Come.' And let the one who is thirsty come; let the one who wishes take the water of life without cost" (**Revelation 22:17**).[541]

—Chuck Smith

> In stark contrast to what we know about God from Scripture, Calvin and his followers have made God out to be the primary and responsible cause of all misery on this planet. While it is difficult (if not impossible to a non-Calvinist), Calvin and Calvinism point a very slanderous finger at God.[542]

—George Bryson

> The God of Calvinism is a far cry from the God of the Bible.[543]

—Tim LaHaye

> Calvinism [portrays] God in a totally unscriptural manner.[544]

—William MacDonald

> Calvinism presents a God who fills hell with those whom He could save but instead damns because He doesn't love them.[545]

—Dave Hunt

---

[541] Smith, Foreword to *The Dark Side of Calvinism*.

[542] Bryson, *The Dark Side of Calvinism*, 371.

[543] Tim LaHaye, Endorsement of *What Love Is This?* by Dave Hunt.

[544] William McDonald, Endorsements of *What Love Is This?* by Dave Hunt.

[545] Hunt, *What Love Is This?*, 116.

Calvinism makes our Heavenly Father look like the worst of despots.[546]

—Joseph R. Chambers

Calvinism incriminates the nature of God.[547]

—Ron Comfort

Different theologies can lead not only to different views of God but to entirely different gods. Although forms of worship may vary within a denomination, theologies do not. A theology is more serious, for it determines what the worship is about and who it is for. As the god of Islam is unlike Jesus, so too is the god of Mormonism because the essential doctrines of Mormonism differ so greatly from those of orthodox Christianity. Since the essential doctrines of Calvinism set themselves against orthodoxy, we can deduce that the god of Calvinism is too different for the Christian to ignore. The orthodox Christian does not separate himself from a Latter-day Saint because of different dress styles, nor does an orthodox Christian distinguish himself from a Jehovah's Witness for merely holding to legalistic opinions. The orthodox Christian separates himself from these two theologies for the more prudent reason—their view of God and His dealings with mankind.

Calvinism is a distinct theology, not likened but more influential than a mere denomination of Christianity. The proclaimed doctrines of Calvinism present such an unbiblical view of God that it is questionable whether Calvinism should remain inside the camp of orthodox Christianity. I do not distinguish my theological convictions from Calvinistic theology merely because of differing tastes in worship styles or teaching methods. I choose to differentiate myself from the Calvinist

---

[546] Joseph R. Chambers, Exceptional endorsements, from Hunt, *What Love Is This?*

[547] Comfort, "The Fruits of Calvinism."

simply because he portrays a fatalistic, discriminatory god who is a far cry from the God of the Bible I know.

The major and salvific doctrines pertaining to salvation in orthodox Christianity that describe God's nature can be summarized succinctly as follows:

God desires, wills, and intends to save all.

Compare this to the Calvinist doctrines of salvation:

God only desired, willed, and intended to save some.

When Calvinistic doctrine is summarized plainly, its cultish side is apparent. When compared to the caricatured god of Jehovah's Witnesses and Mormons, Calvinism's portrayal of God is even more confusing and frightening.

- The god of Calvinism commands his followers to love all people equally, while he loves only the elect with a *certain* love.
- The god of Calvinism commands his followers to show no partiality to any people, but he withholds "saving grace" from a majority of the world.
- The god of Calvinism begs people to repent and seek holiness while at the same time withholding from them the free will to do so.
- The god of Calvinism demands that his followers evangelize even though their efforts are ultimately useless.
- The god of Calvinism desires that all men should be saved but also finds it within his "good pleasure" to punish the unfortunate to Hell.[548]

These examples alone should be sufficient for anyone to see that the god of Calvinism cannot be made compatible with the true God of the Bible. Yet, the cultic features of Calvinism have been defended by double talk, flawed rhetoric, and twisted terminology for many years.

---

[548] Calvin, *Institutes*, 3.23.10.

Recently I talked with a pastor and friend who likes to think of himself as "somewhat" of a Calvinist. He said, "If God only chose to save some people . . . You know . . . He can do what He wants." Obviously, I agree. God *can* do what He wants, but refuting a point of Calvinist doctrine is not equivalent to arguing for the opposite. No matter how strongly I believe that all people have a chance to be saved, I must conclude that if indeed there is a God, by His very nature, He can do whatever He wants. Any Christian must admit this. God is God, above all and over all, bound by nothing, and He is completely sovereign. Thus, if God intended to save some and damn some, I would not contend differently. However, based on the divine revelation of the Holy Bible I must fervently contest the belief that God intended to save some and damn some, and show the fallacy of such a notion.

Many Calvinists believe that people reject their doctrines because they are simply unpleasant. In the case above, my Calvinist friend assumed (as many often do) that I have rejected Calvinist theology because of my unwillingness to believe the unpleasant notion that God could actually choose not to save some. This "unpleasantness" is considered by Calvinists as a "tough truth," but acceptance of it often becomes a Calvinist's source of spiritual pride. On the outward appearance, the message of Calvinism is a hard gospel to swallow. Yet Calvinists do swallow it and then boast of their deep adoration and commitment to God, regardless of His supposed tough truth!

The basic "tough truth" of Calvinism is that God does not desire to save everyone. In this day and age of watered-down, seeker-friendly Christianity, Calvinists stand out as those who have not compromised biblical truth. This is what makes Calvinism so distinguished. It claims to be for those who are spiritually mature. It is for those who have the spiritual enlightenment and humility to worship God when their own ideas of justice and universal love are not met. Many Calvinists take pride in showing their humility to set their own humanistic philosophies down and accept God on His own terms. Calvinism boasts of being the only theology opposed to:

. . . the superficial, seeker-sensitive theology that predominates in many churches in America . . . [where] God is often reduced to a "cosmic bellhop" whose only concern is to meet whatever needs contemporary people feel in their lives. Doctrine is dismissed as irrelevant, Scripture is used as a self-help manual, and worship is replaced by various forms of entertainment.

. . . the God of Calvinism is far from a cosmic bellhop. He is not obliged to do anything for you except send you to hell, and, if he chooses to do so, he is glorified by your damnation. Calvinism is, if anything, serious about doctrine, passionate about the Bible, and zealous for the glory of God.[549]

We must make an important note here about Calvinists being passionate about the glory of God. Although it is an obviously good thing to desire God's glory, this holy aspiration cannot be at the expense of truth. Geisler sees this error as a "theologism," a term coined by the French philosopher, Étienne Gilson. Geisler explains:

Briefly, this is the fallacy of assuming that the view that seems to give the most glory to God is true. Extreme Calvinists resort time and again to this position . . . argu[ing] that the less credit given to man, the more glory given to God. And, God will get the most glory if creatures have absolutely nothing to do with their salvation, not even exercising their free choice to receive it. However, this does not follow, since truth is not determined by what appears to glorify God but by what actually fits with the facts.[550]

---

[549] Walls and Dongell, *Why I Am Not a Calvinist*, 17.

[550] Geisler, *Chosen but Free*, 255.

I believe Geisler's insight explains why Calvinists believe what they do. Although from a heart and mind sincerely aiming to please God, the theologism not only proves illogical but can often lead to an inflated view of one's spiritual maturity. Thus, when people do not accept Calvinist theology, Calvinists usually assume that the reason is simply spiritual immaturity. Yet, I do not distinguish my theology from Calvinism because I am not humble enough to lay down my own fabricated thoughts and philosophies of God. And I do not refute Calvinism because I feel that God should love and give everyone a chance. I do not contest the tenets of Calvinism because I lack the spiritual maturity to say honestly, as Job did, "Though He slay me, yet will I trust Him (**Job 13:15a**, NKVJ)."[551] I am against Calvinism because like a cult, its god is not derived from the Scripture's plain teachings but rather from the systemized thoughts of a young and charismatic lawyer in the wake of the greatest religious reformation ever. Through hundreds of years, having been "masqueraded as sound Biblical doctrine"[552] Calvinists worship a god that I do not know. This truth has also led author Louis Ruggiero to write a rebuttal of Calvinism, which is rightly entitled, *The God of Calvinism*. As Brown writes, "The Bible tells us that God not only permits evil, He even ordains it."[553] That view of God is why I am not a Calvinist.

Geisler seems to agree, stating that

> hyper-Calvinism makes God the direct author of evil. For God does not merely permit evil, He causes it. But we know that God is absolutely good (**Matt. 5:48**), and He cannot do, promote, or produce evil (**Hab. 1:13**; **James 1:13**). Second, hyper-Calvinists explicitly confess not only that God is not all-loving but that He also hates the non-elect.[554]

---

[551] NKLV, Job 13:15.

[552] Vance, *The Other Side of Calvinism*, Preface ix.

[553] Brown, *The Five Dilemmas of Calvinism*, 91.

[554] Geisler, *Chosen but Free*, 218.

The consistent Calvinist is dangerously close to worshiping another god whose gospel and spirit differs much from those of the God of orthodox Christianity. Dave Hunt has even compared the god of Calvinism to the pagan god of Baal:

> The Bible contrasts the truth, purity, love, and mercy of the true God with the capricious destructiveness of pagan gods. In the process, the prophets appeal to our reason and to the conscience God has given us. Baal is exposed as a false god not worthy of worship because of its demand that children be sacrificed in the sacred fires on its altars. Would the true God cause billions to burn Whom He could deliver? If it is legitimate to appeal to conscience and reason in exposing false gods, surely no lesser standard should be applied to determine which is the true God. And if He is presented as being less gracious, less loving, less kind and merciful than He expects mankind to be, then surely there is a legitimate reason for declaring that the one depicted cannot be the true God. To attribute to Him any lack of love and mercy is surely to misrepresent the true God.[555]

A Good and Merciful God?

The stark truth of the matter is that the God of extreme Calvinism is not all-loving. . . . In a redemptive sense, He loves only the elect.[556]

—Norman Geisler

One question regarding Calvinism that remains up for grabs is the nature of God's goodness. In one way or another, this question is

---

[555] Hunt, *What Love Is This?*, 374.

[556] Geisler, *Chosen but Free*, 88.

A CULTISH SIDE OF CALVINISM

quietly pondered in the Calvinist's thoughts: how can an all-loving and merciful God choose to not save some? This inquiry is quite different than the typical question posed to all Christians: how can an all-loving and merciful God allow the unsaved to go to Hell? Understanding the difference between the two questions is paramount. The first places the ultimate destiny of mankind in the will of the Creator, while the latter places the ultimate destiny in the free will of the creation. Both views correctly rest upon the biblical "grace through faith" doctrines, but only one acknowledges the free will of man. So, when an unbeliever asks a Christian how a loving God can send people to Hell for their unbelief, a reasonable and biblical answer is that people themselves choose not to believe and thus send themselves to Hell. This same question when posed to a Calvinist can be answered that God simply chose some for eternal life. Thus, an appropriate question that still seems to mystify Calvinists is how can an all-loving and merciful God choose not to save some?

The usual response given by the Calvinist when asked how a good and merciful God can stay true to His nature despite being ultimately responsible for dooming the "un-elect" is fairly consistent among Calvinists: "He didn't have to save any of us." Joshua Harris explains:

> If you really understand Reformed Theology, we should just sit around shaking our heads going, "It's unbelievable. Why would God choose any of us?" You are so amazed, you're not picking a fight with anyone, you're just crying tears of amazement that should lead to a heart for lost people that God does indeed save, when He doesn't have to save anybody.[557]

Although the point is true that God didn't have to save any of us, Harris's logic is far from biblical. Imagine if a killer walked into a church of 300 members, including young children, adults, and the elderly, and

---

[557] Quoted by Collin Hansen in "Young, Restless, Reformed."

held them hostage at gunpoint. With reasons unknown to anyone in the church, the killer approaches a middle-aged man, and pulls the trigger. The killer repeats this action over and over, killing many people within the church: men, women, kids, babies, and the elderly. Finally, after he has murdered 275 of the churchgoers, he tells the remaining that not only are they free to go, but that they are invited to his house for a celebratory feast. Would the survivors be rejoicing over the gunman's graciousness upon them, or horror-stricken by his cruelty toward the others? Would they be filled with joy that they were set free, or would they be so plagued by what happened that they wished death upon themselves? Would they take his invitation? Would they run into the killer's arms, or run from him?

Note the logic that "he didn't have to save anyone" applies to this scenario. The few people who had nothing to do with their deliverance or salvation would most likely not be too thrilled to take the invitation to the killer's banquet feast. Although the reasoning that God didn't have to save any of us is true, it fails to make coherent sense of an all-loving god.

In debating George Bryson, a leading Calvinist admitted to Calvinism's view of God. The following is Calvinist John Rabe's "loose paraphrase" from this debate:

> BRYSON: Calvinists believe that God is an evil potentate who causes sin and tyrannically damns people and for no good reason causes babies to be raped.
>
> CALVINIST: Yes, and here's why I believe that. Genesis 50 says . . .
>
> COMMENTATOR: Yikes! With friends like this who needs enemies? [558]

---

[558] Bryson, *The Dark Side of Calvinism*, 372.

While this leading Calvinist's response is shocking, I deeply appreciate his honesty in acknowledging the "sovereign" attributes of his god. Because Calvinist theology has misinterpreted certain verses of the Bible for 400 years, they have essentially created a totally new and totally foreign god.

CHAPTER FOUR

More Division in the Body of Christ / The Expense of Truth

> There is no pillow so soft as a clear conscience.[559]
>
> —French Proverb

> Failure to embrace and act upon truth will always result in deception.[560]
>
> —Tom Drout

In our closing chapter, we will consider the cost of defending truth. At what point does a denomination cross the line from Christianity to unorthodoxy? If an unstructured religion is open to every sort of doctrine and belief, it will become nothing more than a Unitarian Universalist Church[561], full of contradictions. Yet if a Christian

---

[559] French Proverb, [online]; accessed 2 February 2010; available from http://thinkexist.com/quotation/there_is_no_pillow_so_soft_as_a_clear/167219.html; Internet.

[560] Tom Drout, quotation included under the heading "Truth," The Jesus Site [online]; accessed 2 February 2010; available from http://www.jesussite.com/quotes/truth.html; Internet.

[561] "Unitarian Universalism is a caring, open-minded religion that encourages seekers to follow their own spiritual paths. [Their] faith draws on many religious sources, welcoming people with different beliefs. [They] are united by

denomination is too strict in its beliefs and separates itself from every other Christian who does not share them, the result will be a host of sects that lack the cohesive essentials of the Christian body. Thus, while orthodox Christians are correct to clarify their differences on essential matters from groups such as Mormons and Jehovah's Witnesses, it can be problematic to create new denominations over every petty theological difference.

By now, it should be evident whether the doctrines of Calvinism are essential or secondary to orthodox Christianity. We should be of the understanding that the Calvinist's perspective of God is relatively new and different from the orthodox one. Finally, we should ask ourselves if these particular beliefs are important enough to pursue a deeper investigation and possibly allow them to be a source of division within the body of Christ. At what cost should Christians maintain biblical truth?

We should also note a stark contradiction made by many Calvinists. Though they typically desire to distinguish themselves within Christianity as being "Reformed," we find them ironically charging anyone who disagrees with their theology as being divisive. We see this irony exemplified in the debate between Dave Hunt and Calvinist apologists Doug VanderMeulin and Steve Watkins. VanderMeulin and Watkins commented that Hunt's book had the effect of negatively polarizing Christians within the church.[562] If "polarizing" means plainly laying out the differences between Calvinism and orthodoxy, then Dave Hunt should probably be found guilty. Hunt's book, *What Love Is This?* is simply an honest and frank discussion of how he understands Calvinism. I find it absurd that VanderMeulin and Watkins would accuse Hunt's book of polarizing Christians, as their own ambassadors are infiltrating

---

shared values, not by creed or dogma." Taken from the *Unitarian Universalist Association of Congregations* website [online]; accessed 28 December 2010; available from http://www.uua.org/visitors/index.shtml; Internet.

[562] Hunt, *Conversation on Calvinism.*

ignorant churches from the pulpit in order to convert them to Calvinism. If there is any such "polarizing" surrounding the Reformed faith, it would be hard to place real blame on the non-Calvinists.

What is truly polarizing in Reformed circles is that Calvinists want to spread their "superior" and "intellectual" theology to all churches, regardless of how it is accepted. For example, John Piper, who "has more than anyone else, contributed to a resurgence of Reformed theology among young people," states:

> One of the most common things I deal with in younger pastors is conflict with their senior pastors. They're a youth pastor, and they've gone to Trinity or read something Sproul or I wrote, and they say, "We're really out of step. What should we do?"

Piper advises these young pastors to be "totally candid and ask permission to teach according to their newfound convictions, even if they are in Wesleyan-Arminian churches."[563]

Although Piper encourages his young audience to "ask permission" to "evangelize," some Calvinists do not. The following story illustrates this problem:

> The pastor of First Baptist Church in Pauls Valley, Oklahoma, for 27 years, Joe Elam only encountered Calvinism once during his ministry—and it left a bitter taste in his mouth. Though forbidden to do so, a former youth pastor at his church secretly taught predestination to teens, Elam said, sowing seeds of lingering division among several families.
>
> "It was a wake-up call for us," said Elam, who recently led the Arbuckle Baptist Association to adopt a motion

---

[563] Hansen, "Young, Restless, and Reformed," p. 35.

calling on the Baptist General Convention of Oklahoma to rebuke Reformed theology. It sent copies of the motion to all members of the Southern Baptist Convention's executive committee.[564]

The reason for such heated debates and the "lingering division" mentioned by Elam is the radical differences between Calvinism and Christian orthodoxy. There is a great disparity between not only the gospel of Calvinism and the gospel of orthodox Christianity but also between the god of Calvinism and the God of the Bible. Fearing that the Corinthian Church was following "another gospel," Paul wrote (**2 Corinthians 11:3–4**, NKJV):

> But I fear, lest somehow, as the serpent deceived Eve by his craftiness, so your minds may be corrupted from the simplicity that is in Christ. For if he who comes preaches another Jesus whom we have not preached, or *if* you receive a different spirit which you have not received, or a different gospel which you have not accepted—you may well put up with it.[565]

There are noteworthy similarities between Calvinism and this "different gospel" that Paul addressed: Calvinism, too, has deceived its followers by intellectual "craftiness" from the "simplicity" of the true gospel. The gospel of Calvinism preaches "another Jesus" (Who never meant to save all), a "different spirit" (Who never meant to convict and sanctify all), and a "different gospel" (that is not "good news" to all) than what the orthodox gospel message has always taught.

---

[564] Ken Walker, "TULIP Blooming: Southern Baptist Seminaries Re-introduce Calvinism to a Wary Denomination," *Christianity Today* 52, no. 2 (February 2008) [online]; accessed 2 February 2010; available from http://www.christianitytoday.com/ct/2008/february/8.19.html?start=1; Internet.

[565] NKJV, 2 Corinthians 11:3–4.

The doctrines of Calvinism and Reformed Theology are, by their very nature, a threat to the body of Christ, and separation from such a theology would be more than a "last resort"—it would be a biblical mandate. Noticing the divisive disposition of Calvinism, Ron Comfort, president and founder of Ambassador Baptist College, has said:

> In forty-two years of ministry, I have been in thousands of churches. I have never been in one that was built on Calvinism. I have been in many that have been divided by Calvinism, but never one that was built on Calvinism. I told my wife that the only thing that is attractive to me about Calvinism is that if I were a Calvinist, I would never have to go through a building program.[566]

As I began thinking and writing about the topic of this book, I had to seriously ask myself, *Am I trying to divide the already divided body of Christ over this topic?* Well, no. Another question I asked myself was, *Am I writing a book that will bring division among Christians over matters that don't really matter?* Again, no. Salvation is no small matter. The purpose of the book has been to point out the doctrinal differences between Calvinism and orthodox Christianity, of which many people are unaware, and to challenge the reader to question whether Calvinism has anything in common with cults. If this challenge somehow plays a part in bringing division within Christianity, may it be for nothing less than the essential matters of the faith. We should understand that it was in the hope of bringing a Calvinistic reformation to the entire body of Christ that Reformed Theology has itself divided the body of Christ. Although this hope may be founded on good intentions for Christian unity, its progress and unorthodoxy have shown themselves to be a necessary cause of division. Calvinism is hardly embraced by those who are really

---

[566] Comfort, "The Fruits of Calvinism."

familiar with it, yet it is a theology fervently welcomed by many young and unknowing Christian minds.

As we consider possible division in the body of Christ over doctrinal issues, we should remember that doctrine divides. Doctrine, by its very nature and purpose, separates. Its very inception with the apostles and church fathers clarified the fundamental differences between true followers of Jesus and the Gnostics; between those who held that Jesus was a man and those who believed he was not. It divided those people who believed that Jesus was a mixture of both man and God from those who held that he was both fully man and fully God. As time passed and new issues arose, doctrine became more specific and detailed and, in turn, more copious. The doctrine of the Trinity might have been one of the largest theological battles of church history. But after much time and argument, at least two groups emerged. And close to the same time, this doctrine also divided the Roman Church from the Byzantine.

While a majority of debates within the first centuries of the church were over the essential beliefs of Christianity, almost all denominational squabbles did not come until much later. Some of these differences gave way to Lutheran, Wesleyan, Baptist, and Pentecostal churches, each with their own conservative and liberal branches—and the list can go on. Though not generally considered essential issues even the differences between these groups are doctrinal.

Today is no different. While we stand on two thousand years of church growth brought through much struggle, we still must compare any doctrine to that of sound biblical theology—not systematic theology. When John Calvin wrote and finished his *Institutes* and his followers ratified TULIP as the acronym for their official doctrinal statement to the church and world, their intent was to divide those who agreed with their particular doctrine from those who did not. To believe that the pattern is different today would be naïve. Contemporary theologians supporting Calvinism—such as Sproul, Piper, White, Grudem, and many more—are writing scores of books ranging anywhere from devotionals and footnotes in the *Reformation Study Bible* to 1200-page treatises of systematic theology. These are all helping to form not only the church but the world's theological view. Whether indirectly or not, promoters of Calvinism are bisecting those who align themselves with Calvin's theology from those who do not.

This book's thesis is not intended to be divisive, but I am aware that some readers will not only disagree but also take offense. Nevertheless, I have intentionally avoided softening the positions argued here, knowing that because the content is primarily doctrinal, it will undoubtedly be used by some in divisive ways. No matter how "polite" or how "politically correct" we may want to be and despite how nonjudgmental and inclusive the contemporary Christian has been taught to act by social norms, those serious about their faith in Christ must recognize that doctrine divides. Division was one of Jesus' main teaching themes. Even nondenominational churches, whose greatest strength might be their openness to various types of people and theologies, must come to grips with the particular doctrines of Calvinism. Nondenominational churches have been growing rapidly and are liked so much by so many because they provide a haven from church authorities that bicker and divide over nonessentials. Yet sadly, the essential claims of Calvinism have come to churches known to be liberally open to the nonessentials of Christianity.

This book does not itself divide—doctrine divides. If nondenominational churches are wrestling with Calvinism in their body (as the Calvary Chapel movement did, and later took a stand) it should not automatically be viewed as a bad thing but rather as a clarification and refinement process for church doctrine. Church leaders should not ask if Calvinism will divide the church but rather how it will and, therefore, how to maintain unity, if practically possible, without sacrificing biblical truth.

It is not my place to direct the reader how to respond to the differences between Calvinistic and orthodox doctrine. My hope is that readers will compare the essential claims about whom Jesus intended to save with Calvinism's theology of Limited Atonement, all the while "endeavoring to keep the unity of the Spirit in the bond of peace" (**Ephesians 4:3**, KJV).

In closing this chapter, I leave you with the example of Pastor Tom Stipe of the Crossroads Church in Denver, who stood for truth and counted the cost. In the late 1970s, when Tom Stripe was the director of the Association of Vineyard Churches (AVC), uncertain and unbiblical practices started to infiltrate these churches. After much time and thought, Tom was convinced that much of the AVC's teachings, practices, and attendees were straying from biblical truth. Knowing the difficulty of standing for truth in the company of friends, he confessed that he and his wife "didn't want to cause trouble. We had formed close relationships with these people, loved them, and considered them an important part of our lives. But we could no longer remain silent concerning the truth."[567] Shortly after, he wrote, "Frustrated, I returned to my own church in Denver. I had just witnessed close friends, co-laborers in Christ, legitimate Christian leaders being 'tossed to and fro by every wind of doctrine.' . . . At that moment, truth became more important to me than relationships." [568]

Tom Stipe's story shows how even legitimate Christian leaders can fall for unbiblical doctrines, and his example of standing up for the truth should move other pastors and influential Christians to do the same regarding Calvinism. Stipe understood that some of the extreme charismatic practices of the Vineyard leaders were not only unhealthy for their congregations but were misrepresentations of God. As special ambassadors for Christ, Christian leaders cannot allow their view or understanding of God to be less or more than what the Bible reveals. Unfortunately, the proclamation of Calvinism as a biblically sound theology has had its effect by misrepresenting God.

---

[567] Tom Stipe, Foreword in *Counterfeit Revival: Looking for God in All the Wrong Places* by Hank Hanegraaff (Nashville: Word Publishing, 2001), xv.

[568] Ibid., xvi.

Calvinism's Misrepresentation of God

What comes into our minds when we think about God is the
most important thing about us.[569]

—A. W. Tozer

Because Calvinism has had a large and influential role in history,
having cloaked itself in scriptural half-truths and having been long
supported by "Christian intellects," many people from the secular world
accept this theology as a faithful interpretation of the Bible. With only a
relatively small number of Christian leaders criticizing Calvinist
theology—such as George Bryson, Dave Hunt, Laurence Vance, and
Walls and Dongell—people from both outside and within the church
remain in the dark regarding the facts of Calvinism. Vance rightly notes
in his preface that there are "but a few . . . major books against
Calvinism."[570] One need not go to the bookstore to verify this lack of
awareness but only to observe the secular environment. Calvinism's
misrepresentation of God has not only tainted how some Christians view
God but how unbelievers have come to understand Him.

If Calvinism's claims were correct, I could not confidently say
with Paul, "For I know whom I have believed and am persuaded that He
is able to keep what I have committed to Him" (**1 Timothy 2:12**,
NKJV).[571] Calvinism distorts the very words and character of God, calls
into question my own salvation, and ultimately justifies the hatred
towards Him that many non-Christians feel. When I encounter or read
about people who are anti-God, I often find that their view of God is

---

[569] A. W. Tozer, *The Knowledge of the Holy. The Attributes of God: Their Meaning in the Christian Life* (New York: HarperCollins, 1961), 7.

[570] Vance, *The Other Side of Calvinism*, Preface ix; See Vance's footnote 4 for his list of works.

[571] NKJV, 1 Timothy 2:12.

Calvinistically distorted. The influence is noticeable in a number of prominent atheists, but we will first consider a rock star with an almost cult-like following.

James Maynard Keenan is a songwriter and singer with a large and loyal cult-like following. He currently sings for the bands A Perfect Circle and Tool. Anyone familiar with music knows of his hostile lyrics towards God and particularly Jesus. In one song called "Eulogy," Keenan sings about the death of Jesus:

Standing above the crowd,
he had a voice that was strong and loud
and I swallowed his façade cuz I'm so eager to identify
with someone above the ground,
someone who seemed to feel the same,
someone prepared to lead the way,
with someone who would die for me.

James continues on, no longer singing *of* Jesus but *to* him, yelling,

Will you? Will you now?
*Would you die for me? Don't you f***ing lie.*
*Don't you step out of line. Don't you f***ing lie.*
You've claimed all this time that you would die for me.[572]

What is the message of Maynard's "eulogy"? In the first phrase, we read that he wants to believe that "someone" will die for him. Yet, in the second phrase the writer not only questions the authenticity of the human sacrifice but calls him a liar ("You've claimed all this time that you would die for me"). Keenan concludes that Jesus' offer to die for him is not trustworthy. This perception of Jesus' atonement can only be ascertained by Calvinism's theology. I find it very ironic that Christians abhor these lyrics while seeming not to care that Sproul, White, Piper, and other leading Calvinists not only preach the same message (sparing

---

[572] James Maynard Keenan, song title: 'eulogy', Aenima, [compact sound disk], Ocean Way, Hollywood, California, The Hook, 1996.

the curse words) but also cloak it in scriptural quasi-truths presented as "pure biblical Christianity."[573] That a Christian with any admiration for Calvinism might think James Keenan's lyrics are wrong is inconsistent. However, if the doctrines of Calvinism are correct, then Keenan paints an accurate picture of God as taught in TULIP theology. According to Calvinism, how could I, or Keenan, or anybody else, truly know that the Christ died for us? When Jesus said, "This is my blood . . . which is shed for many for the remission of sins" (**Matthew 26:28**, NKJV),[574] how can one really determine if he or she is one of the "many"? As Calvinists believe that Jesus was offering salvation only to a select few, one can only ask: Was Jesus being dishonest? Was He lying when he stated the following?

> *John 6:51: "I am the living bread which came down from heaven. If anyone eats of this bread, he will live forever; and the bread that I shall give is My flesh, which I shall give for the life of the world."*

> *John 3:16: "For God so loved the world that He gave His only begotten Son, that whoever believes in Him should not perish but have everlasting life."*

> *John 12:47: ". . . for I did not come to judge the world but to save the world."*

Calvinism actually justifies Keenan's view of Jesus and also brings into question C. S. Lewis's "Lunatic, Liar, or Lord" argument.[575] Lewis proposed that out of the many views of Jesus, He must have been either a lunatic, a liar, or the Lord He claimed to be. By process of elimination, Lewis concluded that Jesus had to have been the Lord He claimed to be, a far more believable and scripturally accurate option than the other two.

---

[573] Coppes, *Are the Five Points Enough*, 16.

[574] NKJV, Matthew 26:28.

[575] C. S. Lewis, *Mere Christianity* (New York: HarperCollins, 1980), 52–53.

Yet somehow the TULIP doctrine of Calvinism misinterprets the above verses to portray Jesus more as liar than as Lord.

The theology of Calvinism has long dominated the world's view of Christianity and has influenced countless people, like James Maynard Keenan, into believing a lie. Dave Hunt writes that Calvinism's misinterpretation of God has given atheists an "excuse . . . not to believe in Him."[576] He asks:

> How many unbelievers have rejected God because of this deplorable distortion we do not know—but may that excuse be denied every reader from this time forth! And may believers, in confidence that the gospel is indeed glad tidings for *all* people, take God's good news to the whole world![577]

Unfortunately, Dave Hunt's assertion that Calvinism can be blamed for being the atheist's excuse is not hypothetical. All of Charles Templeton's arguments against the Bible and its God, as recounted in his book *Farewell To God: My Reasons For Rejecting the Christian Faith*, revolve around the central issue of God's love. Although most of Templeton's opinions can be rebutted with relative ease, one cannot. When Templeton interprets Exodus 10 (the hardening of Pharaoh's heart), he thinks and writes like a Calvinist:

> The incredible part of the story is that these punishments were inflicted despite the fact that—as the text makes clear—Pharaoh could not assent to Moses' entreaties. He had no option: Yahweh himself had made Pharaoh adamant . . . Can one believe that a loving God, the Father of all humankind, could do such a despicable

---

[576] Hunt, *What Love Is This?*, 533.

[577] Ibid.

thing? This is from a God of love, the God who is "no respecter of persons."[578]

So we ask the question again, *How many unbelievers have rejected God because of this deplorable distortion?* A number of atheists and biologists seem to agree with Calvinism's contention that free will is only an illusion. Addressing claims that mankind essentially has no soul or free will, Christian apologist Dinesh D'Souza notes:

> Many scientific atheists portray man as simply a carbon-based machine, a purely material object whose belief in immaterial things is a kind of epiphenomenon or illusion. Biologist Francis Crick, who helped to discover the structure of DNA, writes that all biology is reducible to the laws of physics and chemistry. Life is the product of the same mechanical operations as the inanimate matter in nature. Conscience is "no more than the behavior of the vast assembly of nerve cells and their associated molecules."[579]

Calvinist Tim Warner came to the same conclusion, stating that free will is a mere "illusion." He writes:

> . . . it becomes obvious that man's apparent free will is somewhat of an illusion. That is, man only appears to have free will. God ultimately decides who is to be saved and who is to be lost totally apart from any kind of decision on the part of the individual. Before the creation, God sovereignty decided whom He would save and

---

[578] Charles Templeton, *Farewell to God: My Reasons for Rejecting the Christian Faith* (Toronto, Canada: McClelland & Stewart, Inc., 1996), 66-67.

[579] Dinesh D'Souza, *What's So Great about Christianity?* (Washington, DC: Regnery Publishing, Inc., 2007), 25.

whom He would not. Man has no independent choice in the matter at all.[580]

A formidable opponent to faith is self-proclaimed "anti-theist" Christopher Hitchens, who does not believe that God exists. In a debate with Dinesh D'Souza, Hitchens accurately but unknowingly describes the god of Calvinism:

> Christianity . . . attacks us in our deepest integrity, it says that you and I wouldn't know a right . . . thought without the permission of a celestial dictatorship—that guards us while we sleep, that can convict us of thought crime . . . and . . . will continue to judge us, persecute us, and supervise us even after we were dead. How horrible it would be if we were condemned to live in this posture of gratitude . . . to an unalterable dictatorship in whose installation we had had no say.[581]

In Hitchens' description of God, we see Calvin's distinct interpretation of Total Depravity and the total Calvinistic denial of man's free will. Hitchens' description of deity in his book, *God Is Not Great: How Religion Poisons Everything*, accurately reflects Calvinism and Hitchens' disdain for John Calvin:

> According to the really extreme religious totalitarians, such as John Calvin, who borrowed his awful doctrine

---

[580] Tim Warner, "Calvinism: Introduction" (10/2003), The Pristine Faith Restoration Society web site [online]; accessed 2 February 2010; available from http://www.pfrs.org/calvinism/index.html; Internet.

[581] Christopher Hitchens, in a "Debate between Christopher Hitchens and Dinesh D'Souza: 'Is Christianity the Problem?'," at The King's College, moderated by Marvin Olasky, posted on *The Richard Dawkins Foundation for Reason and Science* Web site [online]; accessed 2 February 2010; available from http://richarddawkins.net/videos/1776-debate-between-christopher-hitchens-and-dinesh-d-39-souza; Internet.

from Augustine, an infinity of punishment can be awaiting you even before you are born. Long ago it was written which souls would be chosen or "elected" when the time came to divide the sheep from the goats. No appeal against this primordial sentence is possible, and no good works or professions of faith can save one who has not been fortunate enough to be picked. Calvin's Geneva was a prototypical totalitarian state, and Calvin himself a sadist and torturer and killer, who burned Servetus (one of the great thinkers and questioners of the day) while the man was still alive. The lesser wretchedness induced in Calvin's followers, compelled to waste their lives worrying if they had been "elected" or not, is well caught in George Eliot's Adam Bede, and in an old English plebeian satire against the other sects, from Jehovah's Witnesses to Plymouth Brethren, who dare to claim that they are of the elect, and that they alone know the exact number of those who will be plucked from the burning:

We are the pure and chosen few, and all the rest are damned. There's room enough in hell for you—we don't want heaven crammed.

I had an innocuous but weak-spirited uncle whose life was ruined and made miserable in just this way. Calvin may seem like a far-off figure to us, but those who used to grab and use power in his name are still among us and go by the softer names of Presbyterians and Baptists. The urge to ban and censor books, silence dissenters, condemn outsiders, invade the private sphere, and invoke an exclusive salvation is the very essence of the totalitarian. The fatalism of Islam, which believes that all is arranged by Allah in advance, has some points of resemblance in its utter denial of human autonomy and liberty, as well as in its arrogant and insufferable belief that its faith already contains everything that anyone might ever need to know.[582]

I am not surprised when Hitchens confesses in his book that his father was brought up with a "strict Baptist/Calvinist upbringing."[583]

These voices of Christian hate in the secular world should not go unnoticed or unchallenged. Atheists both past and present usually have a warped view of God, one that is apparently complicated, at least, by Calvinism. As cults usually do, Calvinism misrepresents God to the world. Although orthodox Christians have countered the mistaken concepts of God found in the classic cults, they have seldom openly opposed similar ideas found in Calvinism. It is my hope that both Christians and non-Christians will become more informed about the aspects of Calvinist theology that are too cultish for comfort. It is my hope that those who have ties to Calvinism or any other cult will seek better to understand their unbalanced theology in light of the Scriptures. For all of the good and correct doctrine that might be found in Calvinism, its essential message of salvation skews the character of God. The fruit of this misrepresentation can be seen in the examples noted above.

If, as A. W. Tozer believed, "What comes into our minds when we think about God is the most important thing about us," may the theology and doctrines that make up our view of God and His son Jesus be far from John Calvin's.

John 3:16

On Easter morning 1986, I was sitting in a kitchen chair waiting for my family as they prepared to leave for our church's morning

---

[582] Christopher Hitchens, *God Is Not Great: How Religion Poisons Everything* (New York: Twelve Hachette Book Group, 2007), 233–34.

[583] Ibid., 11.

service. I was reading a pocket Bible, and my eyes noticed the words of **John 3:16**. I read and re-read them, first to myself and then under my breath. Finally, as my family was just about ready to go, I jumped up from my chair and ran into my parents' room, where I recited the verse with pride and joy. This was the first verse I memorized. Although my parents' enthusiasm was somewhat limited due to their concern about running late, my excitement was untouched. Soon after, as much as my young mind could comprehend, I received the grace of God as I prayed with my father in his room.

Twenty-two years later, I heard *New York Times* best-selling author Max Lucado being interviewed on national radio. He was describing the contents of his new book, which he simply and appropriately titled *3:16: The Numbers of Hope*.[584] The book focuses on the powerfully simple truth of John 3:16—that because God loved the world, He gave His Son so that whoever believes in Him will have everlasting life. The following quotes were all collected from the introduction to Lucado's *3:16: Numbers of Hope*:

> "**John 3:16** is the North Star of the Bible. If you align your life with it, you can find The Way home" (Anne Graham Lotz, AnGel Ministries).

> "I remember vividly that I walked down an aisle in a church one night, without prompting by my parents, and knelt at a humble altar. There through my tears, I gave my heart to Jesus. I was three years old. That night proved to be the highlight of my entire life. The 'whosoever' in **John 3:16** even extended to a little toddler. Praise the Lord!" (Dr. James Dobson, founder of Focus on the Family).

---

[584] Max Lucado, *3:16: The Numbers of Hope* (Nashville: Thomas Nelson, 2007).

"To me, **John 3:16** is the very foundation of my faith. It is because of God's love that He gave and it's because of God's love that I am saved forever" (CeCe Winans, gospel music artist).

"This is the first verse that I learned as a child and it changed my life. To most 10-year-olds, these would be sweet words to recite to Mom and Dad to make them smile. To me they were a lighthouse in the darkness, a concrete promise when everything else seemed untrue and a hope that could not be extinguished. Over forty years later I wrap the truth of these words around me every day as I look for others who are lost at sea, betrayed and hopeless. All the literature in the world cannot compete with the treasure contained in these twenty-five words" (Sheila Walsh, author of *God Has a Dream for Your Life*).

"We can *all* endure a great deal of pain and grief, and general 'life-is-not-fair' experiences when we know who *loves* us, and how incredible and incomprehensible the *joy* is that awaits us" (Michael Blanton, of Blanton Entertainment, a musical artist development group).

"Out of great need is born great faith. I have seen both. 3:16 brings life and faith to a hope-starved world. May we embrace its message anew" (Bishop John K. Rucyahana, Anglican Bishop of Shyira Diocese of northwest Rwanda).

"**John 3:16** is the foundation of my faith. A picture of undeserved, unconditional, and unwavering love from a Father to his kids" (Ernie Johnson, Sportscaster for TNT/TBS).

"I love **John 3:16** because it is the gospel in a nutshell. It shares God's great love for us, and our great need for him" (Mac Powell, lead singer of Third Day).

"There are hundreds of verses in scripture that are of significant importance to me. But this is the most important verse in the Bible" (John Smoltz, Atlanta Braves Pitcher).

"**John 3:16** is the Mount Everest of Scripture passages from God's Word. In this great verse, we see the highest statement of Theology as it portrays God's nature as a God who deeply loves. It portrays the genius of Soteriology as it shows how God planned to rescue mankind through the gift of His Son, Jesus. **John 3:16** sums up God's nature, God's plan, and God's intent" (Frank S. Page, president of the Southern Baptist Convention's Executive Committee).

"By twenty I was visibly unraveling mentally and emotionally. It would take the harrowing experience of living as an agoraphobic before I considered God's intervening love and relinquished my heart to Christ. 3:16 is the undeniable address my sanity, safety, and eternal security takes refuge in" (Patsy Clairmont, best-selling author and Women of Faith speaker).

"God's love is not some mere sentiment, but rather something that He showed in a tangible way. God offers to us the gift of eternal life. To receive a gift, you must reach out to accept it, and then open it" (Greg Laurie, pastor and evangelist).

"**John 3:16**. What an amazing scripture—God loved us while we were quite unlovable people. He reached out to us when we were unreach-able. Knowing that we would fail Him, deny Him, and spurn this unconditional love, He still gave . . . unconditionally!" (Don Moen, singer and songwriter).

"God gave his son as payment for our sins, everyone's sins—the payment was as horrible as anything you can imagine. Beyond the physical pain, the experience of separation from his Father was a pain that cannot be described. But Jesus endured this for us so that we can enjoy eternal life" (Ned Yost, manager of the Kansas City Royals baseball team).

"Without hope, the fear of death is overwhelming. But as Christians, the Bible verse **John 3:16** assures us that there is everlasting life—and this promise alone should give all of us hope at the time of death" (Kenneth Cooper, M.D., M.P.H.).

The collective thoughts about **John 3:16** and Lucado's book are overwhelming. From theologians, artists and entertainers the truth and comfort found within the twenty-five-word verse proves to be the heart and soul of the Christian message. Jerry Vines records just how timeless the verse was and remains:

In the 1870's archeologists uncovered a giant, red granite obelisk in the sands of Egypt. The Egyptians named it "Cleopatra's Needle" and gave it to Great Britain. "Cleopatra's Needle" was erected along London's Thames River. At the base of the shaft was a time vault. In it were placed several items of the day: coins, clothing, children's toys, newspapers, and photographs. A committee was appointed to include the greatest single verse in the Bible. The committee unanimously chose to place into the vault **John 3:16**, which had been translated into the 215 known languages of the day.[585]

Because of this, no other verse exposes the truth and practical consequences of maintaining the doctrines of Calvinism as does **John 3:16**. Is it by mere chance that the only verse from the Bible's 31,000 verses, often called "the Gospel in a nutshell," happens to be the one that Calvinism clearly and radically changes? Calvinism renders Max Lucado's book, *3:16: The Numbers of Hope*, utterly hopeless. According to Calvinism, *God's love* is something quite less, the vastness of the *world* is diminished to the few elect, *whoever* are only those decreed to be saved, and even their choice to *believe* in Him is by divine compulsion. Yet, of all cults claiming to be Christian, only Calvinism has so maligned the truth and meaning of the world's most well-known verse. While there is hope for the world to find God according to **John 3:16**, the Calvinist must regard the verse and the overall content of Lucado's book as wishful thinking. By the effect of Calvinism, the gospel's good news is turned into a sad message in which hope is turned to despair and free will is anything but free. This is the practical reality of Calvinism and should be revealed as such.

A Balanced View of Calvinism

It is not hard to develop an unbalanced and unfair portrayal of someone or something by extenuating one side of the facts while ignoring the other. Funeral services are usually successful at accomplishing this. They call attention to the good and honorable aspects of the deceased person while glossing over or completely ignoring any immoral behavior or poor life decisions. Because of this, people unfamiliar with the person who has departed are left with an unbalanced view of the legacy the person has left behind. What a challenge it must be

---

[585] Jerry Vines, p. 13.

for the honest minister who conducts funeral services for people who have sown and reaped more pain and sorrow than peace and joy during their lifetimes.

There are always two sides of the story. An accurate explanation of any situation can only be made after both sides have been assessed by a trustworthy source. It is always easier and faster to come to conclusions inadequately instead of patiently weighing both sides and then evaluating. Because this balancing process is difficult and time consuming, we usually take the path of least resistance. Tim Downs explains the results of such decision making:

> All acts of balancing, whether physical or mental, are inherently exhausting . . . As the cost of failure increases, so do the tension and fatigue. Because maintaining balance is so tiring, most people who find themselves on a tightrope instinctively look for the best direction to fall. Better to be at rest in error than to have to maintain the wearisome balance of truth. This has been the source of much of the heresy in the history of the church. How can Jesus be fully God and fully man? I don't know, so I'll just choose which way to fall: He's God or He's man. How can God be sovereign if at the same time man possesses a free will? I can't reconcile the two, so I'll become a hyper-Calvinist or an Arminian. I may be mistaken, but at least I'm off the tightrope.[586]

Every day, people come to both subconscious and conscience conclusions in their life concerning a myriad of things. While some are trivial, others are not. Our understanding of certain people, events, and organizations tends to be, and always begin as, one sided. The mature

---

[586] Tim Downs, *Finding Common Ground: How to Communicate with Those Outside the Christian Community...While We Still Can* (Chicago: Moody Press, 1999), 93.

person waits to make a decision until enough information has been processed. Even if a final ruling has not been made, the person at least can give a two-sided argument. On the other hand, there are those irritating people who are uniformed yet opinionated.

In this book, we have highlighted particular aspects of Calvinism that Calvinists would rather minimize or even conceal. The intent is not to imply that Calvinism is incapable of doing any good nor to suggest that Calvinism has done nothing of eternal value for the last four hundred years. This assessment of Calvinism does not ignore some of the benefits of systematic theology. Rather, the valuable traits of Calvinism have been compared to its harmful ones. As any assessment is made, all sides are evaluated for their worth. In the end, a decision is made. To make a judgment about Calvinism apart from its undesirable aspects would be to judge a man's moral or spiritual heritage based on a dishonest eulogy. More so, the intellectually compromised leaders of Calvinism typically dismiss the incriminating evidence against Calvinism as mere fanatical ranting, and continue to give the unbalanced "eulogy" of Calvinism.

This book has attempted to reveal that side of Calvinism of which many are unaware—*the cultish side*—and ultimately to help balance the view of Calvinism that is held by so many in both the Christian and secular worlds.

APPENDIX of MAIN AUTHORS

These are brief descriptions of the major authors often quoted in this book. The information is taken from either general online dictionaries (Wikipedia) or Web sites at which the authors serve or are employed.

Calvinists

Robert C. Sproul (born 1939 in Pittsburgh, Pennsylvania) is an American Calvinist theologian and pastor. He is the founder and chairman of Ligonier Ministries (named after the Ligonier Valley just outside of Pittsburgh, where the ministry started as a study center for college and seminary students) and can be heard daily on the *Renewing Your Mind* radio broadcast in the United States and throughout sixty countries. Sproul holds degrees from Westminster College, Pennsylvania (B.A., 1961), Pittsburgh Theological Seminary (M.Div., 1964), the Free University of Amsterdam (Drs., 1969), and Whitefield Theological Seminary (Ph.D., 2001), and he has taught at numerous colleges and seminaries, including Reformed Theological Seminary in Orlando and Jackson, Mississippi, and Knox Theological Seminary in Ft. Lauderdale. Currently, he is Senior Minister of Preaching and Teaching at Saint Andrews Chapel in Sanford, Florida. Sproul was ordained as an elder in the United Presbyterian Church in the USA in 1965 but left that denomination because of liberalism around 1975 and joined the Presbyterian Church in America. (St. Andrews Chapel, however, is independent and not affiliated with that or any other denomination.) Sproul is a council member of the Alliance of Confessing Evangelicals.[587]

---

[587] Wikipedia, s.v., "R. C. Sproul"

John Piper was born in Chattanooga, Tennessee. Piper attended Wheaton College (1964–68), where he majored in literature and minored in philosophy. Following college, he completed a Bachelor of Divinity degree at Fuller Theological Seminary in Pasadena, California (1968–71). While at Fuller, he took as many courses as he could from Daniel Fuller, the most influential living teacher in his life, and through Fuller he discovered the writings of Jonathan Edwards, his most influential nonliving teacher. Piper did his doctoral work in New Testament Studies at the University of Munich in Munich, West Germany (1971–74). Upon completion of his doctorate, he taught Biblical Studies at Bethel University and Seminary in Saint Paul, Minnesota for six years (1974–80). In 1980, after what he described as an irresistible call of the Lord to preach, Piper became Senior Pastor of Bethlehem Baptist Church in Minneapolis, Minnesota, where he has been ministering ever since.[588]

James R. White (born 1962) is the director of Alpha and Omega Ministries, a Christian apologetics organization based in Phoenix, Arizona. He is the author of more than twenty books, a professor, a prolific debater, and an elder of the Phoenix Reformed Baptist Church. He received a B.A. from Grand Canyon College, an M.A. from Fuller Theological Seminary, and a Th.M., a Th.D., and a D.Min. from the Columbia Evangelical Seminary (formerly Faraston Seminary). He is a professor of Greek, Hebrew, systematic theology, and various apologetics topics. White is an avid debater, having participated in over sixty moderated debates since 1990, covering topics such as Calvinism, Roman Catholicism, Islam, Mormonism, and Jehovah's Witnesses.[589]

Charles H. Spurgeon, (June 19, 1834–January 31, 1892) was a British Reformed Baptist preacher who remains highly influential among Christians of different denominations, among whom he is still known as

---

[588] Wikipedia, s.v., "John Piper"

[589] Wikipedia, s.v., "James White"

the "Prince of Preachers." He also founded the charity organization now known as Spurgeon's, which works worldwide with families and children, as well as Spurgeon's College in London. His sermons were translated into many languages in his lifetime. Often, Spurgeon's wife was too ill for her to leave home to hear him preach. Spurgeon, too, suffered ill health toward the end of his life, afflicted by a combination of rheumatism, gout, and Bright's disease. He often recuperated at Menton, near Nice, France, where he eventually died on January 31, 1982. Spurgeon's wife and sons outlived him. His remains were buried at West Norwood Cemetery in London where the tomb is still visited by admirers.[590]

Charles Hodge (1797–1878) was the principal of Princeton Theological Seminary between 1851 and 1878. He was one of the greatest exponents and defenders of historical Calvinism in America during the nineteenth century. He matriculated at the College of New Jersey (now Princeton University) in 1812, and after graduation entered in 1816 the theological seminary in Princeton, having among his classmates his two lifelong friends, John Johns, afterward bishop of Virginia, and Charles P. Mollvaine, afterward bishop of Ohio. In 1819, Hodge was licensed as a minister by the Presbytery of Philadelphia, and he preached regularly at the Falls of Schuylkill, the Philadelphia Arsenal, and Woodbury, New Jersey, over the subsequent months. In 1822, he was appointed by the General Assembly professor of Biblical and Oriental Literature. In 1824, he helped to found the Chi Phi Society along with Robert Baird and Archibald Alexander. In 1825, he founded the *Biblical Repertory and Princeton Review* and during forty years was its editor and the principal contributor to its pages. In 1840, he was transferred to the chair of Didactic Theology, retaining, however, the department of New Testament exegesis, the duties of which he continued to discharge until his death.[591]

---

[590] Wikipedia, s.v., "Charles Spurgeon"

[591] Wikipedia, s.v., "Charles Hodge"

Non-Calvinists

Dave Hunt is a Christian apologist, speaker, radio commentator, and author. He has been in full-time ministry since 1973. The Berean Call ministry, which highlights Hunt's writings, was started in 1990. Hunt has traveled to the Near East, lived in Egypt, and written numerous books on theology, prophecy, cults, and other religions, including critiques of Catholicism, Islam, Mormonism, and Calvinism, among others. His books have sold over 4 million copies and have been translated into at least twenty languages. Theologically, Hunt is evangelical, progressively dispensational, and associated with the Plymouth Brethren Movement. Although he is not a Calvinist, he does hold to eternal security.[592]

Laurence M. Vance is a teacher, an author, a publisher, a freelance writer, the editor of the *Classic Reprints* series, and the director of the Francis Wayland Institute. He holds degrees in history, theology, accounting, and economics. The author of eleven books, he regularly contributes articles and book reviews to both secular and religious periodicals. Dr. Vance's writing interests include free-market economics, taxation, government spending and corruption, the socialism and statism of conservative pundits and Republican politicians, Baptist theology, English Bible history, Greek grammar, and the folly of war. He is a regular columnist for LewRockwell.com, and blogs for LewRockwell.com, Mises.org, and Antiwar.com. Vance is a member of the Society of Biblical Literature, the Grace Evangelical Society, the Society of Dispensational Theology, and the International Society of Bible Collectors, and is an adjunct scholar of the Ludwig von Mises Institute.[593]

---

[592] Wikipedia, s.v., "Dave Hunt"

[593] See Vance's bio; [online] Accessed 28 December 2010; Available from http:// www.vancepublications.com; Internet.

George Bryson is the director of Calvary Chapel Church Planting Mission—an outreach to Russia and the former Soviet Union—and has served in full-time ministry with Calvary Chapel since 1968. In addition to writing a number of pamphlets, George collaborated with Bill Playfair on the book *The Useful Lie*, a challenge to the so-called Christian Recovery Industry. His newest book is *The Gospel of Calvinism*. George and his wife, Debbi, have also written several Bible study guides together.[594]

Jerry L. Walls is a professor of philosophy of religion at Asbury Theological Seminary in Wilmore, Kentucky, where he has taught since 1987. His achievements include a B.A. from Houghton College, 1977; a M.Div. from Princeton Seminary, 1980; a S.T.M. from Yale Divinity School, 1981; and a Ph.D. from Department of Philosophy at the University of Notre Dame, 1989. His books include: *The Problem of Pluralism: Recovering United Methodist Identity; Hell: The Logic of Damnation; C. S. Lewis and Francis Schaeffer: Lessons for a New Century from the Most Influential Apologists of Our Time* (with Scott Burson; *Heaven: The Logic of Eternal Joy; Why I Am Not a Calvinist; The Chronicles of Narnia and Philosophy*; Forthcoming books include *The Oxford Handbook of Eschatology*; and *Basketball and Philosophy*. Dr. Walls is an elder in The United Methodist Church, West Ohio Conference, and is a member of the Society of Christian Philosophers. He is also a member of the Dulles Colloquium of the Institute on Religion and Public Life and is Senior Speaking Fellow for the Morris Institute for Human Values. He has authored a variety of professional and popular articles, on topics ranging from foreknowledge and freedom to Harry Potter.[595]

---

[594] The Berean Call Web site; [online] Accessed 28 December 2010; Available from http://www.thebereancall.org; Internet.

[595] Asbury Theological Seminary Web site; [online] Accessed 28 December 2010; Available from http:// www. Asbury seminary.edu; Internet.

Joseph R. Dongell is a professor of biblical studies at Asbury Theological Seminary in Wilmore, Kentucky. His achievements include a B.A. from Central Wesleyan College, 1978; a M.Div. from Asbury Theological Seminary, 1981; a M.A. from the University of Kentucky, 1986; and a Ph.D. from Union Theological Seminary in Virginia, 1991. Dr. Dongell joined the Asbury Seminary faculty in 1989, and now serves as Professor of Biblical Studies, with primary responsibility in the Inductive Bible Study Department. Prior to 1989, Dongell served as an instructor in various languages (Greek, Hebrew, and Latin) at Asbury Seminary (1981–83), Asbury College (1985–86), and Union Theological Seminary in Richmond, Virginia, (1987). Most recently he has co-authored a book with Asbury Seminary professor, Jerry Walls, entitled *Why I Am Not a Calvinist.* As an ordained elder in the Wesleyan Church, Dongell has maintained an active ministry in that denomination as an associate pastor, a regular adult Sunday School teacher, a one-time director and frequent advisor of the Wesleyan Seminary Foundation on the seminary campus, an instructor in regional Wesleyan ministerial training, and a representative to the annual Graduate Student Theological Seminar.[596]

Dr. Norman Geisler is the author or co-author of some seventy books and hundreds of articles. He has taught theology, philosophy, and apologetics on the college or graduate level for fifty years. He has spoken or debated in at least twenty-six countries on six continents. He has a B.A, M.A., Th.B., and Ph.D (in philosophy). He has taught at some of the top seminaries in the United States, including Trinity Evangelical and Dallas Theological Seminary, and has been guest professor at numerous other schools. He and his wife, Barbara, live in the Charlotte, North Carolina area. He maintains an active writing, speaking, and lecturing

---

[596] Asbury Theological Seminary Web site; [online] Accessed 28 December 2010; Available from http:// www. Asbury seminary.edu; Internet.

ministry across the country.[597] Geisler is noted for his philosophical approach to theology. His four-volume Systematic Theology offers a blend of philosophy and biblical exegesis. Theologically, Geisler is a conservative evangelical. He has dedicated much effort to the cause of biblical inerrancy, and was a contributor to the Chicago Statement on Biblical Inerrancy. Together with William Nix, Geisler wrote General Introduction to the Bible, which is still often used as a textbook by evangelical scholars. Geisler also left the Evangelical Theological Society in 2003, after it did not expel Clark Pinnock, who advocates open theism. He also testified in McLean v. Arkansas, defending creationism. [598]

---

[597] Norman Geisler Web site; [online] Accessed 28 December 2010; Available from http://www.normangeisler.net/; Internet.

[598] Wikipedia, s.v., "Norman Geisler"

BIBLIOGRAPHY

Allen, David, and Steve Lemke. *Whosoever Will: A Biblical Critique of Five-Point Calvinism*. Nashville, TN: B&H Publishing Group, 2010.

Allen, Matthew, and Ernest Reisinger. *A Quite Revolution: A Chronicle of Beginnings of Reformation in the Southern Baptist Convention*. Cape Coral, FL: Founders Press, n.d. [online]. Accessed 28 November 2010. Available from http://www.founders.org/library/quiet/; Internet.

Allen, Jim. *Blessed Hope Ministries*. Website. 2002. <http://www Blessed hope.ws /bibl.html>.

Ascol, Tom. Executive Director of "Founders Ministries," a Reformed Web site, "More Thoughts on the SBC in Greensboro," Founders Ministries Blog, entry posted 15 June 2006; accessed 18 January 2010; available from http://blog.founders.org/2006_06_01_archive.html; Internet.

Baxter, Richard. *The Reformed Pastor*, William, Brown (Editor) Christian Classics Ethreal Library, Grand Rapids, 2002; [online] accessed 28 December 2010; available from http://www.ccel.org/ccel/baxter/pastor.html; CHAPTER 3/APPLICATION/SECTION 1 – THE USE OF HUMILIATION, 62; Internet.

Beek, Joel. *Living for God's Glory: An Introduction to Calvinism*. Orlando, FL: Reformation Trust, 2008.

Benson, Rod. "Why Do People Join Cults?" *John Mark Ministries* Web site [online]. Accessed 16 June 2006. Available from http://www. jmm.aaa.net.au/articles/9498.htm; Internet.

Bettenson, Henry and Chris Maunder. *Documents of the Christian Faith*, 3rd ed. New York: Oxford University Press, 1999.

Boettner, Loraine. *The Reformed Doctrine of Predestination*. Phillipsburg, NJ: Presbyterian and Reformed Publishing Co., 1991.

Brown, Craig R. *The Five Dilemmas of Calvinism*. Orlando: Ligonier Ministries, 2008.

Bryson, George L. *The Five Points of Calvinism: "Weighed and Found Wanting."* Costa Mesa, CA: The Word for Today, 2002.

_____. *The Dark Side of Calvinism: The Calvinist Caste System*. Costa Mesa, CA: The Word for Today, Calvary Chapel Publishing, 2004.

Byrd, James P., Jr. *The Challenges of Roger Williams: Religious Liberty, Violent Persecution, and the Bible*. Macon, GA: Mercer University Press, 2002.

Calvin, John. *God the Creator, God the Redeemer: Institutes of the Christian Religion*. Translated by Henry Beveridge, Gainesville, FL: Bridge-Logos, 2005.

_____. *Concerning the Eternal Predestination of God*. Translated by J. K. S. Reid. London: James Clarke and Co., 1961.

_____. *Institutes of the Christian Religion*. [online]; accessed 27 January 2010; available from http://www.reformed.org/books/institutes/books/book3/bk3ch21.html; Internet.

Carson, D. A. *Jesus' Sermon on the Mount and His Confrontation with the World: An Exposition of Matthew 5–10*. Grand Rapids: Baker Books, 2004.

Chay, Fred and John Correia. *The Faith that Saves: The Nature of Faith in the New Testament*. Grace Line, Inc. United States of America: Schoettle Publishing Company, 2008.

Chesterton, G. K. *Irish Impressions* New York: John Lane Company, 1919.

Cloud, David. "Calvinism on the March Among Evangelicals" *Fundamental Baptist Information Service.* [online]. Accessed 18 October 2010; http://www.wayoflife.org/files/category-calvinism.html; Internet.

Coppes, J. Leonard. *Are the Five Points Enough? Ten Points of Calvinism.* Denver, CO: Leonard J. Coppes, 1980.

Comfort, Ron. "Fruits of Calvinism" [online]. Accessed 18 January 2010. Available from http://www.ambassadors.edu/resources/Fruits_of_Calvinism.pdf; Internet.

Daniel, Curt. "Appendix E: The Practical Applications of Calvinism." In *The Five Points of Calvinism: Defined, Defended, Documented.* 2nd ed., ed. David N. Steele, Curtis C. Thomas, S. Lance Quinn, 187–198, Phillipsburg, NJ: P&R Publishing, 2004.

Dillow, Joseph C. *The Reign of the Servant Kings: A Study of Eternal Security and the Final Significance of Man* (Haysville, NC: Schoettle Publishing Company, 1992.

Downs, Tim. *Finding Common Ground: How to Communicate with Those Outside the Christian Community…While We Still Can.* Chicago: Moody Press, 1999.

Elmquist, Greg. Foreword to "What Should We Think of Evangelism and Calvinism?" by Ernest C. Reisinger [online]. Accessed 1 February 2010. Available from http://www.reformedreader.org/e&c.htm; Internet.

Engelsma, David J. "A Defense of Calvinism" [online]. Accessed 28 November 2010. Available from http://www.prca.org/pamphlets/pamphlet_31.html; Internet.

Ewald, Dan, "The Call of Caedmon." Interview with Derek Webb and members of Caedmon's Call. *All Access* November 2000.

Frame, John M. *The Doctrine of the Christian Life: A Theology of Lordship.* Phillipsburg, NJ: P&R Publishing, 2008.

Freeman, L. Paul. "What's Wrong with Five-Point Calvinism?" *Wholesome Words* Web site [online]. Accessed 18 January 2010. Available from http://www.wholesomewords.org/etexts/freeman/pfcalvin.html; Internet.

Geisler, Norman L. *Chosen but Free.* Minneapolis: Bethany House Publishers, 2001.

Geisler, Norman L., and Ron Rhodes. *Correcting the Cults: Expert Responses to Their Scripture Twisting.* Grand Rapids: Baker Books, 1997.

George, Timothy. "John Calvin: Comeback Kid." *Christianity Today* 53, no. 9 (September 2009): 1-8 [online]. Accessed 28 September 2010. Available from http://www.christianitytoday.com/ct/2009/september/14.27.html; Internet.

Giaquinto, Brian. "Calvinism debated at Southern Baptist Convention." *Spero News.* Website, 14 June 2006. [online]. Accessed 28 December 2010. Available from http://www.speroforum.com/site/article.asp?idCategory=33&idsub=134&id=4013.

Gill, John. "John 6:44," In *John Gill's Exposition of the Bible* [online]. Accessed 15 July 2006. Available from http://www.biblestudytools.com/commentaries/gills-exposition-of-the-bible/john-6-44.html; Internet.

Godfrey, W. Robert. *An Unexpected Journey: Discovering Reformed Christianity.* Phillipsburg, NJ: P&R Publishing, 2004.

Gonzalez, Marco. "an_interview_with_vern_poythre" 2005/12/ See, www.reformationtheology.com, [online] accessed on 21 December 2010; Internet.

Hanko, Herman, Homer Hoeksema, and Gise J. Van Baren. *The Five Points of Calvinism.* Grandville, MI: Reformed Free Publishing Association, 1967 [online]. Accessed January 2010; Available from http://www.prca.org/ fivepoints/chapter5.html; Internet.

Haden, Jeffery. Institute for the Study of American Religion, [online]accessed; January 26, 2010; at www.americanreligion.org; Internet.

Hanegraaff, Hank. "What Are Some Common Marks of a Cult?" Christian Research Institute (CRI) Statement: CP0201 [online]. Accessed 26 January 2010. Available from http://www.equip.org/perspectives/common-characteristics-of-cults; Internet.

_____. *The Apocalypse Code*. Nashville: Thomas Nelson, 2007.

_____. *Counterfeit Revival: Looking for God in All the Wrong Places*. Nashville: Word Publishing, 2001.

Hancock, Lee. "U.S. Lawyers Detail Sect's Waco Arsenal," *Dallas Morning News* 7 July 2000 [online]; accessed 27 January 2010; available from http://www.cesnur.org/test i/waco99.htm#Anchor-35882; Internet.

Hanko, Herman. *God's Everlasting Covenant of Grace*. Grand Rapids: Reformed Free Publishing Association, 1988.

Hansen, Collin. "Young, Restless, Reformed: Calvinism is Making a Comeback—and Shaking Up the Church." *Christianity Today* 50, no. 9 (September 2006): 1-8 [online]; accessed 27 September 2010; available from http://www.christianity today.com/ct/2006/september/42.32. html; Internet.

Hitchens, Christopher. *God Is Not Great: How Religion Poisons Everything*. New York: Twelve Hachette Book Group, 2007.

Hitchens, Christopher, and Dinesh D'Souza. "Debate between Christopher Hitchens and: 'Is Christianity the Problem?'" Debate conducted at The King's College Provost, moderated by Marvin Olasky. Posted on The Richard Dawkins Foundation for Reason and Science web site [online]; accessed 2 February 2010; available from http://richarddawkins.net/ videos/1776-debate-between-christopher-hitchens-and-dinesh-d-39-souza; Internet.

House, H. Wayne, and Carle Gordon. *Doctrine Twisting: How Core Biblical Truths Are Distorted.* Downers Grove, IL: InterVarsity Press, 2003.

Hunt, Dave, and James White. *Debating Calvinism.* Sisters, OR: Multnomah Publishers, 2004.

Hunt, David. *What Love Is This?* Sisters, OR: Loyal Publishing, 2002.

_____. *Conversation on Calvinism.* Bend, OR: The Berean Call, 2002 [CD-ROM].

Jackson, Wayne. "How to Identify a Cult" [online]. Accessed 28 August 2000. Available from http://courier.com /articles/250-how-to-identify-a-cult; Internet.

Jones, Kristina. "Eyewitness, Why People Join Cults." BBC News 24 March 2000 [online]. Accessed 28 January 2010. Available from http://news. bbc.co.uk/ 2/hi/africa/688317.stm; Internet.

Keenan, James Maynard. "Eulogy." On *Aenima* album. Hollywood, CA: The Hook, 1996 [CD-ROM].

Knechtle, Cliffe. *Help Me Believe: Direct Answers to Real Questions.* Downers Grove, IL: InterVarsity Press, 2000.

LaBaron, Garn, Jr. *A Historical Analysis, Mormon Fundamentalism and Violence* [online]. Accessed 28 January 2010. Available from http://www.exmormon.org/ violence.htm; Internet.

Lalich, Janja and Madaline Tobias. *Take Back Your Life: Recovering from Cults and Abusive Relationships.* Berkeley, CA: Bay Tree Publishing, 2006.

Laston, Broward, "Interview: Missionary Work in Iraq." *Time*, 15 April 2003 [online] accessed 15 December 2010. Available from http://www.time.com/time/world/article/0,8599,443800,00.html.

Lemke, Steve and Allen, David. *Whosoever Will: A Biblical Critique of Five-Point Calvinism.* Nashville, TN: B&H Publishing Group, 2010.

Lewis, C. S. Quote 139, "Calvin, John." In *English Literature in the Sixteenth*, para. 61, p. 42. In *The Quotable Lewis*. ed. Wayne Martindale and Jerry Root Wheaton, IL: Tyndale House Publishers, 1998.

Lucado, Max. *3:16: The Numbers of Hope*. Nashville: Thomas Nelson, 2007.

MacArthur, John F., Jr. *Faith Works: The Gospel According to the Apostles*. Nashville: W Publishing Group, 1993.

Machen, J. Gresham. *The Christian View of Religion*. Volume 3. Edinburgh: The Banner of Trust, 1965.

_____. *The Christian View of Man*. Edinburgh: The Banner of Trust, 1965.

MacCulloch, Diarmaid. *The Reformation: A History*. New York: Penguin Books, 2003.

Matzat, Don. "Martin Luther and the Doctrine of Predestination." *Issues, Etc. Journal*, Volume 1, Number 8; October 1996.

Marsden, George. *Fundamentalism and American Culture*. New York: Oxford, 1980.

Martin, Walter. *The Kingdom of the Cults*. Minneapolis: Bethany House Publishers, 2003.

_____. *Rise of the Cults: A Quick Guide to the Cults*. Capital Heights, MD: Vision House Publishing, 1978.

McCain, Paul, (a Lutheran Reverend posted it on his blog) [online] Accessed 2 July 2008 from http://cyberbrethren.com; Internet.

McDowell, Josh, Don Steward, *Handbook of Today's Religions*, Thomas Nelson, 1983.

McGuire, James. "Appendix A: 'A Kinder Gentler Calvinism.'" In *The Five Points of Calvinism: Defined, Defended, Documented*, 2nd. ed., ed.

David N. Steele, Curtis C. Thomas, S. Lance Quinn, ##-##. Phillipsburg, NJ: P&R Publishing Company, 2004.

McGrath, Alister. *A Life of John Calvin*. Oxford, England: Basil Blackwell, 1990.

McKim, Donald K. *Westminster Dictionary of Theological Terms*. Louisville, KY: Westminster John Knox Press, 1996.

McNeill, John T. *The History and Character of Calvinism*. New York: Oxford University Press, 1967.

Milton, John. From "On Christian Doctrine." *Milton—The Major Works*. New York: Oxford University Press, 2003.

Murray, John. *Redemption Accomplished and Applied*. Grand Rapids: Eerdmans, 1955.

Mouw, Richard J. *Calvinism in the Las Vegas Airport: Making Connections in Today's World*. Grand Rapids: Zondervan, 2004.

Neste, Ray V. "John Calvin on Evangelism and Missions." *Founders Journal* 33 (Summer 1998) [online]. Accessed 1 February 2010. Available from http://www. founders.org/journal/fj33/article2.html; Internet.

Packer, J. I. "Introductory Essay to John Owen's *Death of Death in the Death of Christ* [online]. Accessed 28 January 2010. Available from http://www.all-of grace.org/pub/others/death of death.html; Internet.

Palmer, Edwin. *The Five Points of Calvinism*. Grand Rapids: Baker Book House, 1980.

Parrington, L. Vernon, *Main Currents in American Thought*. Vol. 1 (New York: Harcourt Brace, 1927).

Pink, A. W. *The Sovereignty of God* [online]. Accessed 20 January 2010. Available from http://www.reformed.org/books/pink/index.html? Main frame=/ books/pink/pink_sov_08.html; Internet.

_____. *Eternal Security* [online]. Accessed 28 January 2010. Available from http://www.theologue.org/Eternal Security-AWPink.html; Internet.

Piper, John. "Irresistible Grace" [online]. Accessed 20 January 2010. Available from http://www.monergism. com/thethreshold/articles/ piper/ irresistable.html; Internet.

_____. *The Pleasures of God*. Sisters, OR: Multnomah Publishers, 2000.

Piper, John, and Bethlehem Baptist Church Staff. "What We Believe about the Five Points of Calvinism" [online]. Accessed 5 January 2008; Available from http://www.desiringgod.org/ resource-library/resources/what-we-believe-about-the-five-points-of-calvinism; Internet.

Plass, Ewald M. *What Luther Says*. St. Louis, MO: Concordia Publishing House, 2006.

Reisinger, Ernest. "What Should We Think of Evangelism and Calvinism?" [online]. Accessed 1 February 2010. Available from http://www.reformedreader.org/e&c.htm; Internet.

Reisinger, Ernest C., and Matthew Allen. *A Quiet Revolution: A Chronicle of Beginnings of Reformation in the Southern Baptist Convention* [online]. Accessed 1 February 2010. Available from http://www.founders. org/ library/quiet4/; Internet.

Rice, John R. *Some Serious, Popular False Doctrines Answered from the Scriptures*. Murfreesboro, TN: Sword of the Lord Publishers, 1970.

Rieske, Kent R. "Calvinism: False Doctrines of the "Pope" of Geneva / Total Depravity, Unconditional Election, Limited Atonement, Irresistible Grace and Perseverance" [online]. Accessed 22 January 2010. Available from http://www.biblelife .org/calvinism.htm; Internet.

Rigdon, Sidney. "Oration, Delivered by Mr. S. Rigdon, On the 4th of July, 1838 [online]. Accessed 28 January 2010. Available from http://sidneyrigdon.com/rigd1838.htm; Internet.

Row, Jonathan. "Pastore Won't Let Up." Post on Positive Liberty blog, 29 April 2007 [online]. Accessed 29 April 2007. Available from positiveliberty.com/2007/04/pastore-wont-let-up.html; Internet.

Schaff, Phillip. *History of the Christian Church*. Volume 8, History of the Reformation, "The Swiss Reformation." Grand Rapids: Christian Classics Ethereal Library, 2002 [online at Christian Classics Ethereal Library (Dallas, TX: Electronic Bible Society, 2002). Accessed 27 September 2010; available from http://www.ccel.org/s/schaff/ history/8_toc.htm; Internet.

Seaton, W. J. *The Five Points of Calvinism*. Edinburgh: The Banner of Truth Trust, 1970.

Shedd, William G. T. *Calvinism: Pure and Mixed*. Edinburgh: The Banner of Truth Trust, 1986.

Smith, Chuck. Foreword to *The Dark Side of Calvinism: "Weighed and Found Wanting"* by George Bryson. Costa Mesa, CA: The Word for Today, 2002.

Smith, James. *Letters to a Young Calvinist—An Invitation to the Reformed Tradition*, Grand Rapids: Brazos Press, 2010.

Smith, Joseph. *The Book of Mormon*. Salt Lake City: The Church of Latter-day Saints, S1948.

D'Souza, Dinesh. *What's So Great about Christianity?* Washington, DC: Regnery Publishing, Inc., 2007.

Spencer, Duane Edwards. *TULIP: The Five Points of Calvinism in Light of Scripture*. Grand Rapids: Baker Book House, 1979.

Sproul, R. C. *Chosen by God*. Wheaton, IL: Tyndale Publishing House, 1986.

_____. *Defending Your Faith: An Introduction to Apologetics*. Wheaton, IL: Crossway Books, 2003.

_____. *Essential Truths of the Christian Faith*. Wheaton, IL: Tyndale Publishers, Inc., 1992.

_____, ed. *The Reformation Study Bible, English Standard Version*. Orlando: Ligonier Ministries, 2005.

_____. *What Is Reformed Theology? Understanding the Basics*. Grand Rapids: Baker Books, 1997.

_____. *Willing to Believe: The Controversy over Free Will*. Grand Rapids: Baker Books, 1997.

Spurgeon, Charles Haddon. "A Defense of Calvinism." *The Spurgeon Archive* [online]. Accessed 15 January 2010. Available http:// www. Spurgeon .org/calvinism.htm; Internet.

_____. *Expositions of the Doctrines of Grace*. Pasadena, TX: Pilgrim Publications, n.d.

_____. *The Soul Winner*. Grand Rapids: Eerdmans, 1963.

Steele, David N., Curtis C. Thomas, and S. Lance Quinn. *The Five Points of Calvinism: Defined, Defended, and Documented*. 2nd ed. Phillipsburg, New Jersey: P&R Publishing Company, 2004.

Stipe, Tom. Foreword to *Counterfeit Revival: Looking for God in All the Wrong Places* by Hank Hanegraaff. Nashville: Word Publishing Group, 2001.

Streiker, Lowell D. *Cults: The Continuing Threat*. Nashville: Abingdon Press, 1983.

Strong, James. *The New Strong's Exhaustive Concordance of the Bible*, Nashville: Thomas Nelson Publishers, 1995, 1996.

Tanner, Jerald and Sandra, "Mormon Blood Atonement: Fact or Fiction?" *The Salt Lake City Messenger*, Issue 92, April 1997 [online]. Accessed 28 January 2010. Available from http://1857massacre.com/MMM/bloodatonement.htm; Internet.

Templeton, Charles. *Farewell to God: My Reasons for Rejecting the Christian Faith*. Toronto: McClelland & Stewart Inc., 1996.

Thorn, Joe. "Reformed Motivation." Blog entry 22 February 2006 at JoeThorn.net [online]. Accessed 28 November 2010. Available from http://www. joethorn.net/2006/02/22/reformed-motivation/; Internet.

Tozer, A. W. *The Knowledge of the Holy. The Attributes of God: Their Meaning in the Christian Life*. New York: HarperCollins, 1961.

Van Neste, Ray, "John Calvin on Evangelism and Missions." *Founders Journal* 33 (Summer 1998) [online]. Accessed 1 February 2010. Available from http://www. founders.org/journal /fj33/article2.html; Internet.

Van Baren, Gise J. "Limited Atonement" [online]. Accessed 28 January 2010. Available from http://www.prca.org/pamphlets /pamphlet_46.html; Internet.

_____. "The Perseverance of the Saints." In *The Five Points of Calvinism*. Grandville, MI: Reformed Free Publishing Association, 1976) [online]. Accessed 28 January 2010. Available from http://www.prca.org/fivepoints/chapter5.html; Internet.

Vance, Laurence M. *The Other Side of Calvinism*. Pensacola, FL: Vance Publications, 2002.

Walker, Ken "TULIP Blooming, Southern Baptist Seminaries Re-introduce Calvinism to a Wary Denomination," *Christianity Today* 52, no. 2 (February 2008) [online];

accessed 2 February 2010; available from http://www. christianitytoday.com/ct/2008/february/8.19.html?start=1; Internet.

Walls, Jerry L., and Joseph R. Dongell. *Why I Am Not a Calvinist.* Downers Grove, IL: InterVarsity Press, 2004.

Warner, Tim. "Calvinism: Introduction" (10/2003). The Pristine Faith Restoration Society [online]. Accessed 2 February 2010. Available from http://www.pfrs.org/calvinism/index.html; Internet. available from http://www.pfrs.org/calvinism/index.html; Internet

White, Ellen G. *Testimonies for the Church Volume 5, 67* [online]. Accessed 2 February 2010. Available from http://www.truth fortheendtime.com/SOPText/Testimonies_for_the_Church/T estimonies%20for%20the%20Church%20Volume%205.pdf; Internet.

White, James R. "Blinded By Tradition: An Open Letter to Dave Hunt Regarding His Newly Published Attack Upon the Reformation, *What Love Is This? Calvin's Misrepresentation of God* [online]. Accessed 13 July 2007. Available from http:// vintage.aomin.org/DHOpenLetter.html; Internet.

_____. *Debating Calvinism.* See Hunt, David.

_____. *The Potter's Freedom: A Defense of the Reformation and the Rebuttal of Norman Geisler's Chosen but Free.* Amityville, NY: Calvary Press, 2000.

Williamson, G. I. *The Westminster Confession of Faith: For Study Classes.* Philadelphia: P&R Publishing Co., 1964, 2004.

Witherington, Ben, III. *The Problems with Evangelical Theology: Testing the Exegetical Foundations of Calvinism, Dispensationalism, and Wesleyanism.* Waco, TX: Baylor University Press, 2005.

Wood, L. Charles, *The Mormon Conspiracy: A Review of Present Day and Historical Conspiracies to Mormonize America and the World.* Chula Vista, CA: Black Forest Press, 2004.

Worthen, Molly, "Who Would Jesus Smack Down?" *The New York Times* 6 January 2009 [online]. Accessed 28 September 2010]. Available from http://www. nytimes. com/2009/01/11/magazine/11punk-t.html.

_____. "The Reformer - How Al Mohler transformed a seminary, helped change a denomination, and challenges a secular culture." *Christianity Today* 1 October 2010 [online]. Accessed 15 December 2010]. Available from http://www.christianitytoday .com/ct/2010/october/3.18.html.

Yancey, Philip. *What's So Amazing About Grace?* Nashville: Thomas Nelson, 2007.

Zweig, Stefan. "The Right to Heresy." In *Dark Side of Calvinism: The Calvinist Caste System* by George Bryson, Costa Mesa, CA: The Word for Today, Calvary Chapel Publishing, 2004.

www.ingramcontent.com/pod-product-compliance
Lightning Source LLC
Chambersburg PA
CBHW031234090426
42742CB00007B/195